GCSE ART AND DESIGN

LONGMAN

LONGMAN REVISE GUIDES

SERIES EDITORS:
Geoff Black and Stuart Wall

TITLES AVAILABLE:
Art and Design
Biology
Business Studies
C.D.T. – Design and Realisation
Chemistry
Economics
English
English Literature
French
Geography
German
Mathematics
Physics
World History

FORTHCOMING:
British and European History
C.D.T. – Technology
Computer Studies
Commerce
Home Economics
Human Biology
Music
Office Studies and Keyboarding
Religious Studies
Science
Social and Economic History

GCSE
ART AND
DESIGN

LONGMAN
REVISE
GUIDES

Bill Read

Longman

Longman Group UK Limited,
Longman House, Burnt Mill, Harlow,
Essex CM20 2JE, England
and Associated Companies throughout the world.

© Longman Group UK Limited 1988

First published 1988

British Library Cataloguing in Publication Data

Read, William
    Art and Design. — (Longman GCSE revise
    guides).
    1. England. Secondary schools. Curriculum
    subjects: Design. GCSE examinations.
    I. Title
    745.4'076

    ISBN 0–582–01884–6

Produced by The Pen and Ink Book Company,
Huntingdon, Cambridgeshire.

Set in 10/12 Century Old Style
Printed and bound in Great Britain at
The University Printing House, Oxford.

CONTENTS

EDITORS' PREFACE

Longman GCSE Guides are written by experienced examiners and teachers, and aim to give you the best possible foundation for success in examinations and other modes of assessment. Examiners are well aware that the performance of many candidates falls well short of their true potential, and this series of books aims to remedy this, by encouraging thorough study and a full understanding of the concepts involved. The Revise Guides should be seen as course companions and study aids to be used throughout the year, not just for last minute revision.

Examiners are in no doubt that a structured approach in preparing for examinations and in presenting coursework can, together with hard work and diligent application, substantially improve performance.

The largely self-contained nature of each chapter gives the book a useful degree of flexibility. After starting with the opening general chapters on the background to the GCSE, and the syllabus coverage, all other chapters can be read selectively, in any order appropriate to the stage you have reached in your course.

We believe that this book, and the series as a whole, will help you establish a solid platform of basic knowledge and examination techniques on which to build.

Geoff Black and Stuart Wall

AUTHOR'S PREFACE

I hope this book will help you to improve the standard of your work in Art and Design and thereby enable you to gain a higher level of success in your GCSE examination.

In Art and Design there are no correct, or expected, solutions to the problems which confront you in your work. Rather than seeking such model examples, it is more important for you to concentrate on developing a sound *working method* which allows you to explore fully all that might be said to be associated with the study of Art and Design. Alongside such a working method will necessarily be an equally sound *working habit*. It will be no good you knowing how to work, but not working! If this were to be the case, the likelihood is that you would fall back upon trying to produce the 'correct' answer at the eleventh hour in your studies.

This all means that the PROCESS in Art and Design is the basis for the most successful work. Process does not mean how you make a lino-cut, or throw a pot, although this is part of it. It will be likely to include how extensively you investigate a particular problem and how many alternative solutions and pieces of related information you uncover as you do so. Some of this related information may not be obviously about Art and Design. All of this will be dealt with in this book.

Concentrating on the Process does not mean that the PRODUCTS in Art and Design are unimportant. The things that you make and the things that you draw contain within them some of the *evidence* of what it is you have considered in your studies. But the Products are not the whole story. Your teachers and your examiner will want to see all that it is you have done, even that which you did not use eventually! In this book you will be helped to understand how necessary it is to present *all* your work for the GCSE examination.

The advantages of concentrating on the Process and allowing the Product to evolve from your studies will be demonstrated to you. Even if you are one of the so-called 'good at art' people, your level of achievement will improve by *attending to* the Process in your Art and Design studies. If you are *not* one of those people, then your level of achievement will improve by *concentrating on* the Process in your Art and Design studies.

One important aspect of the Process in Art and Design is the Historical content of the subject. I have tended to use many historical references throughout this book. This I have done because I believe sincerely that it is one of the important ways in which you can readily improve your own work and understanding in Art and Design. Even if you are only able to use books and reproductions, rather than visiting Museums and Galleries, such historical study will quickly lead you into other contexts which surround the making and the forms of the Products in Art and Design. The book will help you to understand this.

The pictures in this book do not necessarily illustrate what is said in the text. They are often chosen because they help to explain an idea by broadening and developing that idea. Do not fall into the trap of regarding them as the pictures you should copy if you want to achieve a high mark in your GCSE. If you follow the *argument* in the text I expect you to produce good work of your own which will be personal, original and fresh. To do this, and to enjoy it, is after all, one of the prime joys and reasons for doing Art and Design in the first place!

Bill Read.

ACKNOWLEDGEMENTS

I am grateful to the following Examination Groups for permission to quote from their examination syllabuses and to reproduce questions in their specimen examination papers. Whilst the Examining Groups have granted permission to reproduce the questions, I accept full responsibility for the solutions provided.

The London and East Anglian Examining Group
The Midland Examining Group
The Northern Examining Association
The Northern Ireland Schools Examinations Council
The Welsh Joint Examining Council
The International General Certificate of Secondary Education

I am grateful to the following for permission to produce further copyright material.

The Tate Gallery, London.
The Trustees of the National Gallery, London.
The Courtauld Institute Galleries, London.
The Trustees of the Wallace Collection, London.
The National Portrait Gallery, London.
The Castle Museum, Norwich.

Great Cornard Upper School, Sudbury, Suffolk and The Robert Smyth School, Market Harborough, Leicestershire, for permission to include students' work. Shenley Court School, Birmingham, West Midlands, for help in producing photographs of students' work.

Whilst I have received help in formulating my ideas about Art and Design from too many people for me to name them individually, I am grateful to the team behind this publication, to the many colleagues and friends I have worked with, and the astronomical number of pupils and students I have taught and learnt from. Gratitude is also due to my wife, without whose tolerance and understanding this book would never have been completed.

GCSE IN ART AND DESIGN

NATIONAL & GENERAL CRITERIA
GCSE GRADES
GRADE RELATIONSHIPS
CRITERIA-RELATED GRADES
GRADE DESCRIPTIONS
SKILLS REQUIRED
DOMAINS IN ART AND DESIGN
UNENDORSED AND ENDORSED CERTIFICATES
ASSESSMENT
EXTERNAL CANDIDATES

GETTING STARTED

This chapter aims to help you understand what is required of you in GCSE Art and Design. It introduces you to the national criteria for the GCSE, as well as the Art and Design syllabuses of all the Examining Groups responsible for the examination.

Two major documents, each published by the Schools Examination Council (SEC), explain the GCSE. They are, in order of publication:

1 General Certificate of Secondary Education.
   The General Criteria.
   HMSO, 1985.
2 General Certificate of Secondary Education.
   The National Criteria for Art and Design.
   HMSO, 1985.

The first of these documents deals with the standards and requirements which *all* subjects in the school curriculum have to fulfil. The second interprets and applies those standards and requirements in terms of *Art and Design* only.

ESSENTIAL PRINCIPLES

1 > NATIONAL AND GENERAL CRITERIA

Of the two documents, whilst the former has considerable bearing on *what it is you do* in your Art and Design studies, and *how you do it*, the latter is more important to you and probably easier to understand. It has been the responsibility of those who compiled the national criteria for *Art and Design* to take into account the specific requirements of the general criteria, and to *apply them* to Art and Design itself. So, it is possible for you to get by on a study of the national criteria for Art and Design only.

Of course, you could choose to *ignore* both these documents. After all, the *Examining Group* whose Art and Design examination syllabus you are using has had to make sure that their syllabus takes into account the content of *both* documents. That this has been so is checked by the SEC, which approves *all* GCSE examination syllabuses. So, you could decide that if you obey the *examination syllabus* you are using, you are by definition fulfilling *all* the requirements of *all* criteria surrounding the GCSE.

> **Understand fully what is required of you, and you will gain a higher reward for your work.**

You could also convince yourself that you do *not* even have to read the examination syllabus concerned. After all, your teachers should understand the requirements of the examination syllabus, otherwise they would not be in a position to design an appropriate course of study for you to follow!

No doubt your teachers *have* designed a highly appropriate course of study for you to follow, but if you do *no more* than go along blindly with what it is you are told to do, then your level of understanding is likely to be fairly minimal. If you *are* a serious student, and presumably you are, otherwise you would not be interested in this book, you should take it upon *yourself* to find out just what *is* expected of you in your Art and Design GCSE examination.

So follow your course of study in a diligent manner, but *do* get hold of a copy of the *examination syllabus* and read it. Try also to borrow, or buy from HMSO, a copy of the *National Criteria for Art and Design*, at least. This document will help to explain *why* your examination syllabus looks like it does.

2 > GCSE GRADES

The GCSE sets out to describe and reward an **absolute** level of performance. It is intended that each grade in the GCSE examination will describe levels of achievement ranging from the most basic level of competence to the highest levels of achievement in each subject. It is intended that the *grade* you achieve should accurately reflect the standards of ability *you* show in your *Coursework* and the *Externally Set Examination*. In turn, every other candidate is assessed and rewarded according to what *they* have done, *without any reference or comparison between one candidate and another*.

One of the means to achieve this ambition, to reward an *absolute* level of performance, depends upon the fact that no-one is barred from taking the examination. The GCSE is to be designed for all candidates, *whatever their ability relative to other candidates*, who are able to reach the standards required for the award of particular grades.

Because your performance is *not* to be compared with others, and because the GCSE examination is *not* designed for only a limited percentage of the school population at the age of 16+, you are able to earn an absolute reward for what you *actually do* in the course and examination.

This might be difficult for you to understand. Perhaps the only way to explain it is to describe what could happen in the examinations which existed *before* the GCSE. The intention in the examinations before GCSE was that only a *limited number* of candidates could pass the particular examination in any one year. So your work *was* compared with that of candidates of similar ability. This meant that the work of the candidates taking the examination each year was put into an *order* of level of comparative achievement. If it was then known *how many* candidates should pass the examination, *at what grades*, this could be achieved by striking lines under every 'so-many' candidates, in order to end up with the required distribution of passes in the examination.

> **The GCSE rewards you for the work you *actually do*, not for how well you compare with others.**

Of course, this is a crude generalisation of what happened, and does the previous examinations and those administering them an injustice. Familiarity with the practice probably meant that this did not happen in so mechanical a way. Nevertheless, if an examination is planned so that only a specific proportion of the population can pass it at any one time, then work which would *pass* one year would *fail* another, *if* the standard of students was higher the second year. This means that reward for an *absolute level of performance* could not exist under the examinations prior to the GCSE, whereas this is one of the positive qualities that the GCSE is setting out to introduce.

The intention in GCSE is that comparisons will only be made in order to *confirm* that your work fulfils the *standard required* for the award of a particular grade, in the same way as another candidate's work does. This will constitute *positive* comparison and will mean that *your* work will receive the grade it is worth, regardless of the value of any other candidate's work.

3 GRADE RELATIONSHIPS

Now that mention has been made of the examinations *prior* to the GCSE, it might be as well to use those examinations and their grade awards, in order to explain the values of the GCSE grades.

The two previous examinations, the General Certificate of Education (GCE) Ordinary Level, and the Certificate of Secondary Education (CSE), were related to each other insofar as their grade boundaries deliberately *coincided* at one point. The minimum mark required for a Grade C pass at the GCE O level was the same as the minimum mark required for a CSE Grade 1 pass.

The grades which the GCE O level and the CSE examinations covered between them were to accommodate only 60% of the school population at the age of 16+. The GCSE has to accommodate, theoretically at least, the whole of the 16+ age group in schools. To do so it will require a larger range of grades than either of the two previous examinations.

Again, the GCSE has been directly related to the GCE O level and the CSE. A Grade C in the GCSE is to be comparable to the GCE O level Grade C, and the CSE Grade 1. This has set up a table of relationships between all three of the examinations. This is explained in Table 1.1.

EXAMINATION	GCE O LEVEL	CSE	GCSE
GRADE LEVEL	A		A
	B		B
	C	1	C
		2	D
		3	E
		4	F
		5	G

Table 1.1 The relationship between GCE O level, CSE and GCSE grades

In the early days of the GCSE it is likely that the users of the examination will compare a grade you get in your examination with those in the previous GCE O level and CSE examinations. A 'user' of the examination is taken to be those who might offer you a job, for instance, or a place on a more advanced educational course. It is to be hoped that eventually, all those associated with the GCSE, that is to say you, other candidates now and in the future, parents, teachers and users will come to understand that the GCSE grades have *absolute* values of their own. *The GCSE grades, unlike any previous examination, will state specifically what it is you have achieved, and what it is you can do.*

4 CRITERIA-RELATED GRADES

The GCSE uses a scale of seven pass grades, A to G. As we have seen the GCSE aims to use *absolute standards* for grading. These standards are known as 'Criteria-Related Grading'. In practice some subjects have so far had difficulty in defining these seven absolute levels of ability which will describe achievement for each grade. Art and Design is one such subject. Nevertheless, *all* subjects must have **criteria-related grades** in the end. As a *step* along the way to this goal, the Exam Groups have established **grade descriptions**.

5 GRADE DESCRIPTIONS

At the moment each GCSE examination syllabus must include, if the subject has not *yet* got criteria-related grades, certain **grade descriptions**.

At least *two* grade descriptions must be published in each syllabus. These two grade descriptions must be for Grade C, and Grade F. Other grade descriptions can be included if the Examining Group responsible for the particular syllabus so wishes.

If you refer back to Table 1.1, Grades C and F can be seen to have particular significance. They each correspond to *trigger points* in the previous examinations.

The **GCSE Grade** C coincides with the old GCE O level Grade C, *and* the CSE Grade 1. Both of these were considered to represent a minimum level of pass *appropriate to going forward to more advanced educational courses*.

In turn, the **GCSE Grade F** coincides with the old CSE Grade 4. This CSE grade was regarded as representing the level of achievement equal to the *average level of ability of all the pupils in schools at the age of 16+*.

So, you can see *why* it was insisted that the *grade descriptions* for the GCSE Grades C and F should be included in each syllabus, if the subject did *not* have criteria-related grades ready at the time of publication.

Reading the grade descriptions in your syllabus will help *you* begin to judge your own level of ability and your standing within the subject. For this reason, if no other, it is important that you get hold of a copy of the syllabus you are using, *and read it*.

NEA	GRADE F
	Candidates awarded this grade will normally be able to demonstrate:
	1 a basic knowledge and understanding of elementary visual concepts but within certain limitations. Many of the more difficult problems attempted by more able candidates are avoided;
	2 drawing skills which may be bold and vigorous but will lack consistency, coherence and accuracy. There will be evidence, for example, of difficulty in controlling and expressing forms related in space with confidence and fluency;
	3 image making, recorded or visualised, which tends to lack organisation, diversity and variety, although they may appear refreshingly direct;
	4 interest and enjoyment although the candidate might lack continuity and concentration and the ability to sequence ideas and images;
	5 the use of pattern making and colour work which may be limited in range and subtlety;
	6 through completed work that they only rarely make independent judgements and/or sustained independent activity. The ability to research and select relevant information will be minimal;
	7 a modest range of craft skills and that the candidate only works comfortably within them. The work may still be lively and appear robust, but lack structural sensibility, refinement and judgement.
NEA	**GRADE C**
	Candidates awarded this grade will normally be able to demonstrate:
	1 a clear evidence of their basic knowledge and understanding of the visual elements with a good sense of their relationships and unity;
	2 through drawing skills, reasonable confidence, consistency, coherence and accuracy. There will be evidence, for example, of an ability to convey the sense of forms related in space with a reasonable degree of fluency in articulation and expression. Preparatory studies, when relevant, will also provide clear evidence of these qualities as well as the candidate's own personal involvement;
	3 image making, recorded or visualised, which shows evidence of organisation, diversity and variety. When secondary source material is used it will be minimal and will always show evidence of development and extension;
	4 the use of colour with some understanding and sensitivity; for example, the ability to express form through colour will be evident;
	5 evidence of the ability to research and select information. All candidates will have been able to sustain independent work and interest;
	6 the quality and range of work, in response to the syllabus followed, which will show attainment clearly above average and will represent the candidate's own authentic creative effort.
IGCSE	**GRADE A**
	Candidates awarded Grade A will have met all of the Curriculum Objectives. They will have demonstrated a firm grasp of skills and a superior creative ability in the options chosen. Their work will show a high degree of organisation, extensive investigation and will be characterised by an interpretation which is highly personal and perceptive, reflecting informed and considered judgement.

Table 1.2 An illustration of grade descriptions

66 Grade Descriptions
help you understand what is
required of you for the
GCSE. 99

Your *teachers*, if you are in full-time education, are likely to be well aware of the standard represented by Grade F. It is one of the means by which they begin to evaluate your chances of *succeeding* in the examination and, indeed, if it is appropriate to *enter* you for it.

If *you* understand what is represented by Grade F, then you can also begin to grasp what might be required of you if you are to improve enough to get one of the *higher* grades. Indeed, you can then go on to look closely at the description for Grade C. You can work out the levels required for *other* grades from the grade descriptions for F and C published in your syllabus.

To help you to understand this, and your chances in the examination, Table 1.2., shows you what the Northern Examining Association (NEA) syllabus says with regard to grade descriptions for, first, Grade F, and then Grade C. You should of course check with your own syllabus. The International General Certificate of Secondary Education (IGCSE) has provided a grade description for Grade A, and this also is shown in Table 1.2.

6 SKILLS REQUIRED

You will see from the various grade descriptions that there are some references to:

- the ability to use techniques and materials;
- reaching certain levels of achievement in your work.

These are skills or qualities which you might have reasonably supposed to be necessary in Art and Design. They are about *producing* Art and Design items or articles.

What you might *not* have expected to find in the grade descriptions are references to:

- producing work which demonstrates a personal response;
- showing certain personal qualities in your work;
- showing genuine signs of interest;
- having made real effort.

These are things which might have surprised you. This second batch of qualities represents one of the ways in which the GCSE really is unique.

66 So *how* you work is as
important as *what* you do,
and how *well* you do it. 99

In the past it was not possible to take any account of the way you worked for your examination. It was often said, particularly by examiners, that 'you cannot measure and reward attitude'. Of course, in fact, you did receive some reward for working hard. It showed in the standard of work you achieved as the result of much practice. There was also some assessed *coursework* in the CSE, but little or none in GCE O level. However, in **GCSE** you are examined *at least* as much on your work from your course of study as you are at the time of your externally set examination. This will be explained more fully later.

As most of the evidence about how you work will come from the period of your course of study rather than your externally set examination, it must be evident from reading the grade descriptions that it is vital that you perform well from day one of your GCSE course of study and not leave it all until your externally set examination.

This is something your teachers might tell you repeatedly. But unless *you* read it for yourself, and understand the need for it, you may not pay much heed to your teachers' advice in this respect. You will probably not have thought it possible that your level of *interest* and your degree of *effort* was going to be measured alongside your ability as an artist or a designer.

OTHER QUALITIES

If you refer to the extract for Grade F, taken from the Northern Examining Association (NEA) syllabus (Table 1.2) you will detect qualities *other than* the personal ones of interest and effort, and those relevant to producing good art and design work. There is *much more* to being even competent at Art and Design in the GCSE than just *how you work* and the *quality of the work you produce*. These further qualities are common to the examinations of all the Examining Groups.

What then, are these *further qualities*, and what significance do they have for *you* and your work in the GCSE, no matter which examination syllabus you may be using?

The following are some of the terms used to describe these 'other' qualities in the NEA syllabus.

i) Visual Concepts (Grade F 1)

- What is a visual concept?
- How many are there?
- Where can they be observed, and how can they be learnt?

Visual Concepts are more or less the ways in which you translate the things which you see or imagine into, for example, paintings, sculptures, or your own ideas.

Visual concepts deal with the way you, perhaps, create *recession* in your picture, or the way that you create a *sense of weight* in a sculpture, or the way you give *shape* to your designs for a newly planned kitchen, and so on. One of the best ways of understanding what visual concepts are, and the way in which they work for you in art and design, is to study the work of *recognised artists and designers*, taking the examples you study from a *variety of historical times* and from a *number of countries*.

ii) Accuracy (Grade F 2)

- What is an accurate drawing?
- Is there only one kind of accuracy?

Accuracy seems to be a highly definitive term. After all, a thing is either accurate, or it is not. Accuracy in Art and Design is only a *relative* term. For instance, if you are drawing the plans for the *kitchen design* mentioned above, you would expect your drawing to be accurately measured, down to the last millimetre. However, if you are doing a drawing of some *flowers*, from a bowl of flowers in front of you, there are a number of 'accuracies' you could be concerned with. You could be doing an accurate *botanical* drawing. Or you could be doing an accurate *representation of the colours* in each flower. Or you could be concerned with so-called *photographic* accuracy. If these possibilities did not exist, why is it that drawings can look so different, not in *what* they depict, but in the *way* in which they depict it?

iii) Organisation (Grade F 3)

- Does organisation mean what it *appears* to mean?

The term, **organisation**, is used alongside 'diversity' and 'variety'. There is also a reference to 'refreshingly direct'. Would your work, being organised, mean that you have *abandoned* 'directness', or 'variety', or 'diversity'? It is clear that, if you *did* abandon these other qualities, your work would be hardly likely to merit much reward in this section of the grade description. Therefore, the term 'organisation' must mean something *other than* it appears to on its face value. It might be that reference to other areas of the examination syllabuses would provide you with the answer. This is why it is important for you to read your examination syllabus.

iv) Sequence ideas and images (Grade F 4)

- Are not all ideas and images sequenced?
- How else do your ideas come to you, except one after another?
- How can you make one image at the same time as another?

There can be no denying that, no matter how the human brain computes your ideas, you can only recognise and visualise them *one at a time*. It might be that 'sequencing' means here one of a number of things. It could be that you are expected to show that you understand that 'one idea leads to another'. Perhaps you are expected to show how you 'develop' one piece of work into another. Or maybe you are expected to gather and present your work in such a way that it 'explains' what it is you have done in a particular programme of study.

v) Independence (Grade F 6)

- Does this mean that you should ignore your teachers?
- Can it be that, if you obey all the proposals above, you will lose marks for your work?

If you have read and understood the syllabus, you would be most unlikely to want to ignore your teachers. You would realise that what they asked you to do *was* important in terms of your result in the examination.

Even an apparent 'weakness' in your work *might* be an illustration of your level of independence. It might be that you have made a *rational* decision to present your work in the way that it is. For instance, you might have decided to leave a drawing as 'inaccurate' because there was *no need* for you to improve its accuracy; the drawing might have been used by you as a *means* to an end, whereby you developed a *further* piece of work from it.

vi) R e f i n e m e n t   a n d   j u d g e m e n t (Grade F 7)

- How many ways can you show refinement?
- How do you convey to others the nature and extent of your judgements?

The trouble here is that refinements are often the *result* of judgements. Some of this dual process goes on in your 'mind's eye', and it is not automatically documented in any way. Your concern in this respect is to make *evident* the **judgements** you make, and the *ways* in which your ideas develop, so that the *process* may be evaluated and rewarded. It is clearly a means of access to a better mark in the examination if you do so.

If you do 'document' your judgements in some way, your **refinements** should be self-evident in your work.

What should become apparent to you from an analysis of this nature is that *you* need to read and understand the syllabus you are using. It is no use leaving it all to your teacher, or to this book. You must help yourself to gain the fullest understanding possible. To help you to do this, by *acquiring* a copy of the syllabus you are using, the names and addresses of the various Examining Groups are provided at the end of this chapter. When you obtain a copy of your syllabus, you will find that the sections of it entitled 'Assessment Objectives', 'Assessment Criteria', or 'Scheme of Assessment', will be most helpful in guiding you and helping you to answer many of the questions you might have.

If you can begin to understand enough to ask the 'right' questions, you will find that the answers come easily to hand. If you sit around waiting for somebody else to ask you the questions, or give you the answers, you will wait a long time, and risk getting nowhere in the end.

**DOMAINS IN
ART AND
DESIGN**

Some work has already gone on towards writing the **criteria-related** grades in Art and Design. The basis for this work in Art and Design, as in all subjects, evolves around the **DOMAINS** which are considered essential to worthwhile study of the subject. The idea behind the 'domains' is that your study in the subject should involve *you* in showing *your ability* in a number of *areas* of learning and creativity which it is *generally agreed* are covered by art and design education.

The domains currently envisaged for Art and Design include,

- **The Conceptual domain:**
  how you *form* your ideas, *make decisions* about them, and *develop* them;
- **The Productive domain:**
  the demonstration of your ability to *select*, *control* and *use* both the,
     formal elements of Art and Design,
  and the,
     technical aspects surrounding the *production* of forms and images used to express your ideas and decisions;
- **The Critical domain:**
  how you are able to *justify* your decisions in your own work;
  how you are able to *express* the insights you may have into the work of others;
  how you are able to *compare and relate* your own work with that of others.

These descriptions of each domain might be expressed in slightly different ways by various people, but they offer you a *generally agreed* interpretation of what is meant by each domain. It might be easier for you to understand them if the above interpretations are explained more fully.

THE CONCEPTUAL DOMAIN

The **conceptual domain** is concerned with *how you obtain* your ideas, your ability to *gather information* which will support and enrich them, and how you *choose* between them. This domain is also concerned with how you mould and develop your ideas in the light of the information you gather and the choices you make.

THE PRODUCTIVE DOMAIN

In the **productive domain** the *'formal elements'* means things such as line, shape, colour, light and dark, texture, and contrast. Their use might be explained by considering how you might show a sense of movement in a piece of work by means of a broken, or jagged line, or by repeating and overlapping a shape, or by contrasting warm and cool colours.

The *'technical aspects'* means your skills and technical abilities *and* your *technical knowledge*. This could mean that you not only *use* tools and materials in a sound and competent way, but that you know *which* tools and materials to choose in order to give form to your ideas in the way that you intended.

THE CRITICAL DOMAIN

Making decisions, i.e. choosing between alternatives which present themselves to you, can be seen to be *not enough* in Art and Design in the GCSE. The **critical domain** shows that you should be able to *justify* what it is you choose to do.

Sometimes this justification and its explanation will be contained in your *final result*, and will be entirely visual. At other times it will be contained in your *sketches*, which again are visual traces of your thoughts and decisions. Even so, you should not lose sight of the fact that in Art and Design part of the way in which you work involves you in a *dialogue* with your teachers. It will pay you to get to know the *vocabulary* associated with the subject and to learn how to use it. At the same time, at the age of 16+, more of your education will involve you in *writing* rather than drawing. As a consequence, you should be well able to *write down* important points from your Art and Design lessons, and to keep these notes as *traces* of your thoughts and decisions.

The above, more detailed explanation of the domains will show you that there are a number of *ways* in which you can show evidence of your involvement in all three areas of learning and creativity represented by the domains.

> ❝ In Art and Design the *Domains* help to give *shape* and *form* to your work. ❞

If you are careful to *record and save* everything that you think of and do, you will find that instead of having only a 'finished' piece of work to show for all your efforts in a particular study, you will have a number of other drawings and notes. These drawings and notes will, *with* your finished piece of work, demonstrate much better how you have worked in *all* the areas of learning and creativity, than would your finished piece of work alone.

At the same time, *not all* your work will be original, and your own. Some of it might well be in the form of collected information, gleaned from magazines and newspapers, copied from books, or obtained using examples from the History of Art and Design. Nevertheless, the way you have gone about choosing, finding and interpreting work and material of this nature will also be part of your *personal* response to a problem. This too can be saved, documented and presented when the time comes to be assessed.

---

8 ⟩ UNENDORSED AND ENDORSED CERTIFICATES

GCSE Art and Design provides you with the opportunity to take your certificate under either an **UNENDORSED** title, or one or more of five **ENDORSED** titles. The type of course and examination which covers a **broad** system of study, without specifying any particular area of Art and Design, is known as **'unendorsed'**. On the other hand, those courses of study and examination which *do* specify a **particular area**, are known as **'endorsed'**.

The five endorsed titles are:

- DRAWING AND PAINTING;
- GRAPHICS;
- PHOTOGRAPHY;
- TEXTILES;
- THREE-DIMENSIONAL STUDIES.

Table 1.3 gives an outline of what is likely to be included in each endorsed area of study. The table is adapted from details included in the Midland Examining Group (MEG) Art and Design examination syllabus. The points made do however apply to all the Examining Groups, although each might express them differently.

ENDORSED TITLE	DESCRIPTION
Drawing and painting	■ To involve activities such as, oil painting, water-colour, spray-gun, overlay, collage, frottage, mixed-media.
	■ Knowledge and skills may include, using drawings to observe, record, analyse, communicate, express, recognise, explore, develop – ideas.
	■ Applications might include, illustration, murals, stage-sets, portraiture, still life, landscape, etc.
Graphics	■ To involve activities such as, printing, lettering, computer graphics.
	■ Knowledge and skills may include, layout and presentation, depicting and interpreting graphic images, composing, etc.
	■ Applications might include, fine-art prints, packaging and display, presentation lettering, advertising design and layouts, technical graphics, experimental printmaking, film and video credits and graphics, heraldry signs, etc.
Photography	■ To involve activities such as, developing and printing, montage, toning, video, etc.
	■ Knowledge and skills may include, use of a camera, effects of light and exposure of film, selection of viewpoint, lighting and background, prints and enlargements, etc.
	■ Applications might include, photo-journalism, fashion, still life, portraiture, animation, micro – and macro – photography, etc.
Textiles	■ To involve activities such as, macrame, weaving, knitting, printing, tie-dye, embroidery, collage, applique, patchwork, etc.
	■ Knowledge and skills may include, use of pattern drafts, handling of materials, surface and textural qualities, structures, etc.
	■ Applications might include, textile design, tapestry, theatre, sculpture, puppetry, costume making, fashion and dress design, etc.
Three-dimensional Studies	■ To involve activities such as, modelling, carving, constructing, casting, throwing, etc.
	■ Knowledge and skills may include, modelling, carving, constructing, casting, throwing methods, vacuum-forming, surface and decoration treatments, composing, form in relation to function, etc.
	■ Applications might include, jewellery, sculpture, stage and theatre design, product design, etc.

Table 1.3 Possible contents of Endorsed Certificate courses of study

	LEAG	MEG	NEA	NISEC	SEG	WJEC	IGCSE
■ Specific syllabuses	No	No	Yes	*	Yes	No	**
■ Specific mark schemes	No	No	No	No	Yes	No	**

* NISEC do not have 'endorsed certificate titles' in their examination, but it is possible to study in areas which more or less coincide with any of the endorsed certificate titles.

** IGCSE do not have endorsed certificates in their examination.

Table 1.4 The Endorsed Certificates

SYLLABUSES AND MARK SCHEMES

The first thing that you must find out, in the case of the endorsed titles, is whether your published Art and Design examination syllabus includes *separate* syllabuses for *each* of the endorsed titles, as well as the syllabus for the unendorsed title. If it *does*, then does each separate syllabus have its own scheme of assessment? Table 1.4 will help you answer these questions.

DIFFERENCES BETWEEN 'UNENDORSED' AND 'ENDORSED' CERTIFICATES

In an **endorsed** certificate you will be expected to acquire a much *higher* level of skill and technical ability in the use of a *particular* material, and the tools and technology associated with it, than you would if you used the same things in an unendorsed course of study. You will then have to ask yourself if you are *capable* of this higher standard. Your teacher will help you to come to a decision of this kind.

MIXING UNENDORSED AND ENDORSED CERTIFICATES

In the same period of examination you **CANNOT** take an *unendorsed* certificate with one, or more, of the *endorsed* certificates, from the *same* Examining Group. You **CAN**, however, take *more than one* of the *endorsed* certificate titles from the same Examining Group in the same period of examination. But you will need *separate sets* of coursework for each title that you take. This will most probably mean that you will have to be taking Art and Design at least twice on *your* school time-table, otherwise you will not be able to produce the required, separate sets of coursework for each different title that you intend to take.

THE RELATIVE STATUS OF UNENDORSED AND ENDORSED CERTIFICATES

There is no difference in the *level* of qualification between an unendorsed certificate and an endorsed certificate. Both are of equal standing and have the same currency so far as the level of the qualification is concerned. So do not start to read 'hidden', but not present, meanings into the two words, unendorsed and endorsed.

Your choice as to which *type of certificate*, and, in the case of the endorsed certificates, which *title* you take, is dependent upon:

- the opportunities which exist in your school;
- your interests and abilities;
- your future ambitions.

One of the reasons why you might choose to take one or more endorsed titles, might be because of your *future intentions*. For instance, it might be that you intend to leave school at the end of your examinations at the age of 16+. You might know that you are likely to start work in either a Photographic Shop or a Boutique. In circumstances such as these, it could be to your advantage to take either an *endorsed* certificate entitled *Photography*, or one entitled *Textiles*.

It is up to *you* to make your future intentions known to your *teachers*, and to discuss with them the best path for you to take. If they do not know of your intentions until it is too late, then they will be unable to help you to use the marvellous opportunities which exist in the GCSE to your fullest advantage.

MODES OF EXAMINATION

In the GCSE there is the opportunity for assessment to be by a variety of ways or 'modes'. In fact there are *three* modes of assessment, each differing in terms of:

- *who* sets the examination syllabus;

and

- *how* work is assessed.

Table 1.5 tells you more about each mode.

MODE	EXAMINATION SYLLABUS	ASSESSMENT
1	Set by GCSE Examining Group	Assessed externally by the GCSE Examining Group
2	Set by the school(s)	Assessed externally by the GCSE Examining Group which has approved the syllabus
3	Set by the school(s)	Assessed internally by the school(s) and then moderated by the GCSE Examining Group which has approved the syllabus

Table 1.5 Alternative modes of examination in the GCSE

9 ASSESSMENT In Chapter 2 we look more carefully at the *weighting* given to the two parts of the Art and Design assessment by each of the Examining Groups.

The 'two parts' of the assessment are:

- the coursework presented to the examiners;
- the externally set examination.

The 'externally set examination' consists of two parts (see Chapter 2),

- PREPARATORY STUDIES;
- CONTROLLED TEST.

TEACHER ASSESSORS

Your *teachers* also 'assess' your work.

In the first place, your teachers will probably assess your coursework *as it goes on*. This is sometimes referred to as **CONTINUOUS ASSESSMENT**. At the *end* of your coursework, your teachers will re-evaluate *all* your coursework and award it a final mark for the examination.

When you complete your work for the **externally set examination**, again your teachers will be involved in its assessment.

Both your coursework *and* your work for the externally set examination will be considered together, and your *teachers* will place you into a grade for the certificate, which they *recommend* to the examiner. The *examiner's* task is to survey the decisions made by your teachers about you, and every other candidate in your school.

The examiner will be looking to see if the marks your teachers have awarded you for your work contain any bias. Bias might be in your favour, or against you. It is usual for the examiner to do this by comparing the marks *you* have been awarded against those awarded for the work of *other* candidates in your school. The examiner will be trying to see that *similar work* has been awarded *similar grades*.

If the examiner is *not* satisfied in respect of you, or any other individual candidates in your school, then your teachers will be asked to agree to an *amendment* of your mark and grade.

The second, and most important task that the examiner has, is to judge if the same quality of work in *your school* gets the *same grade* as the same quality of work in *another school*. The examiner knows the 'National Standard' for the examination and is trying to get the work of your school in line with that. This process is known as **MODERATION**, and it is a vital function of the examiner, along with 'assessing' the work of individual candidates during a visit to a school.

Assessment and moderation in Art and Design can go on *in* your school, or your teachers can elect to send the work of your school's candidates *away* for the same purpose. In either event, your *teachers* will mark your work *first*, as described above. If your work is seen by an examiner in your school, then you will probably be asked to display your work in a small exhibition.

We have now described the *process* of assessment. What is more important to you, and your result in the examination, is how *you* gain access to the whole range of marks available for your work. To understand this, you need to *know* and *understand* the:

- ASSESSMENT AIMS AND OBJECTIVES;
and the
- ASSESSMENT CRITERIA,

which are contained in your syllabus.

AIMS

You will find in your syllabus, first of all, the **AIMS** of the course. It is hoped that these aims will be met as a result of following the syllabus. Aims are therefore 'good intentions', but it is generally understood that they might *not* end up as tangible qualities which you and every other candidate might display.

ASSESSMENT OBJECTIVES

On the other hand, the **ASSESSMENT OBJECTIVES** are qualities that it is necessary for you to both *work towards* and to *display* in your work in the examination. Of course, not every candidate will reach the same level of achievement in these assessment objectives. This is why different grades result from the examination. What is important from your point of view is that you know fully what is *expected* of you, and that you make sure that you *display clearly* in your work how well you have worked towards each of the assessment objectives.

For instance, all the Art and Design examination syllabuses available require that you should show your ability to '*record from direct experience*'. At its baldest this means that you should show that you are able to make a *representational drawing from a portion of the three-dimensional world in front of you*. If you did *not* know that this is required of you, it would be very easy to do only 'imaginative' work, where you 'make everything up'. It should now be clear to you that you must do *some* drawing from *direct observation*, no matter where your interests might lie.

You should note that the examination syllabuses rarely place any emphasis on the various assessment objectives. That is to say, they do *not* state that one particular assessment objective is considered *more important* than another, and is consequently a means to *more of the marks available* in your examination.

In fact, the tendency for all the syllabuses is to state that *you* should 'weight' the assessment objectives, according to the intentions and purpose contained within *your* work. This means that in *some* of your work you will be dealing with a *particular selection* of the assessment objectives, and in other work you will be dealing with a *different selection*. Your teacher will probably control this aspect of your work, but *you* should know what is at stake at any time.

What is important is that you should ensure that your work contains within it *evidence* that you have attended to *all* the assessment objectives *at some time or another*. You must show that you have *developed* your performance in these to the best of your ability.

ASSESSMENT CRITERIA

In your syllabus, the **ASSESSMENT CRITERIA** spells out *how* your level of achievement towards any of the assessment objectives will be rewarded in terms of contributing towards the ultimate grade you receive for the examination. By studying the assessment criteria you can see how, and in what ways, you can improve your level of performance, and thus gain a higher grade in the examination.

Remember, in order to get the best possible reward for your work it is necessary to:

- *know* what the examination is *looking for*;
- make certain that you have covered *all aspects* of everything that is required of you;
- *develop* to the best of your ability those things which are required of you;
- *present* your work so that it is *evident* where, and how, you have covered those requirements.

The assessment objectives and the assessment criteria of *your* syllabus will help you meet each of these requirements.

DIFFERENTIATION BY OUTCOME

It has been said already that the GCSE covers an extremely wide ability range. Setting a single examination to cover this wide range of abilities is a difficult task. Each subject has tackled the problem in its own way, often by building 'hurdles' into the examination. A *hurdle* is a cut-off point in an examination representing a set standard of performance. If you *do not reach* that standard in your work, then you *cannot proceed* any further, that is to say, to the *higher grades* in the examination. There are *no* hurdles in Art and Design in the GCSE.

In Art and Design the method used to distinguish between levels of performance is known as **Differentiation by Outcome**. This does not represent a 'hurdle'. Differentiation by outcome means that *all* the candidates taking the examination at any one time receive the *same set of questions*. Each candidate can choose to answer whatever question they wish, subject to it being part of their examination.

In the GCSE, the fact that every candidate can choose to tackle any of the questions in Art and Design, is described as responding to *Neutral Stimulus*. With differentiation by outcome it is the *quality* of what it is you do, rather than *which level of question* you are allowed to tackle, which determines the level of your result.

Assessment Objectives and *Assessment Criteria* explain how *good grades* may be obtained.

10	**EXTERNAL CANDIDATES**

All that has been explained so far applies to those of you in *full-time education*, where you are following a taught and organised course of study, usually of two years' duration. This will usually mean that you are attending either a Secondary School, or a Further Education Institution, or perhaps Adult Evening Classes.

Provided you have satisfied your teachers, your *entry* for the examination will be automatic in most cases. However, if you do attend Adult Evening Classes, you should enquire whether your entry for the examination is automatic, or whether you need to enter for the examination as an External Candidate.

EXAMINING GROUP	COURSEWORK?	EXAMINATION DETAILS FOR EXTERNAL CANDIDATES	INFORMATION AVAILABLE
LONDON and EAST ANGLIAN GROUP	No	Candidates receive a 'candidates' paper' which specifies two themes. Both themes must be responded to during the period of the externally set examination, and in the same time given to full-time candidates to respond to one theme only.	In a separate examination syllabus from the Examining Group
MIDLAND EXAMINING GROUP	No	Candidates receive a list of 'Starting Points', with instructions on how to proceed in the examination	In the Examining Group's Art and Design examination syllabus
NORTHERN EXAMINING ASSOCIATION	Yes	You must give the Examining Group a brief outline of the course of study you intend, for their approval. The work intended must be equivalent in quantity to that from a two year course of study in full-time education. In addition, candidates must comply with the Group's requirements for their externally set examination.	In the Examining Group's Art and Design examination syllabus
NORTHERN IRELAND SCHOOLS EXAMINATION COUNCIL	Yes	Coursework will be validated by an appointee of the Group. Otherwise, candidates must comply with the arrangements for the Group's externally set examination.	From the Examining Group
WELSH JOINT EDUCATION COMMITTEE	No	Candidates will take two externally set controlled tests	In the Examining Group's Art and Design examination syllabus
INTERNATIONAL GCSE	Yes	Candidates will follow exactly the same arrangements as for the full-time candidates	In the Examining Group's Art and Design examination syllabus

Table 1.6 Details of provision for external candidates in the GCSE

APPLYING FOR ENTRY

To make an application as an external candidate you need to:

- get the name, location, and full address of an accepted EXAMINATION CENTRE from the Examining Group whose syllabus and examination you wish to take;
- contact that Examination Centre and check that you can take the examination with them and under their supervision;
- complete and send in all the necessary ENTRY FORMS for the examination, which will usually be provided for you by the Examining Group in question;
- pay the fees when, and as, instructed;
- note when, and how, you will receive your copy of the EXAMINATION PAPER for the examination.

When you contact the Examination Centre, check that they have the facilities for you to take the examination in the way you intend. For instance, it would be silly for you to register with an Examination Centre which has *no darkroom facilities*, if you knew that you would be using *creative photography* in your examination. You should also check if you will have to supply your *own* materials for your examination, or whether the Examination Centre, or the Examining Group will supply you with materials.

If you are an external candidate, each Examining Group has its own way of dealing with the *coursework* aspect of your examination. Because it is difficult to guarantee that the work you might submit as your coursework is genuinely your own, some Examining Groups have *alternatives* to coursework in their examination. If you find it difficult to consider producing the required quantity of coursework for the examination, this might guide your selection of Examining Group. But remember, if you choose a syllabus from an Examining Group not in your geographical region, you might find it impossible to find a local Examination Centre which would allow you to *take* that Examining Group's syllabus. It might mean you have to travel many miles to an Examination Centre in another part of the country.

Table 1.6 explains the situation with regard to how each Examining Group deals with the question of *coursework* and gives you a breakdown of their arrangements for external candidates. Again, this table cannot replace the information contained in the syllabus available from each Examining Group at a small cost.

EXAMINING GROUPS

Between them, the Examining *Groups* cover the whole of England, Northern Ireland and Wales. In addition, the International GCSE (IGCSE) caters for Overseas Candidates. Each Examining Group contains within it a number of Examining *Boards* which have been grouped together largely on the basis of their geographical location. These Examining Boards used to administer the GCE O level and the CSE examinations. They still operate under their original names within the new Examining Groups. The original Examining Boards are sometimes referred to as the 'Parent Boards' within an Examining Group.

To know the name and address of the Parent Boards can be important to you, should you need to contact the Examining Group direct. The Examining Board *nearest your own geographical location* is known as your 'Home Board'. If you are in any doubt as to whom to contact in an Examining Group, this *Home Board* will be nearest to hand to answer your enquiries.

The Examining Board within an Examining Group which actually *takes the responsibility for the administration of a particular subject syllabus* is known as the '**Servicing Board**'. This is the Examining Board you *should contact* if you have any query about *your examination*.

Different Parent Boards within an Examining Group have responsibility for different subject syllabuses in this way. Those marked with an asterisk in Table 1.7 are those known to be the *Servicing Board* for Art and Design in each case.

Remember that any Examining Group is an extremely busy organisation, particularly at the times surrounding the externally set examination. Your enquiries should be kept to a minimum, be precise, and preferably be in the form of a letter. A letter can be filed by an Examining Group and it is in your interests that this should be so if you need to show that you have done a particular thing. You will find that each Examining Group is at pains to help, and to explain all the requirements of their examination syllabuses.

Table 1.7 gives you the names and addresses relevant to each Examining Group, and identifies the *Servicing Board* within each Group.

■ **LONDON and EAST ANGLIAN GROUP (LEAG)**

EAST ANGLIAN EXAMINATIONS BOARD	'The Lindens' Lexden Road Colchester CO3 3RL
*LONDON REGIONAL EXAMINING BOARD	Lyon House 104 Wandsworth High Street London SW18 4LF
UNIVERSITY OF LONDON SCHOOL EXAMINATIONS BOARD	Stewart House 32 Russell Square London WC1B 5DN

■ **MIDLAND EXAMINING GROUP (MEG)**

EAST MIDLAND REGIONAL EXAMINING BOARD	Robins Wood House Robins Wood Road Aspley Nottingham NG8 3NR
OXFORD and CAMBRIDGE SCHOOL EXAMINATION BOARD	*Cambridge Office* 10 Trumpington Street Cambridge CB2 1QB *Oxford Office* Elsfield Way Oxford OX2 8EP
SOUTHERN UNIVERSITIES' JOINT BOARD for SCHOOL EXAMINATIONS	Cotham Road Bristol BS6 6DD
*THE WEST MIDLANDS EXAMINATIONS BOARD	Norfolk House Smallbrook Queensway Birmingham B5 4NJ
UNIVERSITY OF CAMBRIDGE LOCAL EXAMINATIONS SYNDICATE	Syndicate Buildings 1 Hills Road CB1 2EU

■ **NORTHERN EXAMINING ASSOCIATION (NEA)**

ASSOCIATED LANCASHIRE SCHOOLS EXAMINING BOARD	12 Harter Street Manchester M1 6HL
JOINT MATRICULATION BOARD	Manchester M15 6EU
* NORTH REGIONAL EXAMINATIONS BOARD	Wheatfield Road Westerhope Newcastle upon Tyne NE5 5JZ
NORTH WEST REGIONAL EXAMINATIONS BOARD	Orbit House Albert Street Eccles Manchester M30 0WL
YORKSHIRE and HUMBERSIDE REGIONAL EXAMINATIONS BOARDS	*Harrogate Office* 31–33 Springfield Avenue Harrogate HG1 2HW *Sheffield Office* Scarsdale House 136 Derbyshire Lane Sheffield S8 8SE

■ *NORTHERN IRELAND SCHOOLS EXAMINATIONS COUNCIL (NISEC)	Beechill House 42 Beechill Road Belfast BT8 4RS
■ SOUTHERN EXAMINING GROUP (SEG)	
*THE ASSOCIATED EXAMINING BOARD (AEB)	Wellington House Station Road Aldershot GU11 1BQ
THE OXFORD DELEGACY of LOCAL EXAMINATIONS (OLE)	Ewert Place Banbury Road Summertown Oxford OX2 7BZ
THE SOUTH-EAST REGIONAL EXAMINATIONS BOARD (SEREB)	Beloe House 2/10 Mount Ephraim Road Royal Tunbridge Wells TN1 1EU
THE SOUTHERN REGIONAL EXAMINATIONS BOARD (SREB)	Avondale House 33 Carlton Crescent Southampton SO9 4YL
THE SOUTH WESTERN EXAMINATIONS BOARD (SWExB)	23/29 Marsh Street Bristol BS1 4BP
■ *WELSH JOINT EDUCATION COMMITTEE (WJEC)	245 Western Avenue Cardiff CF5 2YX
■ INTERNATIONAL GENERAL CERTIFICATE OF SECONDARY EDUCATION (IGCSE)	
UNIVERSITY OF CAMBRIDGE LOCAL EXAMINATIONS SYNDICATE: INTERNATIONAL EXAMINATIONS	Syndicate Buildings 1 Hills Road Cambridge CB1 2EU United Kingdom

Table 1.7 Names and addresses of each Examining Board in the Examining Groups

* denotes *Servicing Board* within each Examining Group.

G L O S S A R Y   O F   T E R M S   U S E D

Continuous assessment	The term given to the practice of marking your work at times *throughout* your course.
Controlled test	That portion of the externally set examination in GCSE Art and Design which is carried out unaided and within a set number of hours.
Coursework	That evidence of study in Art and Design, practical and theoretical, visual and verbal, which is produced *during the course*. This work constitutes a large percentage of the final examination mark in GCSE Art and Design.
Criteria-related grades	The seven grades of pass in the GCSE Art and Design examination will, eventually, each have their own set standards of performance. These will, as far as possible, represent *absolute* levels of achievement.
Differentiation by outcome	All candidates will receive the *same* set of questions from any one Examining Group, and will be able to respond to *any* of them. The work that each candidate *produces* as their response will put them into their grade level for the examination. There will be no hurdles to overcome, nor will comparisons be made between candidates.
Domains	The areas of knowledge, learning, understanding and skill, thought appropriate to the worthwhile study of Art and Design.

Endorsed certificate	The certificate awarded in one of the five restricted areas of study in Art and Design which are approved by the SEC.
Externally set examination	That section of the GCSE which is conducted as an examination at the *end* of the course, and set by the Examining Group responsible.
Examiner	The person appointed by the Examining Group to monitor the mark and grade given to your work by your teachers, and to moderate that mark and grade if necessary.
Examining group	Regional groupings of existing Examining Boards. Each Examining *Group* is responsible for the GCSE in a *region* of the United Kingdom, with the exception of Scotland. The International GCSE is available for overseas candidates.
External candidate	A candidate unable to follow a taught course of study. Usually someone outside full-time education.
GCSE	The General Certificate of Secondary Education. First debated in 1984, courses began in 1986, with the first examinations held in 1988.
Grade descriptions	An *account* of the type of skills and ability considered to be appropriate to a *particular* level of achievement. Two or three such descriptions only are published in each syllabus. You can get an idea of other grades from these. Grade descriptions will disappear in Art and Design syllabuses once criteria-related grades are introduced.
Modes of examination	A description of the *type* of course and *means* by which it is assessed.
Moderation	The moving up, or down, of the marks awarded candidates by their teachers in order to *match* the *particular work* to the agreed *national* standards.
National criteria	Nationally set standards for Art and Design that your course and assessment must meet. These contain the general criteria, for all subjects, and the subject-specific criteria for each subject, here Art and Design.
Preparatory studies	Those *exploratory, investigative* and *developmental* studies which accompany any work in Art and Design. They include the visual forms and images, the written and verbal responses, as well as the thought processes involved in the production of Art and Design. They constitute part of the externally set examination but are also essential in course-work.
SEC	The Secondary Examinations Council. This body is in overall control of the GCSE and its examination.
Targeted candidature	The percentage of the school population, here at the age of 16+, for which an examination is designed. The GCSE in Art and Design is intended for *all* levels of ability.
Teachers	In the GCSE, teachers are those who both decide and control the course of study, and initially mark and grade a candidate's work.
Unendorsed certificate	The certificate awarded examination work from an unrestricted course of study.

BIBLIOGRAPHY

SEC (1985). *The General National Criteria*. HMSO.
SEC (1985). *The National Criteria for Art and Design*. HMSO.
The Various Examining Groups. Art and Design Examination Syllabuses.

ASSESSMENT IN ART AND DESIGN

GETTING STARTED

Your *overall* assessment has two elements:

COURSEWORK

That work done by you *during* your course of study. *What* you do, and *how* you do it, is a matter between you and your teachers, provided it satisfies the demands of the syllabus in question.

EXTERNALLY SET EXAMINATION

That work done by you in response to questions, starting points or any other stimulus *provided by the Examining Group* whose syllabus you are using.

The **externally set** examination is usually referred to as the **Controlled Test**, but remember that it has *two parts*;

- PREPARATORY STUDIES;

and

- CONTROLLED TEST.

In GCSE Art and Design your assessment begins with the first day of your course of study. Unless you work consistently *throughout* your course of study, you will jeopardise your chances of a high grade. Your coursework not only prepares you to cope with your externally set examination, it also accounts for a very large proportion of the marks you will get for your final grade. Therefore you cannot afford to slack at any time during your course of study.

ESSENTIAL PRINCIPLES

1 ⟩ WEIGHTING

Table 2.1 shows how the total marks are divided between your coursework and your externally set examination. You can see from this table that the Examining Groups consider your coursework to be *at least* as important as your externally set examination.

EXAMINATION GROUP	COURSEWORK	EXTERNALLY SET EXAMINATION (controlled test)
LEAG	33.3% (mimimum)	33.3% (minimum)
MEG	60%	40%
NEA	70%	30%
NISEC	50%	50%
SEG	60%	40%
WJEC	50%	50%

Table 2.1 The distribution of marks between coursework and the externally set examination

The national criteria for Art and Design state that coursework should constitute *no less than* 25% of the total marks for any examination. In reality, the various Examining Groups have given *much more* than the minimum 25% to coursework.

You will see that no Examining Group (we consider LEAG below) gives *less than* 50% of their marks to your coursework. Most give *more than* 50%.

Coursework is one of the means by which *diversity* is encouraged within the GCSE. Because your course of study *interprets* your examination syllabus, and *you*, like all your classmates, *interpret your course of study*, your coursework gives you an opportunity to show your *independence* and *originality*.

In the case of Art and Design, coursework has *always* helped students to develop the practical and creative skills necessary to do original art and design work at the time of the examination. But for the most part this coursework was *hidden* from the examiner. With the GCSE, however, coursework is now *itself* an important part of the overall assessment.

The LEAG syllabus is unusual in that it does not give either the coursework, or the externally set examination, any *particular* weighting in the overall mark. It does however state that each should be worth *at least* one-third of the total marks available. The difference between LEAG and the other Examining Groups is that LEAG assesses your work *as a whole* in order to arrive at your mark, whereas the other Examining Groups mark your coursework, and *then* your externally set examination. The two marks which result are *added together* to arrive at your total mark.

2 ⟩ SYLLABUS PHILOSOPHY

No matter which Art and Design examination syllabus you may be using, if you read it carefully, you will find that it has a 'philosophy' about Art and Design within it.

You can find this philosophy contained largely in the aims, the assessment objectives and the assessment criteria in the syllabus. It will not be that the syllabus states, 'this is our philosophy; and you should do this or that'. Instead it will contain references to the *way* in which you might work, and the *range of knowledge* you might show evidence of in your work.

Of course, your teachers will have sorted this out, in choosing a *particular* syllabus for your school; but *do not be content to leave it at that*. If *you* get hold of a copy of the syllabus and *read* it, *you* will get a better idea of the 'philosophy' behind your course. For instance, your syllabus might state somewhere that, 'you should be aware of the multi-cultural nature of the subject'. It is important that you *be aware* of this, and try to bring this out in your work. You will clearly gain credit for doing so.

❝❝ Study the *Philosophy* of your *Examination Syllabus.* ❞❞

MULTI-CULTURAL NATURE OF ART AND DESIGN

Imagine that you like drawing cats. You may copy them from photographs in books, but hopefully you will also sit and draw your own cat as it sleeps, plays, eats, and so on.

If you do do this, you will be likely to have a very promising project in your coursework for the GCSE. The only trouble is, it will not satisfy all the philosophy contained in the syllabus. To take account of the *multi-cultural* aspect of the philosophy of the syllabus, *provided you know it is there*, you will have to consider how cats, and drawings of them, have been treated in cultures other than your own.

Perhaps you are English, and you might have a classmate from, say, Pakistan. You could talk to that classmate, and exchange remarks about how cats are treated in your different cultures, even discover whether they *are* drawn or sculpted in both cultures. Or, you might have been on holiday in Wales, and realised that cats are an important aspect of Welsh culture. You might be lucky, and discover a book of cat drawings and sculptures which includes some done by, say, Chinese children or African children. If you do, it may become apparent to you that these children 'see' and draw cats in a *different way* to yourself. If they do, this is likely to be a *cultural* effect.

Your enquiries might lead you on to discover how cats have been an important part of various cultures. For instance, the Ancient Egyptians *revered* cats, and they feature strongly in their religious and cultural imagery. You could consider how cats have featured in some cultures as *evil* creatures, often associated with witches. There is no limit to what you might discover once you start on this pathway.

The important thing is that you should *start on it*, provided you know that the syllabus expects you to consider the multi-cultural nature of Art and Design. Making enquiries and following up leads of this nature should be an automatic part of your normal working habit during your course of study.

If it *is*, it will seriously affect your coursework, making *what* you do, and the *way* that you do it, tune with the *philosophy* of the syllabus you are using.

OTHER PHILOSOPHICAL ASPECTS

All the available examination syllabuses stress the importance of multi-cultural considerations in your Art and Design work. Other points also occur in each available syllabus. You should pay particular attention to them in your course of study. Some of them are:

- the historical, social and environmental contexts of Art and Design;
- the development of your critical and analytical faculties;
- economic factors in your work.

There are still others. Some will be common to all the available syllabuses; some will be confined to one of those syllabuses only. It is up to *you* to find out what these points of emphasis are in the syllabus *you* are using.

WHAT IS GCSE ART AND DESIGN?

It should be becoming apparent to you by now that Art and Design is about *much more* than drawing racing cars, or painting pictures of horses, or making pots, or printing textiles, and so on. In Art and Design for the GCSE, drawing, painting, making and printing is a means, not only to *produce* pictures, pots and curtains, but also to take into account these other considerations contained in the *philosophy* behind the examination syllabus you are using.

Art and Design is an excellent way of studying historical, cultural, sociological, and environmental aspects, and of developing your ability to make and justify rational decisions based upon the *evidence* to be gained from such aspects. *Coursework* in particular will give you the opportunity to investigate issues, gather evidence and make decisions and judgements.

3 COURSEWORK REQUIREMENTS

Each Examining Group insists that you do varying amounts of coursework for your assessment. If you do *not* do the required amount, you will not be awarded a certificate at the end of the day.

Table 2.2 shows you the quantity of coursework required of you by each Examining Group.

EXAMINATION GROUP	QUANTITY OF COURSEWORK
LEAG	5 Units (soon there will be no specification)
MEG	4 to 8 pieces
NEA	5 pieces (minimum)
NISEC	5 pieces
SEG	3 units*
WJEC	5 units

Table 2.2 Coursework requirements of each Examining Group

* The SEG use the term 'unit' in a very deliberate and specific way. In their terms a 'unit' should be composed of at least two 'elements' (see the SEG syllabus).

It is already clear that you are expected to include, in your coursework:

- preparatory studies;
- your finished piece(s) of work;
- a variety of considerations, such as the cultural, the historical, and so on.

You might get into a 'rhythm' of work for each piece of coursework. This might include the following stages:

- get the problem;
- do a pencil drawing, find a photograph, experiment with some colour, as part of your preparatory studies;
- try out two ideas, and select one;
- produce a final 'finished' piece of work;
- save the work: start again.

4 > PREPARATORY STUDIES

Every Art and Design examination syllabus refers to *Preparatory Studies*, even if they do not allocate a specific number of marks for them. Chapter 5 looks at preparatory studies in detail. They are the *background* studies that you conduct for a *given* period of time on the topics, and questions set for your controlled test. These preparatory studies are taken into account when your controlled test is marked, and contribute towards the final mark in your externally set examination. Of course we have already seen that the *activities* of investigation and the gathering of evidence are crucial to *most* aspects of *coursework* too. Therefore 'preparatory studies' should, in effect, be a feature of *all* your study, and not just the period before the controlled test.

EXAMINING GROUP	QUESTIONS ISSUED	CONTROLLED TEST DURATION
LEAG	10 – 20 school working days before the controlled test	10 hours
MEG	At least two weeks before the controlled test	10 hours
NEA	Four weeks before the controlled test	12 hours
NISEC	At least six weeks before the controlled test	Paper 1: 12 hours Paper 2: 3 hours
SEG	Six weeks from April 19 or the first appropriate date thereafter	18 hours

WJEC	14 days*	14 days**
IGCSE	2 weeks	3 to 6 hours

Table 2.3 Duration of both the preparatory studies and the controlled test

* Ten marks will be allocated to the preparatory studies work done during these fourteen days.

** Here, fourteen days means, not that you work the equivalent of fourteen days on your controlled test, but that you *finish* your controlled test *within* fourteen days, using the number of hours *necessary* to do so.

Towards the end of your course of study, you will be given the Examining Group's Art and Design *examination paper*. This will be handed out by your teachers. The actual date you will receive this will differ, according to which Examining Group's syllabus you are using. Table 2.3 shows you *when* each Examining Group usually gives out their *examination paper* in relation to the *Controlled Test*. From the moment these questions are issued, preparatory studies for the controlled test can begin.

5 > EXAMINATION PAPERS

The paper you receive for your externally set examination will not necessarily be called an 'examination paper'. Do not be worried by this. Each Examining Group has its own way of referring to the 'questions' that are set you at the time of the externally set examination.

The only Examining Group which does *not* set an examination paper is the NEA. In this examination you, or your teachers, submit your proposed 'STARTING POINT' to the NEA during your course. When this *starting point* is approved by the NEA, it becomes the 'question' you use in the externally controlled part of your examination.

6 > WORKING TIME IN YOUR PREPARATORY STUDIES

The actual date of your controlled test will be later than the date you receive your 'examination paper'. The time *between* the two events is to allow you to *investigate* the problem *behind* the question you wish to answer, and to *gather together* some *reference material*, as well as the *materials you wish to work in*. In other words, to conduct your *preparatory studies* during this period.

In the case of preparatory studies for your externally set examination, you will have to:

- *select* the question you wish to answer;
- *investigate* the problem which confronts you, not forgetting to *follow-up* on any cultural, historical, sociological, and other aspects you decide are relevant;
- make certain that you have the *technical ability* to carry out your ideas, and that your school has the *technical means* for you to carry them out;
- *collect together*, and *organise*, the tools and materials you will require for your work.

As you have seen from Table 2.3, you have only a short amount of time in which to do all these things. This is why it is so necessary for you to develop a sound and comprehensive *working habit* during your course of study. If you *have* done that, in other words practised the activities involved in preparatory studies for the controlled test *throughout your course*, you will find it easier now.

7 > WORKING TIME IN YOUR CONTROLLED TEST

In the same way as each Examining Board has its own time allocation for your preparatory studies in the externally set examination, so they have their own amounts of time for their own controlled test. These varying amounts of time were shown in Table 2.3. During your preparatory studies you must *plan* your work pattern for the controlled test.

If you are allowed ten hours for your controlled test, plan your work for the controlled test so that you use *all* of the ten hours available to you. This does not, however, mean that you should plan to work at a rate which will spread your work out over ten hours!

What then, is significant about a controlled test?

One of the clues lies in the fact that a controlled test is sometimes popularly described as **'unaided work'**. In the national criteria for Art and Design, the description of the controlled test reads,

Controlled Test
A test in which candidates are able to show their ability to work *independently*. The unaided work should also demonstrate the candidate's ability to *work to a brief within a specified time limit*. One form might be a written examination. Where the controlled test is practical work, *preparatory studies must be included* where appropriate.

So, it becomes apparent that it is *not the amount of time* that you spend on your controlled test which is most important, but that you should:

- show your ability to work *independently*, or, *unaided*;
- respond to the stimulus of the question within a *specified amount of time*, but using that time to the full.

It should now be clear to you that it is not 'finishing' your work, alone, which is at stake. More important is that you should show that you can *organise* your activity *yourself*, so that you can fit *your* intentions into the time allowed for the activity. This will, of course, include *finishing* your work within the specified time limit.

If you finish your work in half the time allowed you, you will *not* gain more marks for 'saving time'. The likelihood is, knowing how long you were allowed for your controlled test, that your teachers and the examiner will feel that you did not manage to do much in the time allowed. This could mean that you will lose marks.

The differences in time given to their controlled test by each Examining Group really indicates that Art and Design is an 'open-ended' activity and situation. Each Examining Board is allowing you the time which *they* think appropriate for *their* examination, for *that* age-group.

The logic of this is contained in the fact that, for GCE A level, you are likely to get around *eighteen hours* for your examination piece of work. Here, the Examining Boards concerned are really saying that they consider around eighteen hours is the appropriate amount of time for candidates to display their abilities to the full at the age of 18+. In turn, if you proceed to an Art College, you are likely to get the equivalent of about a *week* to carry out your examination work.

QUANTITIES OF WORK IN THE CONTROLLED TEST

There is nothing that says you should do *only one* piece of work in your controlled test. Or, that once you have finished what you consider to be the piece of work you planned to do in the controlled test, you should pack up and go home. You can choose to do *as many* pieces of work as you like in the controlled test. If you finish what you intended to do, and there is time left, you *can* do more pieces of work to add to your examination.

PLANNING FOR YOUR CONTROLLED TEST

First of all, DO NOT HAVE A 'DUMMY RUN' AT YOUR WORK FOR THE CONTROLLED TEST BEFOREHAND. Long experience has shown teachers and examiners alike that candidates who, for example, paint their picture in full *before* their actual examination, and then go into the examination and try to *repeat* it all again, tend to end up with work which looks stale and unexciting.

Instead of this, try to get yourself into a position immediately before your controlled test where you are 'just bursting' to get on and carry out your final pieces of work for the *first* time. You have enough to do in your preparatory studies, if you are a sensible candidate, *without* wasting time having a *dummy run* at what you intend to do in your controlled test.

Plan your Controlled Test so that it is a *continuation* of your Preparatory Studies.

Do not forget to sort out *which materials* you will need for your controlled test, *and get them together and ready to use before your test starts*. If you need special facilities to carry out your work, such as using a darkroom, remember to tell your teachers of this, and to book *your* use of it during your controlled test. You must then of course make sure that you *plan* your schedule of work during your controlled test, and keep to it, so that you are ready to use the darkroom *when* you have it booked.

In later chapters in this book, you will be taken through sets of preparatory studies, and their accompanying controlled tests, in much more detail and with actual examples. For now, you should be clear what both these parts of the externally set examination demand of you, as well as how you should plan to deal with them.

SUMMARY

Table 2.4 provides a summary of many of the aspects of assessment considered in Chapters 1 and 2.

You should of course gain access to the syllabus of your *own* Examination Group to find out still more about the nature of your assessment.

	LEAG	MEG	NEA	NISEC	SEG	WJEC	IGCSE
WEIGHTING (% OF TOTAL MARK)							
COURSE WORK							
70%			+				
60%		+			+		
50%				+		+	
No weighting	+						+
EXTERNALLY SET EXAMINATION							
50%				+		+	
40%		+			+		
30%			+				
No weighting	+						+
COURSEWORK REQUIREMENTS							
4–8 pieces		+					
5 pieces			+	+			
3 units					+		+
No specification	+						
EXTERNALLY SET EXAMINATION							
PREPARATORY STUDIES TIME ALLOCATION							
6 weeks				+	+		
4 weeks	+		+				
2 weeks		+				+	
CONTROLLED TEST TIME ALLOCATION							
18 hours					+		
12 hours			+	+			
10 hours	+	+					
6 hours							+
3 hours				+			
Other						+	
SYLLABUS TITLES OFFERED							
UNENDORSED: Art and Design	+	+	+		+	+	
ENDORSED: Drawing and Painting	+	+	+		+	+	
ENDORSED: Graphics	+	+	+		+	+	
ENDORSED: Textiles	+	+	+		+	+	
ENDORSED: Three-Dimensional Studies	+	+	+		+	+	
ENDORSED: Photography	+	+	+		+	+	
ALTERNATIVE ARRANGEMENTS				+			+
EXTERNAL CANDIDATES							
INFORMATION							
In Main Art and Design Syllabus		+				+	
In separate Documents	+			+	*		
REQUIREMENTS							
Coursework			+	+			
Single Controlled Test			+				
Two Controlled Tests	+	+			+	+	

Table 2.4 Assessment in GCSE Art and Design

* SEG have not as yet published their arrangements for External Candidates.

GLOSSARY OF TERMS USED

Cultural
The meanings and values which are attached to objects and events according to the values and beliefs held by nations, creeds or civilisations.

Economic factors
In Art and Design, perhaps the 'costing out' of a piece of work, whereby you 'price' time and materials.

Environmental considerations
A study of the effect upon the environment of design decisions. The 'environment' could be very local, rather than general, just as the clothes you wear are an environment local to your body.

Examination paper
The means used by each individual Examining Group to inform you of your choices in your externally set examination.

Externally set examination
A term used in this book to illustrate to you that part of your examination which is set and controlled by your Examining Group. It includes the controlled test and the preparatory studies done prior to it.

Formula
A system, or set of principles, for carrying out a task, which arise out of habit, rather than the analysed need of the moment.

Historical
The references you might make to the products and the accepted meanings of the past, which help you to understand and support what it is that you are doing at the present.

Independence
In GCSE Art and Design 'independence' means developing the means to act and to make decisions *without the support of others*.

Justify (decisions)
Developing the habit of 'explaining' and offering *evidence* in support of your decisions.

Originality
Originality does not necessarily mean 'unique'. That is to say, what you do might well have been done before, but you are doing it in a fresh, personal way, or putting it into a new context or situation.

Philosophy
Simply, the beliefs which are apparently present in the examination syllabus you are using. Such 'beliefs' are usually partially hidden in sections of the syllabus, such as the aims, the assessment objectives and the assessment criteria.

Rational decisions
Those decisions you make, and actions you take, which you are able to justify.

Sociological
The information you find which is explained by reference to the *behaviour* and *customs* of the society from which it originates.

Time limit
A stipulation which has no absolute or natural sense of 'correctness' about it in the case of Art and Design. It is a stipulation decided by each Examining Group, reflecting the amount of time thought to be suitable for *their* controlled test.

Units (coursework)
A complete 'study' in Art and Design. For instance, all the preparatory studies, and the final piece(s) of work in the study.

Weighting
The *proportion* of the whole marks available for the examination *given to one part* of that examination.

3

CONTEXTUAL STUDIES

GETTING STARTED

If you have been following this book closely so far, you will be fully aware by now that there is more to GCSE Art and Design than just painting pictures, doing drawings, throwing pots, constructing sculptures, designing posters, and so on. This 'something more' is usually called **Contextual Studies**. Contextual studies are *all* that you think about, look at, remember, find out, and connect with what you are doing in order to produce your work. In GCSE Art and Design you are asked to *record* your thoughts in some way, and *save all the material* you gather in support of your work.

Of course when you *do* paint a picture, make a pot, and so on, you *do* *record* your thoughts in one way. Your painting, or your pot, is a *record* of the *outcome* of your thoughts and the influences of the material you gathered to help you to produce your 'work'. But GCSE Art and Design is just as interested in the *process* by which you arrived at your finished product.

E S S E N T I A L   P R I N C I P L E S

Whatever it is you *actually do* is *'contextual'* to your work. It is probably easier to understand what constitutes contextual studies by listing some headings which help to 'categorise' the things you might do in creating your work.

1 ⟩ CONTEXTUAL STUDIES: TERMS

The *terms* which give rise to these 'categories' are presented in Table 3.1. These terms have been drawn from the various GCSE Art and Design examination syllabuses. Each term is accompanied with a brief description of its meaning. These descriptions are for the purposes of this book. The descriptions do not exist in the various examination syllabuses.

By creating such a list you are made conscious of *all that you could do* in order to be regarded as conducting high quality *contextual studies* as a basis for your finished item.

AESTHETIC	judgements, values, qualities	Art and design decisions and their outcomes in relation to *widely agreed standards* in art and design
ANALYSIS		Making *judgements* upon the *study*, *research* and *outcomes*, in art and design
CONTEXT(S)		The fullest variety of connected and surrounding circumstances associated with a situation or problem
CRITICAL	awareness, appraisal, evaluation, vocabulary	Being able to arrive at *informed opinions* and *make decisions* about matters according to the amount of *evidence* available
CROSS-CURRICULA		Points of reference which *link* the knowledge and activities of *one subject* with the knowledge and activities of *another subject* in the school time-table
CULTURE(S)		The widely held beliefs and practices common to a *particular* society or nation. Thus an 'alien' or 'alternative' culture is a culture other than one's own
CULTURAL		The state of intellectual, artistic and social development of a group, i.e. what a group produces and treasures as its aesthetic level of expression
ECONOMIC ECONOMY		Associated with the art of careful management of resources. Often to do with producing something at least cost
ENVIRONMENTAL ENVIRONMENTS		The surroundings in which one exists; could be a *general* environment, such as one's country, or a *local* environment, such as one's town or home. Might even refer to one's clothing!
EVALUATION		Give a *reasoned account* of something; often leads to placing items in some *order of priority*
HISTORICAL		The use of *past* events and opinions to throw light on *current* circumstances.
MORAL – ETHICAL		Related to the *rightness* or *wrongness* of human behaviour; often associated with a sense of justice
RECORD		To *retain* and *document* the study, research, and outcomes in art and design
RESEARCH		To *investigate* an event, situation, subject or problem

SELECT	Choose *which* method or outcome to concentrate on, out of a range of possibilities in art and design
SKILLS KNOWLEDGE	Knowing *how* to do something, *why* to adopt that method, and being *proficient* at using it
SOCIAL	The rules, standards, beliefs and values which exist within a society and their resulting *behaviour pattern*
SOCIETY	A *co-operative group* who share the *same* rules and standards
SUBJECT KNOWLEDGE	The facts and ways of knowing which are usually associated with a *particular subject*, such as English, Science, Mathematics, art and design, and so on
UNDERSTANDING	Knowing 'why' and 'how', rather than simply 'what'
VERBAL COMMUNICATION	The *written* or *spoken* content of art and design studies; an important aspect of the GCSE

Table 3.1 References to contextual studies in the various Art and Design examination syllabuses

2 > CONTEXTUAL STUDIES: CATEGORIES

A number of useful *headings* or *categories* can be drawn from these terms:

- Productive Skills and Knowledge;
- Historical Research Skills and Knowledge;
- Cultural Awareness and Knowledge;
- Analytical Skills;
- Critical Awareness.

What do they each mean?

Before they are explained it is vital that you understand and accept that, although they are presented in this list as *separate* areas of skills, knowledge and activities, when working in Art and Design they are *all interdependent* and occur in a thoroughly mixed-up sequence. Your task in the GCSE is to work *naturally*, using and mixing the categories above in the way that professional artists and designers do, but at the same time being conscious of *when* and *how* you are using the various categories.

Of course, unlike the professional artist and designer, you are being *assessed* in GCSE on your method of working. So *you* have to work out your own way of recording and presenting to your teachers and your examiner *evidence* of all that you have done in your work. The simple example given below uses James Watt's Cabinet Steam Engine as a starting point, and from this *begins* to develop some contextual studies.

POWER

Fig. 3.1 James Watt's 'Cabinet' Steam Engine. This, and many other machines, are on display in the Science Museum, London.

Modern machinery is rarely seen in such a raw and powerful state as this. With the age of the micro-chip, everything seems to be boxed in bland cabinets made from some type of plastics material.

The *Industrial Revolution*, which came about through inventions such as Watt's, gave birth to one of the most powerful and energetic outbursts of invention that the world has ever experienced. It is astounding to consider the vast changes brought about by it.

Before the Industrial Revolution the world was largely an 'Agrarian Society', that is to say, societies survived and made their wealth by working the land. After the Industrial Revolution a large portion of that world had become an 'Industrial Society' and remains so today.

Arguably, not even the period of High Renaissance in Italy in the sixteenth century, or the splitting of the atom in the middle of the twentieth century, or the exploration of space in recent years, has had so 'global' an effect as the Industrial Revolution!

What do you think?

You could conduct an experiment to test this theory of the importance of the Industrial Revolution. Try making a *picture* of all the things and events which *you* think are 'powerful' and which have, or might, 'change the world'.

You might write down *your* definition of the term 'Power', and then ask your classmates and others to *judge your pictures* from the 'most powerful' to the 'least powerful', using the definition you have written. This would be a form of 'test' about opinions as to some of the most effective past and present things and events.

It could be interesting to ask each of your classmates to write *their own definition* of the term 'Power', and then to place *your pictures* in an order from 'most' to 'least' powerful, using these alternative definitions.

Doing things like this gives your work a 'context'.

3 > PRODUCTIVE SKILLS AND KNOWLEDGE

Productive skills might be simply described as 'making and doing'. Productive skills should be as 'contextual' as any other skills in Art and Design.

Of course, you might have acquired a number of skills in your earlier years at school. This is highly desirable and all to the good. In the GCSE, however, you have two years only in which to learn and develop your skills in this respect. If you think about the *actual* time in hours this will give you during your course of study for the GCSE, it will become apparent that you can only learn a *limited number* of skills in the time, let alone develop your ability in them to any depth.

If this is so, how do you decide, or how does someone decide for you, *which* skills come first? After all, a hierarchy of skills does not exist in Art and Design. For instance, nobody can say that you must *first* learn to draw in pencil, *then*, when you are proficient at that, you can graduate onto pen and ink, perhaps *ending up* with oil-paints. Instead, bearing in mind the limitations of time, it is probably better if you acquire the skills *relevant to the task* you have in mind.

This means that your *ideas* come first. For instance, you might wish to make a *sculpture* to represent, say, 'power'. After making some drawings and conducting some research into aspects of the meaning of the word 'power', you might well decide that *metal rods* and *pieces of old machinery*, such as cogs and pulleys, best convey one aspect of 'power', and that you want to *work with* such materials. Here you would have identified the *need* for a 'contextual' *skill*, which in this case might be *welding*.

The likelihood that all your classmates will need to learn how to weld is fairly remote. So teaching you and your classmates *how to weld* might be fairly low on your teacher's list of priorities. It will therefore be up to *you* to take the initiative in seeking out every opportunity to develop your skill in welding, since you have identified its importance to *your* work.

In the same way, if any of your classmates start to pick up a skill which is relevant to *their work only*, you should make sure that you *observe* what they do. Make notes if necessary, to help you remember what you have observed and learnt. *You* may need this skill *later* in the course! This process of observing, noting and remembering is called 'shared learning'.

If there are about twenty other students in your class, in addition to yourself, through 'shared learning' you can experience a *vast number* of skills, where these are taught and used on a contextual basis. In fact many more than if your teachers set out to teach *all* of you *every skill* which they thought it necessary for you to learn.

Of course, you, and each of your classmates, will not necessarily *practise* each skill which crops up in this 'contextual' way. But you will learn of its *existence* and be able to *plan* to use it in later work of your own, should the occasion arise.

By picking up in this contextual way those productive skills which *are* directly relevant to your work, you will have the opportunity to *actively use* these skills to analyse, interpret and communicate ideas. This will not only increase your *proficiency* in these skills, but also your *insight* into how they can be applied in different circumstances.

Developing these *contextual skills* means that you are gaining a deep, purposeful and useful *body of knowledge* about skills. Instead of just knowing *how* to do something, you know *what* you want to do and *why* you might choose to use the skill concerned.

4 ▷ HISTORICAL RESEARCH SKILLS AND KNOWLEDGE

If you want to *understand* what you are doing, instead of just 'doing it', then a major part of that understanding must come from the *history* of your subject. This does *not* mean that you should learn all the names and countries of origin of all the major artists and designers the world has ever known, and the dates they lived! If you were to try to do this, and began with Cave Painting, you would be lucky if, at the end of your GCSE course of study, you had reached as far as High Renaissance Italy in about the year 1500! Instead, it is better in GCSE Art and Design that you 'delve back into history' on the basis of what you are doing yourself.

Imagine that your teachers had taken you to a zoo, and that whilst there you had drawn and photographed some of the animals. If you had done so, you might have found it very difficult to draw a *moving* animal, as it paced up and down. Or you may have found it difficult to *represent* skin, fur, feathers, scales, and so on. Even using photography, you may have found it almost impossible to catch the animal in the *pose* which you thought best portrayed its essential qualities. If all this were so, then, when you got back home or to school, you could have set out to improve your own knowledge and ability by 'delving back into history'.

Your teachers could easily tell you that the German artist, **Albrecht Dürer (1471– 1528)**, drew animals, as did the Dutch artist, **Rembrandt van Rijn (1606 – 69)**. So also did the Spanish artist **Pablo Picasso (1881 – 1973)**. With this information to hand, you could begin to conduct your own 'historical research'.

A visit to a library might uncover pictures of the work of these artists. You might be struck by the *differences* in the way that each artist did what was apparently the same thing, such as represent fur. If this were so, you might recognise, through your productive skills knowledge, that the differences were due in part to the *different material* each artist had used to 'draw' their picture.

If you really knew about materials and their uses, you would be aware that each material exercises its *own control* on the way that your work 'looks'. For instance, a drawing done in soft pastel will 'look' different to one done in pencil, or pen and ink, no matter what its subject-matter is.

Historical research might uncover the fact that it was *impossible* for some artists to do a drawing like that of other artists because, during their lifetimes, the material the others used had not been invented.

You might start a *scrapbook of photographs* of animals. 'History' does not have to be 'old' or 'ancient'. If something exists, it is 'historical'. You might start your collection from Colour Supplement Magazines. This might create an interest whereby you go back into time to discover the photographic work of someone such as **Muybridge (1830 – 1904)**, who showed a horse galloping by means of a *series of still-photographs* taken rapidly, one after another.

Gombrich (1984) points out that prior to 'stopped-motion' photography, artists had *incorrectly* depicted horses galloping. When they discovered from stopped-motion photography *how* a horse's legs actually operated in a gallop and put this knowledge into their pictures, their work was strongly criticised as being 'incorrect'. Yet the popular view of 'correct' was itself the result of a mis-conception by artists in the first place! So artists had taught people how 'to see' and when 'reality' became known, it had to overcome the false perceptions created by earlier artists themselves.

Let us now consider an actual *comparative study* as a way of showing *how* historical skills and knowledge can help your contextual studies.

MAKING A COMPARATIVE STUDY

Dürer, Rembrandt and Picasso were suggested to you in this book (page 30) because reproductions of their work appear conveniently in the 'Introduction' in Gombrich, 1984. Gombrich's book is usually readily available in Public Libraries and is often present in either School or Art and Design Departmental Resource Centres. Even if it is not, it is published in paperback form and earlier editions of it, such as that published in 1972, are sometimes available at reduced prices in bookshops.

This book is a good 'reader' for you to use on your course of study. It offers you insights and in-roads to Art, Architecture and Design. It does *not* approach its subject-matter in a formal, matter-of-fact way, such as by concentrating on the dates of certain popular 'mile-stones' in the History of Art, Architecture and Design. Instead it tends to *group together* things and events in a way that comes about through a knowledge of their '**context**'. By this means Gombrich *explains* the work of artists, architects and designers. He shows us how their work both *reflects the age* in which they lived, and how it actually helped to *form that age* and our present-day judgement of it.

A 'reader' leads you *into* your subject, makes you *think*, and offers you *avenues* of further exploration which you might personally decide to follow up. Because of this, as you use Gombrich's book, you will need to follow up points in books which deal with areas, times, artists, architects, or designers in a much more specialised way. This is the value of a good 'reader' in your studies; they are not ends in themselves but help to further direct your studies.

Returning to Dürer, Rembrandt and Picasso, as they are represented in the Introduction to Gombrich's book, Dürer's picture of a hare is done in water colour. Gombrich remarks that the hare '*looks real*' and that this is a quality which many people look for in a work of art. It is, of course, *an* important consideration in making works of art, but it is not the *only* consideration.

Nevertheless, Dürer spent much time trying to make his picture of the hare 'look real'. It cannot be denied that the animal's fur *looks* 'furry', even though you *know* it is only water colour on paper.

Why should he choose to do this? It is no good saying that Dürer painted the way that he did because photography had not been invented and he was concerned to achieve a 'photographic likeness'.

You can see it is not the only way to work as an artist, or even the only way to create a sense of reality. If you study Rembrandt's drawing of an elephant in Gombrich you can see many differences between the way that it is done and the way that Dürer painted his hare.

Apart from the fact that Rembrandt drew his elephant in chalk, it looks 'sketchy' in comparison to Dürer's painting of the hare. Yet, Rembrandt's drawing still 'looks real' in one sense. The 'sketchiness' helps you to recognise that that *is* how an elephant's skin hangs, namely in wrinkly folds over its body. In this sense it is very 'real' as a drawing. Rembrandt was of course fully *capable* of working his drawings up to a similar finish as Dürer did in his picture of the hare. If you look further on in Gombrich you will find examples of Rembrandt doing just this.

Do you think that Rembrandt would have improved his drawing of the elephant if he *had* worked on it further in this way? Would this have improved the appearance of the way that an elephant's skin hangs, looks and 'feels', were you to go up and touch a real elephant?

It is interesting to note that because photography had not been invented in either Rembrandt's or Dürer's time, they faced no pressure to draw and paint in a 'photographic' way. Nor did any other artist working before photography existed. Why, then, did *some* artists work in such a 'photographic' way?

If you are now able to look at Picasso's illustration to Buffon's *Natural History*, a further aspect of appearance and reality appears to creep in. At first glance the work seems to be photographic, like Dürer's painting of a hare. But is it?

As Gombrich says, it certainly looks 'charming' and the chicks look 'fluffy', but do they look 'real' in the same way as Dürer's hare looks 'real', when you study both works more closely?

Picasso's work does not have the same level of 'preciseness' and 'reality' as does Dürer's work. Is the reason because photography *had now been invented*, when Picasso made this drawing?

One reason might be that Picasso's illustration was published in 1942. This was at a time which followed an extended period when, particularly in children's books, it was popular to make drawings of animals have a 'charming', a 'romantic' and even a 'sentimental' air about them. This was true of the Victorians and carried on into the 1930s at least.

Picasso was always keenly aware of the *cultural influences* which gave shape to the appearance of things. Maybe here he was perpetuating a popular form of illustration but elevating it to his own high standards of excellence?

What do you think?

A short historical and contextual study of this kind can show that:

- there are many ways of drawing and representing something;
- those ways are dictated partly by the medium you may use;
- they are also dictated by what it is you intend to do and what it is you wish to achieve;
- they are also influenced by the cultural and social values of the time in which they are made.

❝❝ Contextual Studies are vital to your own practical work and artistic ability. ❞❞

If, as was suggested in this case, you found it difficult to draw animals when you were at a zoo, a study of this kind might lead you to decide what medium you would use if you went back to the zoo. It might make it clear to you that it is very important that you *know* what it is you want to achieve, rather than just having a *vague impression* of what it is you want to do. This comes about by studying and understanding the *alternatives* which exist when you set out to do a drawing. Once you understand what the alternatives are, you can decide what *you* intend to do, and then set about doing it.

SOURCES OF INFORMATION

Learning the *skills* of historical research is learning to operate rather like a detective in a good thriller. You see something and are puzzled, or you recognise that something is missing in your knowledge relevant to your needs at that moment, and you start to investigate, *looking for clues*. As you grow more familiar with the method of historical research, you learn how to go more directly to the best, and most immediate sources of information.

The **sources of information** might be:

- your teachers;
- books;
- libraries, museums and art galleries;
- local newspaper archives;
- persons with particular, or local knowledge;
- your family, relatives and friends.

Let us take each of these sources in turn.

Your teachers

This does not mean your Art and Design teachers alone. It is possible to think of many occasions when your History teachers, or your Science teachers, or your Geography teachers, would be the best and most immediate sources of relevant information.

If you can work out *what* it is you want to know, or where to get information from, you will probably find that your **teachers** are interested in what you are doing and most helpful in helping you to do it. Most teachers would rather be 'asked' how to do a *particular* thing, or how to find something particular out, than to always have to speak in *general* terms to a class, regardless of each pupil's individual needs at that moment.

Books

Using a **book** for research purposes is an art. It does *not* require you to read the book from 'Page One', page by page, through to 'The End'. There are **methods** of using books as research documents:

Contents page: by looking at the contents page, you can find out what the author is *covering* in the book. The title to each chapter gives you a kind of 'précis' of what is dealt with by the author. If you look at the contents page of *this* book you will see what I mean.

Index: from the index you can tell quickly and effectively if the book contains material which is relevant to your needs. If you know some *specific* terms relevant to your field of study, you can check the index to see if they are there. If so, turn to each of the pages listed against the entry in the Index. For instance, you might be looking for some information on 'The Discovery of Oil Painting'. Turning to 'Oil Painting' in the index of your book, you might find:

Oil Painting
　　discovery of, 25

amongst other entries under the title 'Oil Painting'. This will mean that on page 25 of the book it will tell you something about the 'Discovery of Oil Painting '.

In this instance you go *straight* to page 25, and read what it says there. It might say, amongst other valuable things, that the 'van Eycks' are usually credited with the beginning of the use of oil as a painting medium. If so, you *then* look up 'van Eyck' in the index. Under that entry, page 25 will be present, but if there are *other pages mentioned*, you refer to *those* pages in turn. By this means, you will begin to read the *relevant* pieces of the book without wasting time on other issues covered by the author, interesting though they might be.

On the other hand, it might have no more than,

Oil Painting, 25, 55, 103

This means that on each of those pages listed, there will be *something* about Oil Painting.

In this second instance, you need to refer to *each page mentioned in turn*. By this means you will get led into various aspects of oil painting, and might discover, for instance, something about the 'van Eycks' as you go. Again, you will obtain the specific information you need as well as at the same time accumulating a more general knowledge about the subject you are pursuing.

Scanning: some books may *not* contain an index. If this is so, using the contents page as your way into specific parts of the book, you can 'scan' a chapter quickly. Each paragraph should start with what might be called a 'statement of intent'. The opening sentence in a paragraph most often tells you what will be 'opened out', argued, or explained in the *rest* of the paragraph. This is particularly so in well-written 'textbooks'.

Therefore, if you read the *first sentence* of every paragraph in a chapter, you will quickly gain knowledge of what is contained in the chapter and be able to decide if it is worth reading in detail in pursuit of your needs at that moment. *Using books in this way saves time, but does not diminish either the book, or your level of study.*

The thing to remember is that a reference book is *not* a novel. It is not *vital* that you read the book in the way that the author apparently intended you to. You *can* delve into the book at any place, in any sequence. You *can* leave the book, and return to it again, without regard to where you were in it the last time. Of course as you grow familiar with a book by this means, it could well be that you decide out of real interest to read it from beginning to end.

Whenever you *do* use a book, whether you quote from it directly or absorb the argument in it into your own argument, you *must* record and acknowledge the book, or books, you have used. *To do so is not a sign of weakness, or copying on your part, but a sign of mature investigation into a wide range of sources. This quality is looked for and rewarded in GCSE Art and Design.* You will be shown *how to document such references* in the next chapter.

Libraries, Museums and Art Galleries

Libraries: everybody will have access to a **Library** of some sort. This could be your Departmental Library in Art and Design, your School Library and Resources Centre, or your local Public Library, even if it is only a mobile one. *You must learn to use the opportunities offered by your library to the full.* Using a library, and any other form of *information centre*, is a vital life-skill and one which the study of Art and Design helps you to develop.

Bear in mind:

- Libraries are laid out in a manner which makes the information they contain quickly retrievable.

- This retrieval system is usually the 'Dewey System'. Each type of book is allocated and marked with a *number* which allows you to find the *subject* you are looking for.

- If you cannot find what you want, either in the filing or micro-fiche system used to record what the library holds, or on the shelves, there is usually a librarian to hand who will be pleased to help you.

- If the School or Public Library does not have what you want, it may well have access to a *much wider* collection of books. Check with the Librarian.

- Often it is best to look at *all* the books on a subject that are on the library shelves, rather than to concentrate only on the one you went for originally. By this means you might *discover* the unexpected, and achieve something unique in your work.

Museums and Art Galleries: you might be extremely fortunate, and live where it's easy to visit either a **Museum** or an **Art Gallery**. Sometimes you may have to travel some distance to one which holds the materials you are interested in.

Whatever the situation, you should *plan* your visit in advance so that you use the opportunity to the full:

- Go knowing *what* it is you want to find out about.
- Be alert to *other relevant things* which you may see when you are there.
- You may be able to see the *original* works which you wish to study. Then you may be able to buy a postcard or other representation of what you are studying.
- Again, the people in charge will be only too willing to help you to find the things you wish to see, and give you any other information you may need.
- When you are in the building, use your *notebook* to *make sketches* and *write notes*.
- When you get home, *write up your discoveries more fully*, incorporating your sketches, notes and any postcards you might have. But do *not* destroy *any* of the material you have gathered.

> 66 In GCSE Art and Design you must save and present everything you do during your studies. 99

Local Newspaper Archives

It is not always easy to gain access to your **local newspaper archives**, but your Public Library may keep copies of old editions of newspapers which you can use. It is usually easier to gain access to such archives if you can *identify clearly* what it is you want to find out. This will mean that you need to undertake some close and intelligent planning so that your request makes sense to the person in charge of the particular archive.

Do not be put off by this. Your local newspaper archives will undoubtedly contain some immensely interesting and valuable information on a number of subjects which you might be investigating and could well reward your perseverance in gaining access to it.

Persons with particular, or local, knowledge

A look through your local newspaper, a visit to your local library, or a word with your teachers could well unearth the fact that there is **someone** living in your area who has:

- *expert knowledge* on the subject of Art and Design, or the problem you are investigating;
- a deep and possibly wide-ranging knowledge of *local* matters.

If you can discover people such as these, provided they are not too busy and provided that your interest is obviously a keen and genuine one, they will often be willing to help you. The thing to remember is to be polite, be sensible, and be thankful – even if no help is actually forthcoming.

Your Family, Relatives and Friends

It is all too easy to *fail* to recognise just how much knowledge and experience exists *within* your immediate circle of family, relatives and friends. A *grandparent* will be able to tell you things which otherwise might exist only in history books, and will probably be able to produce fading photographs of the past. If you take a tape-recorder to talk to older persons you will gain a lot of information which can be followed up later on.

It may still be popular to think of your parents as 'squares' but, whether you like it or not, they could well be a source of unexpected knowledge and experience on matters which might well surprise you. In years to come, you would be offended if *your* children believed that *you* knew nothing about music, football, dancing or computers. In other words, everyone and everything is a source of potential knowledge and experience to you. Learn how to use this great source of possible information.

5 ▷ CULTURAL AWARENESS AND KNOWLEDGE

Culture is a difficult term to explain and define. This is because it has come to have a number of connections which warp and confuse its use. The biggest danger is that the word is used in a variety of ways without explanation, as if in each case it had the same meaning.

There is a strong tendency to mean 'highbrow', when the word culture is used. It is also usual to use the term 'sub-culture' when referring to the activities of a group which construct their own small cultural code within the more general culture of a particular society.

It will probably be best if you think of *culture* as meaning a group of people who can be *identified* by observing:

- the way in which they live and behave;
- the beliefs they hold;
- the objects and images they produce;
- the methods of communication they employ.

This means that *you* belong to a culture. That culture is part of the general society *you* live in. For instance, if you live in the United Kingdom, you are part of the general 'British' culture. How you live, what you believe in, the things that you own, the way you communicate, are all governed to some extent by the institutions and people around you, whether you like it or not. In other words, you are influenced to a greater or lesser extent by *British* culture.

At the same time, you may be part of a *sub-culture* within that general culture, such as a minority group living in the United Kingdom. For instance, the fact that you are in your mid-teens will inevitably mean that you will be part of one or more of the various 'Teenage' sub-cultures which exist. Your own interests or hobbies may bring you into contact with many other sub-cultures in Britain; Christian Youth, 'Bikers', Naturalists, Vegetarians, etc.

MULTI-CULTURAL

In the same way that you can see the differences between the *teenage* sub-culture and the *general* culture you live in, so you can identify differences between that general culture and the general cultures *of other nations*.

In Art and Design terms, you are likely to be aware of the various ('cultural') patterns and colours used on their blankets by individual North American Indian Tribes. You will probably recognise that both the patterns and the colours *differ* from those used traditionally in the United Kingdom.

Each Art and Design examination syllabus specifies that you should be aware of the *multi-cultural* nature of Art and Design. It is therefore vital that within *your* work, there is *some* content which shows an awareness *and understanding of this matter*.

This might mean that you:

- show your understanding of the *meaning* of words, forms, images and customs within your *own* culture, as well as within *other* cultures;
- show that you can recognise and understand ways in which different cultures *overlap*, as well as the *contrasts* and alternatives which exist;
- are able to *use* this knowledge and appreciation in your *own practical work*;
- can *critically evaluate* the things you observe and use in terms of their cultural significance.

6 ⟩ **ANALYTICAL SKILLS**

When you are sat in front of a landscape, or a still life, or a figure, making a drawing of what it is you can see, you are conducting an **analysis**. Therefore, you are using your 'analytical skills'.

You are conducting an analysis because you *cannot* hope to record everything you see in all its individual and fine detail; and anyway, you may not even want to.

If you look at '*Art and Photography*', by A. Scharf (1974), you will begin to see that the great artists of the world pass *judgements* upon the things they observe, make *selections* from the range of phenomena in front of them, and *re-arrange* things to suit their purpose and *aesthetic* values.

No matter what most people might believe and think about 'reality', so far as Art and Design is concerned, artists mostly depict 'what they *want* to see' at least as much as 'what they *actually* see'.

In '*Art and Photography*', Scharf has collected photographs of the *actual* scenes that an artist such as the Frenchman, **Paul Cézanne (1839 – 1906)** drew and painted. By putting the relevant reproduction of *Cézanne's work* against the *photograph* it is possible to see *how* the artist has 'analysed' what he saw and made a number of sophisticated changes in how he painted and represented it.

You might think that when you use a *camera* you are *not* selecting or making analytical abbreviations of what it is you see. But even by pointing the camera at 'A' and *not* at 'B', you *are* conducting an analysis. In turn, although *you* do not do it, the camera and the film within it themselves *condense* what is seen into a *limited range* of tones or colours which do not measure up to the range your eye can distinguish.

So you can see that you *do* use analytical skills in the most basic of Art and Design activities, and that what you are doing is in the best Art and Design traditions. This tradition means that in Art and Design, the *analysis* of subject-matter, forms, images, environments and ideas is *expressed visually* as much as verbally.

To the artist and designer it is natural to explore and to analyse a situation, a problem, or an idea through drawing, colour studies, photographs, models, and so on. It is also natural for them to refer to, and analyse, the work of others, and to use the *results* of previous exploration in their own work.

In Science, the results of one person's 'Research' is used most legitimately by another person interested in the same area of study. All that is needed is that the second person *acknowledges* that they have used the work of the former person. It would be considered unnecessary to spend time 're-inventing the wheel' each time work in a particular area of study went on.

Such principles can be properly adopted in *Art and Design*. Here, 'using the work of others' means that you should not only *refer* to the works of others, but also find a way of *showing* your teachers and the examiner how you have changed *your* activities or attitudes as a result of that work. This may mean that you will need to explain your reasons and decisions in *written* or *verbal* form.

Therefore, in *analysis* in Art and Design, visual *and* verbal communication about your actions is a necessary part of your studies.

DEFINITION

Analysis can be seen to involve certain **practices**. These are:

- observing;
- researching;
- thinking;
- discrimination;
- decision-making.

All of these things have material, or concrete, *outcomes* in Art and Design. In your GCSE examination your task and responsibility will be to make it clear:

- that they *have* occurred in your work;
- *what it is* you have done in this respect;
- *why you chose* to do it.

Observing

This might appear to need no discussion. To paraphrase that great analytical observer, Sherlock Holmes, many people *look*, but they do not *see*. *Observing* itself requires analytical skills if you *are* to 'see' what is before you, and to interpret and portray it in art and design form.

Researching

What has already been said about historical research will apply here. The only difference is in terms of scope and degree. You will not necessarily restrain yourself to *history alone* in order to understand the things you see and how you might portray them in Art and Design.

You will need to consider *cultural effects*. For instance, you might be struck by the difficulty of showing *water* in your work (see Fig. 3.2). This might lead you to consider how artists from cultures other than your own have portrayed water in Art and Design. For example, if you studied Japanese Art you would see a very different way of representing water in a picture to that used by a French artist such as **Claude Monet (1840 – 1926)**, who painted various pictures of the sea and water-lily ponds (see Plate 1; compare with Plate 2).

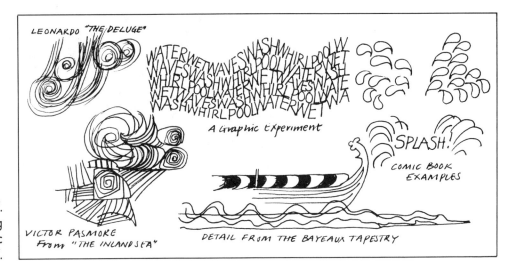

Fig. 3.2 Visual symbols for 'water'. Some ways of showing water, using appropriate visual 'symbolic language'.

Plate 1 Claude Monet, 'Bathers at La Grenouillère'. *Reproduced by courtesy of the Trustees, The National Gallery, London.* In this work Monet has shown water by apparently painting the effect of light upon the rippled surface of the river.

- You are 'researching' when you sit before your subject or work out your designs for a product. By careful study you are trying to *build up your knowledge* relevant to a particular problem.
- You are 'researching' when you learn about the *properties of materials* through their use in your practical work.
- You are 'researching' when you try to find a more *efficient use* of tools and equipment in your practical work.

You can see that the concept of 'research' in Art and Design is wide-ranging. 'Research skills' will be dealt with more fully in the following chapter.

Thinking

It is impossible to act without some kind of thought. Using the phrase 'some kind of thought' suggests immediately that there are different *sorts* of thought. Whatever these different 'sorts of thought' may be, in your Art and Design studies it is vital that you *make your thought processes known.*

- You must learn how to *pause* in your work and register clearly in your mind *what it is* that you have been thinking about.

Plate 2 Paul Cézanne, 'Le Lac d'Annecy'. *The Courtauld Institute Galleries, London.* In contrast, Cézanne shows water by painting the reflections of trees, bushes, houses and the landscape in its surface.

- You must find some way of *recording* your thoughts near the time that they happen.
- You must find some way of *explaining* your thoughts in terms of *how* they have affected your work and your decisions.

Only in this way can your teacher and examiner become *aware* of the reasoning behind your work. What this means is that you must provide *traces of your thoughts* in your work.

Now, this is not as difficult as it may seem. When you paint a picture, make a pot, or design a brooch, what you *actually do* in the practical sense *is* a trace of your thoughts. As was said at the beginning, you cannot act without 'some kind of thought'. Therefore in your *practical work* the *outcomes* of your thoughts *are* recorded. However, in GCSE Art and Design you improve your grade achievement if you can also find ways of showing:

- how *many* thoughts came into your mind;
- *why* you chose *one* to the exclusion of others;
- whether you think that your decisions in this respect are *valid* in the end.
- the *reasons* you give to support this conclusion.

Again, you can show the majority of all this in *visual ways* in your *practical work*. For instance, in investigating a problem in Art and Design and planning your work, you should *sketch out all* the alternative ideas you consider. If you do so, you will show 'how many thoughts came into your mind'.

There is a strong chance that the *work you do* from just one of these sketches will indicate 'why you chose to do what you did to the exclusion of other alternatives present in your exploratory work'. However, it is at *this* stage that it will pay you to find *additional* ways of showing *what* your thoughts were in coming to your decision. A brief *writing down* of possible approaches you considered, and rejected, might help here.

The *finished work* will of course contain within it at least *some* justification for choosing to do what you did. Again, however, you will receive credit for *additional* comment on 'the validity of your decisions in your work'. You need to find some way of *communicating* what your analytical thoughts *were* at the conclusion of your work. A *written* evaluation might be one such way.

Apart from the advantages to your grade in your examination, learning to work in this way is beneficial to you in other directions, any of which will contribute towards your final grade.

Apart from the advantages to your final grade, analysing your final work in this way might:

- help you to see the *strengths* and the *weaknesses* in the way that you have worked, and then to build upon those strengths and avoid those weaknesses in *future* work;

- cause you to go back to one of the alternatives which you rejected previously, and to work on that.

In the next chapter we look more closely at *how* you might 'make more clear' some of your thoughts in ways which are not necessarily contained in your practical work.

Discrimination

When you are *choosing* between one sketch and another in your work, you are exercising 'discrimination'. In GCSE Art and Design it is necessary that you show *how valid* your choice or discrimination was. Once more, part of this validity will be contained in your further practical work. The 'proof of the pudding is in the eating', as it were. However, for *others* to be able to *assess and understand* that validity, and for *you* to be able to conduct a rational and justifiable *analysis* of your results, you need to do more.

For instance, knowing that your grade will be helped if you do one or two *alternatives* in your preparatory studies for a piece of work, you might do *three* sketches. In response to a problem such as 'Excitement', the *first* might be a sketch of a rock climber negotiating a 'chimney' on a difficult mountain. The *second* might be of the sinking of the Titanic. The *third* might be of a lead singer from your favourite group standing in the spotlight on an otherwise darkened stage.

You might decide, after this preparatory work, to choose to work on the *lead singer* picture, painting the singer in a shaft of white light on a black sheet of paper.

It could be that, from the very beginning, you *knew* that you wanted to do this picture. You may only have presented *two alternatives* to satisfy your teachers and what you understood to be the demands of the examination. Be that as it may, the kind of reasons which might make 'sense' to an 'outsider', could be:

- one, you like the group;

- two, their latest single is your favourite at the moment;

- three, you were waiting for the first opportunity to paint such a picture.

Whatever the *actual* reasons, you should make every attempt to *communicate* them.

The above reasons are very *personal* ones, and are *not* based on 'rational' or 'objective' assessment. You could 'improve' on these reasons by trying to identify the *theme* of your work. It is this theme which should provide the basis for subsequent choice. Which alternative best helps you to *express* that theme?

Suppose you have chosen 'excitement' as your theme. Which *terms* describe 'excitement'? These could offer you some basis for your judgements.

Such *terms* might be:

- thrill;

- stimulation;

- drama;

- tenseness;

- fear;

- emotion.

All of these words are associated with 'excitement' in any standard Dictionary.

You can now use these terms as the *standards* or criteria for your analysis of the *three* ideas. This will help you to *discriminate between* those ideas using some level of *rationality* which can later be justified.

Choosing to do the picture of the pop star because 'you like the group, the latest song, and the person' is very *'personal'* and, as a consequence, would be very difficult to justify on a *'public'* level. But now you can reflect on the *three* ideas, using the 'criteria' listed above. It might help if you design and use a 'score chart' to guide your thoughts and decisions.

Suppose you were to *order each idea* from one to three against *each of the criteria*. The result might be,

IDEA CRITERIA	ROCK CLIMBING	TITANIC	POP STAR
Thrilling	1	3	2
Stimulating	2	3	1
Dramatic	3	1	2
Tenseness	1	2	3
Fearful	2	1	3
Emotional	3	1	2
Score	12	11	13

On the basis of this score chart, which analyses the alternative subjects you thought of by setting them against the criteria used to describe the term 'excitement', the *lowest score* represents the probable *first choice*. Therefore, perhaps you should do a picture of the *sinking of the Titanic* if you are to answer the theme most effectively.

Of course *other* considerations will also come into the equation. For instance:

■ What *information* have you got, or could you find, on each subject?

■ Each subject requires you to draw people – *how well* do you do this?

■ Can you cope with the '*background*' in one subject more easily than in another subject?

By answering *self-set* questions of this nature, you will begin to build up a justification for your *discrimination* between the alternative subjects and your final decision on the matter.

Decision-making

What should be clear to you is the need to make your *decisions* upon the basis of:

■ the *criteria* you have identified relative to the problem in hand;

■ the extent and availability of *information* relevant to the particular problem;

■ the extent and level of your *own abilities*;

■ the need for you to *develop* your knowledge, your skills, and your range of work and experiences;

■ the *balance* required in your work at any stage for the purposes of the examination and its requirements.

If you weigh-up these considerations at every point of decision, you will end up making highly relevant, valid and justifiable decisions *throughout* your course of study and your externally set examination.

7 ⟩ CRITICAL AWARENESS

> Knowledge should be obtained within a *critical framework* and received with a *critical stance.* "

The issues raised throughout this chapter are separated only in order to explain them to you. In practice you will incorporate them into your work in an *interdependent* and *interrelated* way which should become automatic to you as you develop 'good' habits in your work.

You combine and use them all within a 'critical framework'. Let's explore this term a little further. If you are *critically aware*, it means that you are *conscious* of the *criteria* you are setting up and using, and that you make every effort to *relate* these to the decisions you have to take. This is what is meant by adopting a 'critical stance' in your work.

Being 'critical' does *not* mean 'knocking' everything that exists, nor accepting blandly everything that you do yourself on the basis that it is 'alright', 'I am pleased with it', 'it was the best I could do with the materials', and so on.

Being *critically aware* and making *critical judgements* means that you should be receptively tolerant of things, judging them on the basis of the *information and knowledge you possess*, rather than the personal 'likes' and 'dislikes' you hold.

For instance, if you return to that picture of a pop star. It might be that your teachers and the examiner do not like pop music, and intensely dislike that particular song. You do *not* expect them to critically judge the value of your picture on their *personal* likes and dislikes. You *do* expect them to weigh-up the *evidence* contained in your work, and judge it on things *other than its subject-matter*.

These things might be:

- the appropriateness of your *choice of materials*;
- the ability you have shown in *handling* those materials;
- how well you *composed* your picture;
- how well you *drew* your picture;
- how much and how good was the *information* you uncovered to help you with your work;
- how well you *discriminated* between the various possible approaches to your work;
- how well you *justified* and *explained* your decisions in your work;
- how well you were able to *criticise* your work in a sound and profitable way;
- whether your criticism and evaluation of your work gave rise to any *development* of your work, perhaps into further pieces of work.

> Criticism deals with justifiable public values rather than *personal opinion*.

In answering all this, your teachers and the examiner will disregard their likes and dislikes of the *subject matter* of your picture. They might consider whether the subject matter was the best *solution* to the problem to hand, but this will *not* influence their evaluation of all the other important qualities in your work.

If this is how you expect others to evaluate your work, it is what *you* should do in respect of your own work and the work of others.

Before leaving the subject of criticism, note that there are *two* distinct types of criticism. These are:

- *Descriptive criticism:* Here you might describe, measure and weigh-up pictures and objects, explaining them as factual accounts.
- *Interpretative criticism:* Here you might set up your *own* criteria to judge pictures and objects in a personal way which could, nevertheless, be understood and justified on a public level.

Artists and designers have always used *both* of these types of criticism in doing their work. When artists draw a scene before them, they might be 'describing' what is there. But in drawing what is there, they may *present it* in such a way that it represents a highly 'personal' view of 'reality'. It has long been a tradition in Art and Design for artists and designers to 'mould the way that others see the world'.

You should try to move your own level of criticism into that of 'interpretative criticism' as your course of study unfolds. This could be in the visual terms described above, or it could be verbal, or some combination of both.

A CONTEXTUAL CASE STUDY – THE HORSE

To help you to understand how all the above might be used in *your own* Art and Design studies, imagine that your teachers have asked you to create some work based upon the theme, 'The Horse'. Here we concentrate on the 'Contextual Studies' relevant to this theme rather than on any practical work. Of course as the contextual studies progress they will guide, alter and develop your intentions so far as your own practical work is concerned.

When you are given the theme by your teachers, you might think it is a good one. This might be because you like horses. That is a reasonable and acceptable attitude to take, after all, your work will at least be 'fired with enthusiasm'. However, can you say *why* you like horses?

Is it because to you they are **strong**, or **graceful**, or **fast**, or **beautiful**, or **friendly** animals? Each adjective in bold type, describing the animal, builds up some *criteria* or standards, which will help you decide *what* to do in your work and *how to justify* your decisions. Or is it because you think that the *shape* of horses will make a good picture or sculpture? Or because you feel that the *surroundings* in which horses are often seen will lend themselves to a good picture? There are many such questions you could *ask yourself* from the start of your consideration of the theme.

Asking questions such as these, you might decide that a picture or a sculpture of a **horse grazing in a meadow** will make a good piece of work in response to the *theme*, and the *criteria* you have decided to adopt.

The next stage might be to seek some **source material** to work from, such as a picture of a horse, or a visit to where you know a horse can be found grazing. Or you could make a start in your contextual studies by deciding to see how *other artists and designers* have treated the horse in their work. As you do so, you must keep your mind open, no matter how far you have got in preparing for your practical work.

8 > INVESTIGATION INTO THE THEME

When do you think the first game of *Polo* was played? You are probably aware that Prince Charles likes the sport. Your contextual studies *research* might have uncovered, to your surprise, that there is a piece of Art and Design work which shows Polo being played at least as far back as 1635. There is in fact a picture of that date painted by a Chinese artist, **Li-Lin**, in water colour on silk, which shows Polo being played.

Because of your Contextual Studies you will probably now know something which you did *not* know before. You might now be wishing you had decided to do a piece of work based upon a game of Polo. It is never too late. Any practical work you may have done so far is all a legitimate part of your *preparatory studies*, and will contribute towards the grade your work is given.

9 > LINEAR PERSPECTIVE

Being surprised, perhaps, by the discovery of this particular picture, you might search further. You could come across the well-known picture by **Paolo Ucello (1397 – 1475)**, called **'The Rout of San Romano'** (see Plate 3). This picture is in the **National Gallery**, London. It was painted at the time when the *Science of Perspective* was being founded. This painting of horses in a battle is popularly known as one of the first examples of 'perspective' in a work of art. It was painted about 1450.

Perspective is the means by which a sense of distance and depth is put into the picture, in this case by the use of what is known as **'Linear Perspective'**. This means that by constructing lines which recede into the picture, Ucello has been able to suggest *depth*.

It should be remembered that at that time most paintings were done on the walls of buildings. This form of art is known as 'Mural Painting'. When **Masaccio (1401–28)** painted his work, **'The Holy Trinity, the Virgin, St John and Donors'**, it appeared as if the wall suddenly had a hole in it! This is a comment on the ability of perspective to create an *effect* of spatial recession.

Spatial recession is something you are probably aware of. The familiar trick of railway lines appearing to meet as they disappear in the distance is generally well known. Of course, you *know* that railway tracks must be consistently parallel to each other, otherwise the train comes off the line! But they *look* as if they meet (Fig 3.3).

In Ucello's painting (Plate 3) he used the fallen lances of the soldiers to show this effect of lines disappearing into the distance and appearing to meet as they did so. The fields in the distance continue this feeling of recession as the lines of their boundaries and hedges appear to converge as they run away from the eye.

He also tried to show that the knights and their horses were solid and in space. This is partially achieved by 'overlapping' some of them.

All of this interest in 'linear perspective' gives Ucello's picture the quality it possesses. It accounts in part for why the men and the horses look like they do, almost like wooden rocking horses and toys out of a Victorian nursery.

If *you* wanted to paint a picture yourself which included horses but showed this effect of linear perspective it might occur to you, from seeing, perhaps, television sports programmes, that the rails at a horse racetrack would provide you with a similar means to achieve your ends.

If you refer to an appropriate Art Book, you are almost certain to find that **Degas (1834 – 1917)** painted scenes reminiscent of this, although he was not pre-occupied with the effect of linear perspective.

It is known that Degas was influenced by the effects of photography. You might almost say that it affected the way that he appeared to see things. If you compare the 'stopped-motion' photographs by Muybridge, and the picture of horses by Degas, you can see how it *might* have come about that Degas painted horses so that they appeared the way that they did.

Fig. 3.3 The 'vanishing' railway line.

Fig. 3.4 After, 'The Races at Longchamp', an original lithograph by Edouard Manet.

Plate 3 Paolo Ucello, 'The Rout of San Romano'. *The National Gallery, London.*

Plate 4 William Frith, 'The Derby Day'. *The Tate Gallery, London.*

Many artists have painted pictures of Racing Horses and some have painted the Race Track in the way that Degas did. For instance, the French artist, **Manet (1832 – 83)** made a 'Lithograph' of **'The Races at Longchamp'** in the 1870s (Fig 3.4).

A **'Lithograph'** is a printmaking medium which was very popular in France, in particular, towards the end of the last century. The French artist, **Henri Toulouse-Lautrec (1864 – 1901)**, was a regular user of the medium. You may have seen prints of his posters for the 'Moulin Rouge', and other Music Halls in Paris at that period.

The British artist, **Frith (1819 – 1909)**, on the other hand painted the Epsom Racecourse on **'Derby Day'** in the late 1850s, showing the crowds and the side-shows that abound there, rather than the 'Race' and the racehorses themselves (see Plate 4).

As you study it, you will become aware that it is telling you something about the *way in which the Victorians behaved*. There are 'Dandies' lounging about, eager to impress 'the Ladies'! There is an acrobatic side-show going on, to the accompaniment of a beating drum. Some people are placing their bets on the horses. One man is using his binoculars, but he is not looking at the race track, it seems! People are dressed in a variety of clothing. From a man in a smock it is possible to derive that the different type of clothing might indicate differing financial, social and working circumstances.

It could occur to you that, using the theme of 'The Horse', you could uncover from this particular painting by Frith *how the Victorians lived*. From *this* you could *compare it with modern times*, perhaps painting your *own* picture of a modern 'Derby Day'. If you did so, you would be discovering much about the *cultural changes* and the *social changes* in England over the past 125 years. In this sense, the painting is a *Social and Historical Document*.

What do *you* think of this way of showing a subject such as 'Derby Day'? Should a picture of the subject show the actual race, or is it alright to show the surroundings and the crowds only?

You have probably seen the 'Derby' on television. It is interesting that in this medium, where they can take a series of separate 'pictures', they often have a feature on the side-shows which still surround the racetrack on 'Derby Day', as well as many pictures of the crowds and the celebrities who are present amongst them.

Even on television they show these different aspects of the event in separate little 'programmes' within the whole transmission. Perhaps artists can be excused for having to do the same thing when they use paint or other graphic media?

Stubbs (1724 – 1806), on the other hand, painted race horses as 'Portraits' for their owners. This required Stubbs to show the horse in a way that did not just show that it was a horse, but that it was a *particular* horse, and as recognisable as any person might be. As a result the appearance of the horse in a Stubbs' picture of this kind takes on its own particular appearance (see Plate 5). The horses often look stiff and 'stilted' because of this.

Seeing this, you might think that he did not know how to draw and paint as well as someone like Frith or Degas, but if you look at another type of 'horse picture' by Stubbs you can see that when he was not painting these 'horse portraits' he could draw and paint horses as well as anyone.

In the painting **'Horse Devoured by a Lion'**, (Plate 6), you can see that he painted his 'non-portraits' in a way that was very different.

Why do you think this was? Try to write an explanation of the differences between these two pictures by Stubbs, giving reasons for why you think they look like they do in each case.

George Morland (1762 – 1804), who was more or less a contemporary of Stubbs, painted his pictures, which often included horses, in a way that was different to either of Stubbs' styles.

Again, he was painting them for very different reasons. It has been suggested and shown throughout this book that the 'reasons' behind a picture most often give rise to the nature of that picture and the way that things appear in it. In the case of Morland, his pictures convey to you his sense of satisfaction and pride in the social order and cultural pattern of his day. Everything in his pictures seems to portray a peaceful rustic existence (see Plate 7). His 'Squires' seem to be benevolent, and his common-people content and respectful. Do you think such a picture of England actually existed?

If you study History in your time-table you might have the relevant contextual knowledge to be able to begin to consider this question. The answer is unlikely to be a

Plate 5 George Stubbs, 'Otho, with John Larkin Up'. *The Tate Gallery, London.*

Plate 6 George Stubbs, 'Horse Devoured by a Lion'. *The Tate Gallery, London.*

Plate 7 George Morland, 'Door of a Village Inn'. *The Tate Gallery, London.*

Plate 8   Paolo Ucello, 'St. George and the Dragon'. *Reproduced by courtesy of the Trustees, The National Gallery, London.*

Plate 9   Jacopo Tintoretto, 'St. George and the Dragon'. *Reproduced by courtesy of the Trustees, The National Gallery, London.*

straight 'Yes' or 'No'. Like Art and Design itself, it is more likely that it is a matter of 'this could be so, but on the other hand it might be that . . .'

There is nothing wrong in answers of this kind. In fact they make you produce reasons and justifications for what you say. It is likely that you have had a 'My Dad is bigger than your Dad' argument at some time in your life. If so, you realise that in such cases the last thing you call upon is reasons and justification for what you are saying. You, and your protagonist, just go on making the same irrational claims that you are correct in your argument: even though, or is it because, the fact at stake can easily be resolved. You just need two Dads and a tape-measure!

If you could get the Dads and the tape-measure together, and you lost by five millimetres, then you might say, 'Ah! But my Dad's heavier than your Dad.' If you did, this would be a breakthrough. You have begun to establish some suitable 'criteria' for the basis of your argument. It might then turn out that the other Dad was 'taller', but your Dad was 'heavier'. Then it is no longer a matter of 'black or white', 'right or wrong', that is to say, an 'either-or' argument, and you are behaving with the critical sensitivity and awareness which is required of you in your GCSE.

Finally, in this selection of pictures which deal with the subject of the 'Horse', here are two pictures of the familiar story of '**St. George and the Dragon**'. The first is by **Ucello** (Plate 8), whom you have met already in this chapter. The second (Plate 9) is by **Tintoretto (1518 – 94)**.

Ucello was born over one hundred years before Tintoretto and died nearly fifty years before Tintoretto was born. This means that, despite the fact that they were both Italians, Ucello a Florentine and Tintoretto a Venetian, they were separated by a century. Does this account for any differences in the way that they each worked? Does it result in identifiable differences in the pictures they each paint?

Having pictures of the *same* subject by both of them provides you with an admirable means to begin to answer such questions.

Some of the differences which you have to begin to explain are:

> 66 Just *recognising* differences is not enough; you must find out the *reasons* for the differences. 99

- why the landscape in the Tintoretto looks different from that in the Ucello;
- the different 'feeling' of light in each picture;
- which picture best shows 'depth' and recession;
- do they both use the same means, linear perspective, to show depth (linear perspective pre-occupied Ucello);
- why the 'hero' is at the back of Tintoretto's picture (this is an unusual device in any historical period: does it 'work');
- which tells the story best;
- which is the most 'dramatic';
- which Dragon is the most 'fearsome';
- are there any differences in the way the horses are drawn and painted in the two pictures;
- are there any differences in the way that Ucello drew and painted the horse in this picture and in the '**Rout of San Romano**'?

There is a lot to be discovered and thought about in Art and Design besides just making your own practical responses to problems. If you *do* set about making these discoveries, it is likely that your *own practical work* will improve dramatically, because it becomes more and more informed.

G L O S S A R Y   O F   T E R M S   U S E D

Analytical skills

The means by which you 'pull a problem apart' as an aid to understanding and explaining it.

Comparative study

A possible unit of work, whereby you analyse a set of works, or ideas, comparing one against the other, in order to arrive at a series of judgements about their relative values.

Critical awareness

The stance you adopt in your work whereby you do not receive anything without questioning it and seeking to understand it.

Cultural awareness

Your knowledge and understanding of the 'way things are' due to the particular circumstances which surround the event or persons.

Decision-making

Not just the decisions you make, but also the *knowledge* and *information* which allow you to form your judgements and take your decisions.

Discrimination

The means and the values by which you *choose between* the alternative opportunities which are before you at any time.

Historical research skills

The means by which you discover and recognise relevant facts from the *past* which help to explain something about the present.

Multi-cultural

A term used in GCSE Art and Design to indicate that Art and Design forms and images differ in appearance and meaning, according to *where* they originate.

Outcomes

In Art and Design, the 'work products' you end up with. These can be written, spoken or visual outcomes.

Personal

The likes and dislikes, and the opinions you hold, *without* justifying them.

Productive skills

The means by which you *produce* your Art and Design responses, plus your ability to be able to understand and use them.

Public

Likes and dislikes, and personal opinions which *are* explained and justified, so that they may be publicly accepted.

BIBLIOGRAPHY

GOMBRICH. E. H (1984). *The Story of Art*. London, Phaidon.
SCHARF. A. (1974). *Art and Photography*. London, Pelican Books.
SETH-SMITH, M. (1978). *The Horse in Art and History*. London, New English Library.
TONY BUZAN. (1974). *Use Your Head*. London, British Broadcasting Corporation.

MATERIALS USE AND STUDY METHODS

GETTING STARTED

Your course of study should provide you with the means for you to work competently, and the means for you to develop and extend your range of knowledge and skills. In this chapter we discuss some **materials** and their use in *a variety of methods*, including *documenting*.

The term '**Documenting**' is taken to mean:

■ committing to any form of *storage system* the material you gather, or the information you use in carrying out your work;

and,

■ designing and using a *retrieval system* whereby you can *find* the material and the information whenever you wish to.

In your *contextual studies* and your *preparatory studies* you will need to document:

■ your *sources* of information;

■ the *information* itself;

■ your *analysis* of the gathered material;

■ your *thoughts and ideas*;

■ your *decisions* and the *reasons* behind them;

■ the *outcome* of your work;

■ your *evaluation* of your results.

To document effectively you must find and use the *means* most relevant and appropriate to the task in hand at any time.

To be able to *do* this will require you to develop:

■ your ability to *use* a variety of *drawing*, *writing* and other 'recording' materials;

■ your knowledge about the *properties* of those materials and their uses;

■ your range of *study methods*.

Your aim should be to present your contextual studies to at least the same standard as you would present any of your other finished Art and Design work.

ESSENTIAL PRINCIPLES

1 ⟩ PENCILS

A **pencil** is a highly convenient *instrument* with which to record things or to explore possibilities. It is, nevertheless, an unfortunate fact that too many pencil drawings offered by Art and Design candidates at the age of 16+ are done with a poor quality pencil and consist usually of a faint outline of the things seen or imagined. If you are going to *use* pencil, and it is to be hoped that you will during your contextual studies and your preparatory studies, then get yourself at least three good quality ones.

Good quality pencils are not cheap, but if you do not tap them, or drop them, they will last a long time. You can get a small metal or plastic tube which holds the ends of pencils in when they get too small to use otherwise.

Pencils range in degrees of hardness or softness each side of the category 'HB'. These categories each side of HB are either 'H' or 'B'. 'H' stands for hardness, and 'B' for softness. Each *letter* is then accompanied by a *number*, for instance, 4H, or 2B. The numbers accompanying **'H'** show *increasing degrees of hardness* from 1 to 7, and so on. The numbers accompanying **'B'** show *increasing degrees of softness* from 1 to 7, and so on. Thus, a 4H is harder than a 2H, and a 4B softer than a 2B. So, for instance, a scale *from* hardness *to* softness might read 4H, 3H, 2H, H, HB, B, 2B, 3B, 4B.

For your studies you should get a good quality HB pencil, a 2H, a B, and a really soft pencil, perhaps a 4B. Between them these will give you a good range of qualities and types of mark.

The 'B' pencil will become your usual drawing instrument, and will require more frequent replacing than the others. The 2H will allow you to make *detailed* drawings, such as plans and working drawings for constructions. Your 4B pencil will allow you to draw with a rich, velvety blackness in some areas of your work. This is particularly useful if you are doing a drawing which represents the effect of light and dark. The HB is useful as a pencil to 'map-in' at the start of your work, or to write with.

2 ⟩ GRAPHIC STICK-MEDIA

A pencil is a **stick-medium**. It is not the only one. Drawings can, and should be made in a variety of other stick-media. In the category of stick-media come pen and ink, ball-pens, crayons, conte crayon, pastels, and oil pastels, for instance.

Each different medium has its own peculiar quality. This quality should be clearly understood by you and be used deliberately in order to achieve the effect you desire in your work.

For instance, a pen dipped in black ink will make a different line and quality of mark from a black stick of conte crayon. If you were drawing *winter trees*, it might be that the *pen and ink* will be ideal to show the stark, black outline of the trunks and branches against the winter sky. On the other hand, you might wish to show how dark and forbidding the same scene appears and you might draw the '*gloom*' with the side of the *conte crayon*, just emphasising the main trunks and branches with the sharp tip of the medium.

Even with a single medium such as *ink*, different effects can be achieved by using different instruments to dip in it and draw with. You might use a stick of wood, a feather, a paint brush, your finger-tip, as much as a fine, steel pen-nib. You might use a toothbrush to 'splatter' ink; a sponge to 'stipple' ink; or a syringe to drop blobs of ink and then straws to blow this around on your paper. Again, each method will give its own distinctive results.

Knowing about the various *qualities* of different marks can be valuable to you in two respects:

- Seeing and understanding the *nature* of different marks and the *medium* which can make each one of them, can help you to 'see' such marks in real objects and scenes. As a consequence you can more accurately *record* the object, or scene, reflecting the marks you can 'see' in its real-life form.

or

- You may want to achieve a certain *effect* in your representation of an object or a scene. Knowing the qualities of various media, you can know *which* to work with to achieve your intentions, instead of using the inevitable pencil and then becoming frustrated because it does not 'work' the way that you want it to.

3 〉 COLOUR

Colour is one of the most emotional and effective aspects of your life. If you have seen the pictures on a black and white television, consider how you feel about those pictures in comparison with the same on a colour receiver.

The stick-media provide access to colour. There are coloured pencils, coloured crayons, coloured pastels, coloured inks, and so on. Make full use of this dimension of the qualities of the stick-media.

Remember that there is also *paint*. Too many people think that when they work with paint they are *not* 'drawing'. This is an unnecessary discouragement! When you 'colour', you draw. You explain what it is you are seeing, or have decided to select by the use of colour, as much as by any other means in your work at the same time.

Look at the work of artists such as Degas, and the French artist, Toulouse-Lautrec. Both these artists used colour as a series of 'lines' in their work. Degas often used pastel, whereas Toulouse-Lautrec often used paint in this way.

> All renderings of objects and ideas are *drawings*.

Similarly, you can see how **Constable (1776 – 1837)** and Monet used a series of various sized 'dabs' of colour to 'draw' with; or how the Russian-born artist, **Nicholas de Staël (1914 – 55)** 'drew' with great 'slabs' of colour; or how the French artist **Georges Seurat (1859 – 91)** used a series of 'dots' in his paintings to 'draw' the things contained in them.

Become familiar with a range of 'wet' colour-media, such as coloured inks, water-colours, and oils, if you can. Each of these different colour-media have their own peculiar qualities which you can use.

Using colour in your *preparatory studies* is a relatively straightforward task. In many ways it involves exactly the same materials and their usage as would apply in your practical work at large. However, using colour in your *contextual studies* is another matter. Suppose you want to *illustrate* a piece of written work; whilst this might include a drawing, it could also include charts, graphs, diagrams, and so on. If you try to '*paint*' these, you might find that your medium is unsuitable for the scale that you are working on. Or it might be that you are using an essentially 'wet' medium and it is causing your paper to 'cockle up'. If this is so you should consider more *appropriate* colouring materials.

These might include coloured paper 'collaged' onto your work; or 'Letratone', which is a sheet of colour which may be 'transferred' by rubbing onto your work; or you might use some of the 'drier' colouring materials, such as coloured pencils, felt-tips or crayons. Be prepared to experiment!

4 〉 OTHER MATERIALS

Once you grasp that *all* renderings of objects and ideas are 'drawings', then there is no limit to the number and range of materials you might use to draw with.

Collage materials such as coloured paper, textured paper, card, string, thread, wool, wire, balsa wood, and so on, can all be used separately, or collectively, to construct 'drawings'. For instance, it might be best to convey your ideas for *pottery* by means of a *paper collage*. The pieces of paper perhaps giving a 'feel' similar to that of working in clay.

You could use clay, or plasticine to draw with. Or even Plaster of Paris, or concrete. Materials such as these are excellent for understanding how an object before you *exists* in 'space', penetrating and enclosing it in its real-life form.

There can be *no limit* to *how* you draw, what you *use* to draw with and what you *consider to be* drawings, only that from your own inhibitions or lack of imagination.

Mix the media you use: Even try using media which will not mix, such as wax and water-colour. Again, the effect is significant and can be useful to your needs in certain circumstances. Be prepared to experiment.

5 〉 PHOTOGRAPHS

Many people seem to have an aversion to including **photography** in Art and Design studies. Try not to share this aversion. Photographs are not, however, substitutes for drawings, or for sitting before the real thing and wrestling to translate a three-dimensional object into two dimensions on paper.

Nevertheless, many artists *have* used the outcomes and effects of photography as an influence upon their work. See if *you* can discover evidence of this and if you can, work out just what it is they have done in this respect. Scharf (1974) is a good guide in exploring and understanding photography.

Taking your *own* photographs can provide you with insights into effects that the *process of photography has* upon the way that it represents things. It can also give you an insight into how photographic images have affected the *way* that things are seen nowadays.

For instance, the familiar black, silhouetted palm tree against the setting, red sun, is almost a contemporary icon. Whilst many art teachers and examiners are 'sick of the sight' of this image in the work of some of their pupils or candidates, there can be no denying that it *is* a contemporary 'cultural' understanding of the *way* that things are (see Fig 4.1). The black palm tree image is now part of the culture of the United Kingdom, even though its imagery is transferred there from the Carribean.

On the other hand, it might be that *knowledge* of the image and how it came about would encourage you to 'see' trees in the country where *you* live as silhouettes against the sunset.

Plate 10 Aubrey Beardsley, 'Cover Design for the Yellow Book'. *The Tate Gallery, London.*

For instance if, unlike the camera, you *were* to see the tree as a black silhouette, you would probably have to take a *rational decision* to do so. The likelihood is that your sophisticated eye would observe slight colour changes and the effect of light and dark in the trees. You *can* 'shut these off', but you should then know and explain *why* you choose to do so, and then *evaluate* whether your decision to do so was valid in the light of your results.

The British artist, **Aubrey Beardsley (1872 – 98)** made decisions about 'seeing' in silhouette in some of his work. This is particularly so in his book illustrations (Plate 10 and Fig 4.1).

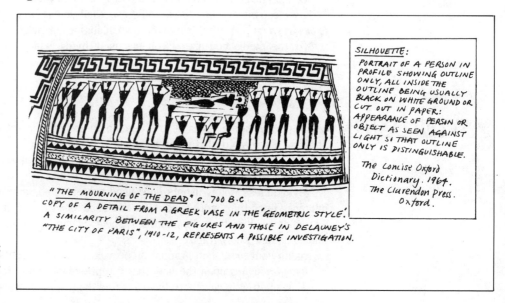

Fig. 4.1 Different 'cultural' uses of the silhouette in the history of art and design.

AUBREY BEARDSLEY "THE PEACOCK SKIRT"
THE COPY ABOVE, OF A BOOK ILLUSTRATION
BY THE ARTIST, SHOWS HOW AN ARTIST
USED THE THEORY OF THE SILHOUETTE TO
CREATE AND FULFIL HIS INTENTIONS.
IT IS NOT STRICTLY, PERHAPS, A
SILHOUETTE, BUT IT OPENS THE DOOR TO
CONSIDER WHETHER ALL BLACK AND
WHITE DRAWINGS ARE FORMS OF THE
SILHOUETTE. WHAT DO YOU THINK?

STAMPS, COINS, MEDALS
AND TOKENS HAVE
TRADITIONALLY
EMPLOYED THE
USE OF SILHOUETTES
IN THEIR VARIOUS
DESIGNS.

DETAIL FROM,
"TOMB WALL - PAINTING, THEBES" c. 1400 B.C.
THE EGYPTIANS MIXED 'PROFILES' AND
'HEAD-ON' VIEWS IN THE SAME FIGURE.
THIS SHOWED THE ESSENTIAL NATURE
OF THE PARTICULAR PART OF THE HUMAN
BODY. IT COULD BE ARGUED THAT THIS
REPRESENTS AN EARLY, INTELLECTUAL
USE OF THE SILHOUETTE.
CAN YOU DETECT A SIMILARITY
BETWEEN THIS THEORY AND THAT OF
CUBISM?

Fig 4.1 (cont)

The essential point about the black silhouetted palm tree is that it has taught you, and other members of your society, to recognise that it represents *one* of the ways of seeing and communicating within your society.

Before the invention of photography it was *less likely* that the silhouette should be one of the ways of seeing, because the *eye* saw things in a different way to that of the *camera lens* and what *was* seen by the *eye* was *recorded* in a different way to that of *photographic film*.

There is of course nothing wrong in using the *knowledge* you have gained from the silhouetted image, but try to demonstrate your *understanding* of the image and the reasons behind it, rather than just copying it into another medium. Above all, try to use it in a personal and creative way.

6 > DRAWINGS

Just think of the different things which you have seen which can be labelled '**drawings**'.

Make a list of them

For instance, there are *plans*:

■ used perhaps to 'describe' the insides of buildings;

■ which might be diagrams of how an army will attack;

■ which might be maps of streets, or countries.

There are also *drawings* of the fronts of buildings:

■ Those which *architects* might do could *explain* the way an intended building will look. In these a number of accepted symbols and textures are used in a traditional and accepted *code* in order to convey information and meaning to those who look at the drawings.

■ A *designer* might make a drawing of the front of a building in order to show what the building *could* look like. The building could be accurate in scale and some detail, but might include the effect of new colours, or plastic additions, and so on.

■ There are also drawings of the fronts of buildings which an *artist* might do. These most often show what the front of a building *actually* looks like. But even then such drawings also convey '*how*' the artist wants the building to be seen.

For instance, sometimes the artist will want to show the effect of light and dark on a building. 'Baroque' buildings were built with the intention of using the effect of *bright sunlight* in their appearance. At other times the artist might be wanting to show the range and qualities of the textures which exist on the front of the building. On yet other occasions the artist might be telling you what effect use and abuse has had on the 'patina' of the building.

INTERNAL CODE

In all these different *types* of drawing of buildings by architects, designers and artists, what is most important is not what is *depicted*, or what *media* is used to produce it, or what it is *meant* to convey. What *is* important is that within each drawing and type of drawing *there is a consistent internal code* which allows people to *read* the particular drawing each time (Fig 4.2).

Fig. 4.2 *Architect's drawing* – top left: (After Frank Lloyd Wright.) Here the architect uses 'symbols' to represent how his building *will* look. *Designer's drawing* – top right: The drawing of the building the designer is 're-designing' might also be a 'technical drawing' (*a*). Often the designer will then produce a transparent 'overlay' (*b*), to show how the building *could* look. In this case, to convey the modern idea of 'multi-screen' cinemas, the designer has suggested calling the cinema a 'Film Factory' and that by the use of false façades, creating the effect of an old industrial building. *Artist's drawing* – bottom: This is a more personal response to how the buildings *do* look, at least to this particular artist.

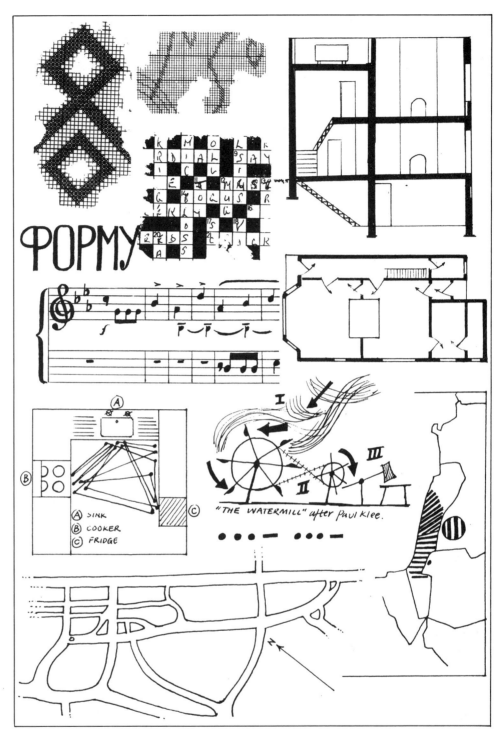

Fig. 4.3 *Drawings.* If drawings do 'convey information and messages', and have an internal code which enables them to be 'read', then a variety of unexpected things can be thought of as 'drawings'.

If you return to the notion of an *architect*'s drawing, it is no use the architect ignoring the *code* already drawn up to indicate 'stone', 'concrete', or 'wood'. In this *code*, certain marks and sequences of marks represent concrete, whilst others represent wood or stone, and so on. The *internal code* would be broken and an observer would be unable to *read*, or understand, the drawing if the architect suddenly started to invent a *new* series of marks to represent such materials.

The *designer* might well use the 'symbols' an architect uses, but a designer's drawings also have their own *internal code*. This is often created by the actual materials a designer uses to represent things. These are materials such as 'colour transfer sheets', 'texture transfer sheets', 'lettering transfer sheets', and acetates, amongst others.

Because of the personal decisions the *artist* has to make, the *code* is often more difficult to invent and establish, and consequently to *read* and understand. The artist has the task of setting up within each drawing the means for it to be *decoded* by an observer, according to what he or she intends to convey in the particular drawing (Fig 4.3). Having done this, the artist might then wish to convey some *other* qualities in a further drawing, so that a *new* internal code has then to be constructed for that drawing.

For instance, suppose you are working in pencil from a still-life made up of a blue jug, a red apple and a lemon, all on a cream cloth against a green wall. You might decide to show the effect of light and dark on the group. To do so you might use your 4B pencil to 'shade in' the *dark* shadows, and other pencils to show the *less dark* shadows.

On the other hand you might choose to show the *relationship* of the various colours present in the group. Taking your 4B pencil, you might 'fill-in' the shape of the red apple in a deep, velvety shading. You might then decide that the blue is lighter than the red, but darker than all the other colours present in the group. So you fill-in the jug in a slightly lighter shade with your pencil. Then, perhaps, the green wall comes next in your decreasing scale of 'darkness' for each of the colours, followed by the lemon, and finally, the cream cloth.

These two drawings of the *same* still-life would *look vastly different*, even though they were both done in 'black and white' with a pencil. The question would be, do they contain the *evidence* within them to allow them to be *decoded*? It might be that they would need to be seen side by side for this to be possible.

If an *internal code* does *not* exist within a drawing, it not only leaves the *observer* confused, at a later date it can even leave the *artist* wondering what was intended in a drawing.

The way that you should attend to your *internal codes* in your drawings should be that you work out *and understand* what it is *you intend* in a drawing. If you *are* clear about this, then you have the means to 'test' whether what you are putting on the paper, or whatever, *is* consistently in accordance with your intentions.

> **If a drawing does not contain *its own internal code* and this internal code is not *used consistently* it is likely to be *unintelligible*.**

In this way you will produce a drawing which contains *within it* the means for *someone else* to read that drawing, decode it, and understand it.

If this is *not* so, then scrub the drawing and try again, because it will be unlikely to have a satisfactory *internal code*.

Sometimes you might put a *key* alongside your drawing. This is something you will be familiar with in maps. There are some types of personal drawings where this is appropriate, but in Art and Design outcomes generally, many of your drawings should be intelligible *without* this device.

Nevertheless, there is another type of drawing which does contain a *key* of a kind, which is not only appropriate but vital in your work. This is known as an *'annotated drawing'*.

> **Drawings record but they also communicate information.**

Just remember that drawings are a way of recording and conveying information and meaning about what you might see, know, or think of. They are not just finished pieces of work in Art and Design which are framed and hung on walls! They are a *message* to yourself and also to others. Therefore, their *meaning* must be clear and intelligible both to yourself *and* to others.

7 ANNOTATED DRAWINGS

An '**annotated drawing**' is a drawn *and* written piece of work. You do a *drawing* showing features which are better and more easily explained in *images*. These might be things such as:

- the *shape* of objects;
- the *relative sizes* of objects;
- the *position and placement* of objects;
- the *selection* you have made from the things before you;
- the *composition* you intend of the things before you.

At the same time you *write* on and around your drawing, as it grows, the things which are more easily explained in *words*. These might be such things as:

- the *colour* of objects;
- the way objects *look against their backgrounds*;
- your *thoughts* about how the work might be *developed* from your drawing at a later date;
- the *'feelings'* and *'emotions'* you might have in response to the things before you.

Annotated drawings are essentially **working drawings**. As such they are very personal. Nevertheless, because you are in an examined position in GCSE Art and Design, you must preserve and present them for your examination.

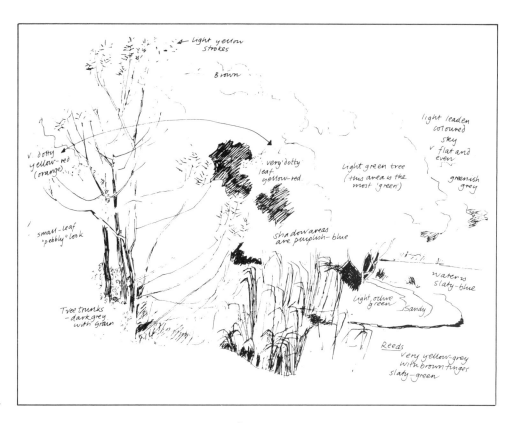

Fig. 4.4 Annotated drawing.

Annotated drawings provide excellent *traces of your thoughts*. Annotated drawings need not be only of things 'seen'. They can record your imaginative ideas and designs as well.

8 > TRACINGS

Making **tracings** is an authentic part of Art and Design activities. Tracings can *speed up* the drawing and designing process. If you want a 'copy' of something in your work, and the original is the correct size for your needs, then it may be sensible to *begin* the drawing by tracing.

For instance, you might be doing a *critical study*, comparing the way in which Rembrandt and Dürer approached the task of *drawing animals*. It would obviously be necessary to include *illustrations* of the work of these two artists in your critical study. *Tracing* would be an excellent way to *obtain* all your illustrations, if you can find sources of the work of the artists. Some of your illustrations might be of *details* of the drawings, and perhaps need to be *magnified* a few times in order to make your point. To get this magnification you could put your tracing through a photocopier with the machine set to 'magnify'. If you then put the first magnified copy through again, you will increase the size of the work, and so on.

9 > WRITTEN WORK

What has been said about *drawing* is applicable to *any* Art and Design activity you may think of. Activities such as designing, sculpting, constructing, carving, painting, printing, photography, and so on, are all subject to the same advice. Do not build up a 'mystique' around the various activities in Art and Design. *Each material* you use, *each idea* you have, *each piece of work* you produce, are *all* governed by the same basic Art and Design principles.

In discussing 'drawing' the emphasis has been upon the *reasons* behind drawings, and how those reasons *shape and form* worthwhile studies in Art and Design. At the same time, the emphasis has been upon the *standards* you should employ in your work.

If you think of the *Ancient Egyptians* you can see that 'writing' is only a form of 'drawing'. In 'writing' you construct *marks* on a surface in such a pattern and sequence that they obey an acknowledged *internal code* and communicate their meaning in a competent and universal manner. In this sense, 'writing' is identical to 'drawing'.

In Art and Design most of your written work is likely to be in the form of *phrases* rather than sentences, *sentences* rather than paragraphs, and *paragraphs* rather than pages. You must therefore try to make each phrase, each sentence, and each paragraph as *concise* and *precise* as you can.

An *exception* to this might occur if you are writing a *critical* piece of work, say on an artist or designer, or an Art and Design product, or a local environment. In writing of this kind you are most likely *constructing an argument*. This will demand that you set out your ground clearly, and then make your point only within the boundaries you have defined. Nevertheless your writing might now take on a form which is more akin to an 'essay' in your English lessons.

WRITING MATERIALS AND TECHNIQUES

There are various ways that you might commit your 'written work' to paper. These are to:

- handwrite with pen, ball-pen, pencil;
- use stencils;
- use 'transfer' lettering;
- use a typewriter;
- use a word processor.

If you have access to either of the last two items and can use them fairly competently, or get someone to use them for you, then the standard of presentation they offer is excellent. If this is not so, then you need to write by hand.

If you **handwrite** your work:

- use *unlined paper* to write on;
- use a *good writing instrument*;
- use a medium which *contrasts well* with your paper;
- write to the *best handwriting* standard you can muster.

Using unlined paper need not mean that your lines slant or wander all over the place. Get a sheet of paper. Using a black felt-tip pen, rule straight, parallel lines across *this* sheet with a distance between them which is suitable for your handwriting. You should experiment with the size which most suits you in this respect. Make the distance between the lines just a little more than you think you need for your handwriting. This lined sheet is your **key sheet**. You can place this 'key sheet' underneath the unlined paper, and use it to guide your writing. DO NOT LOSE YOUR 'KEY SHEET'. KEEP IT CAREFULLY IN A FOLDER. It will make your final work look better and easier to read (Fig 4.5).

Presentation

Try to lay your written work out on the sheet so that the white, or clear, paper around the writing makes a satisfying *pattern*, which encourages someone to *read* what you have written.

- Remember to use *capital letters* to show importance of things such as Headings.
- Use *colour* to make some things stand out, but be carefully selective in deciding what is important in this respect.
- Try to use different *sizes of letters*.
- Use different *letter-forms*.
- If your work emerges something like a small book, put a *'Title page'* in it. This can be illustrated as well as lettered.
- If your work has sections, or chapters, list these on a *'Contents page'*.
- If you have used books in compiling your work, list them in a *'Bibliography'* (see page 63).
- Consider designing a *cover* for your book (Fig 4.6).

ILLUSTRATIONS

If you **illustrate** your written work, and it is to be hoped that you will use this marvellous facility as you are working in Art and Design, make sure that you use a *medium* to draw your illustration which will make a *strong dark line*. A well-sharpened 'B' pencil, indian ink, fibre-tip pen or Rotring pen would be most suitable.

If you use colour, again, use *strong colour* rather than weak washes. You want your teachers, or the examiner, to 'see' your work and be interested enough to read and

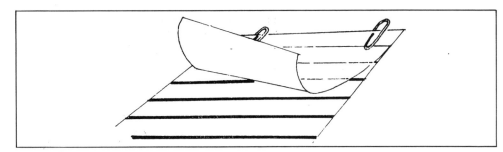

Fig. 4.5 How to construct and use a 'handwriting guide'.

Fig 4.6 Title pages, cover designs for 'book-like' presentations in Art and Design.

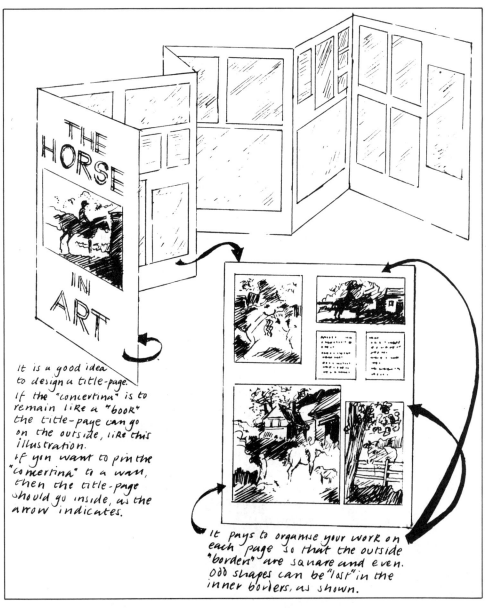

It is a good idea to design a title-page. If the "concertina" is to remain like a "book" the title-page can go on the outside, like this illustration. If you want to pin the "concertina" to a wall, then the title-page should go inside, as the arrow indicates.

It pays to organise your work on each page so that the outside "borders" are square and even. Odd shapes can be "lost" in the inner borders, as shown.

Fig. 4.7 Concertina displays.

understand it to the full. So do not *bore* them with the appearance of your work. Remember what was said earlier in this chapter about the colour media *suitable* for illustrations. It was pointed out that a 'dry' medium is often better for this kind of work, because it does not 'cockle' the paper.

Not all illustrations are 'drawings'. Graphs are an excellent way of putting down a large amount of material into a condensed, precise way. If you *can* use graphs, you will also be demonstrating your ability to use '*Cross-Curricula References*' in your studies. That is to say, techniques and subject-matter which is an important part of *other* school subjects.

10 ❭   DISPLAY   CONCERTINA DISPLAY

The suggestion so far is that your written work will end up on sheets of A4 paper and be like a book. This need not be so. In fact, in Art and Design you would be constraining yourself most inappropriately if you limited yourself to such a format.

It is likely that much of your written work will be done in close harmony with your other *practical* work in Art and Design. This other 'practical work' could be of *any size*. It might even be three-dimensional! To try to make all the possibilities which might exist fit an A4 format is unrealistic. Your examination result would be likely to suffer if you did so.

A *book form* may be most unsuitable in your work, except in certain cases such as a critical study or a sketch book. Some form of presentation which takes the form of a '*display*' might often be more appropriate. For this purpose, a '**Concertina Display**' could prove useful (Fig 4.7).

A 'concertina display' enables you to *complete* a study in Art and Design to the full at the time of its execution, and then to *store* it safely until the time of assessment. A 'concertina display' is simply a number of boards which are hinged together, and fold to the size of just one of the boards. On it you can put sheets of written work and two-dimensional work of any size – subject to the size of the boards being suitably chosen in the first place.

You could even mount work done in 'relief' on a single board which is not hinged to the others but is of the same size. It would be necessary to keep it separated, otherwise the 'concertina' would not fold away.

Adhesives

When 'mounting' your work on the boards you will need to use some form of **adhesive**. Remember that *water*-based adhesives will tend to make your work 'cockle'. *Spirit*-based adhesives are best for this purpose. There are some spirit-based adhesives available which will allow you to move your work if you make an initial mistake in placing it.

When you use an adhesive apply it to the *back of the piece of work*, and not to the board, unless the instructions with the adhesive say that you should apply it to *both* surfaces. When doing so make certain that you cover the back of the work *completely*, paying particular attention to the edges of the work. When you stick the work to the board, gently press the air out from the *centre* of the work towards the edges. You should *protect* your work with a masking sheet of clean paper as you do so.

There are a number of ways of cleaning up the boards when you finish. If you use spirit-based adhesive, any excess adhesive will usually 'rub' off cleanly.

Layout and Design

When you select your work to mount on the boards, you also have to consider what will *go on* each individual board. When arranging this work on each board, make sure that you show your knowledge of **layout and design**. If you have not got any knowledge, then acquire some *before* you commit your work to the boards.

Work usually *looks better* if laid-out with the edges of each piece 'square' to the edges of the board. It pays to try to arrange your work so that it 'creates' an *even border* around it up to the edges of the board.

Your aim is not just to make your work 'look pretty', but to explain *what* it is you have done and *why* you have done it. To do this, apart from *selecting* your work so that it 'creates' a well-designed board in each case, you will have to consider how you '*sequence*' your work.

11 > SEQUENCING

The following two methods are suggested to you as suitable 'starting points' for **sequencing** your work.

CHRONOLOGICAL SEQUENCING

Chronological means, 'in order of time'. In 'chronological sequencing' you arrange your work so that it shows the *order* in which you did things.

In Art and Design it is sometimes difficult to say or remember exactly the order in which you did things, because of the complex thought processes involved in the activity of 'creating' your work. Nevertheless, it *is* possible to put your work into a reasonably accurate 'time sequence'.

Some of the *advantages* of using chronological sequencing are:

- It shows how '*one thing led to another*'.
- It shows how much *you have developed* during a particular study, or throughout your course.

NARRATIVE SEQUENCING

Narrative means, 'telling a story'. In 'narrative sequencing' you arrange your work so that it '*explains*' what it is that you have done.

This means that you do *not* concentrate on 'what came first', but, rather, that you *select* the order in which you present your work so that *other people* can 'read' it and understand it.

Some of the *advantages* of using narrative sequencing are that it is easier:

- to explain your *reasons* for what you did;
- to *justify* your decisions;
- to *come to a logical conclusion* at the end.

For instance, using the example of the 'Horse in Art' from Chapter 3, you might decide to produce all your work on that theme in a *narrative sequence*, rather than a *chronological sequence*.

To do so:

- Get *all* your work on the 'Horse' together.
- Shuffle it around to see if it 'tells a story'.
- When it begins to do so, try to identify distinct 'parts' to the story.
- Try to put these 'parts' into an *order* which makes sense to a reader or listener. There should obviously be a beginning, middle and end, i.e. some *development* in the story.
- Try to tie the parts together by *writing* a few 'linking' words in large felt-tip on separate pieces of paper.

These words will begin to *explain* your point of view, *show* your decisions and the *reasons* behind them, bring in the *alternatives* which occurred in your work, and end up with some *conclusions* you have made. All that you then need to do is to write the 'story' down more fully. In the case of the 'Horse in Art', you might begin:

> In the history of Art and Design the horse has been a popular subject. Artists have drawn, painted and sculpted the animal throughout time. The reasons for doing so vary, according to the particular time and the society the artist has lived in.
>
> For instance, the Arab Stallion is an important part of Middle Eastern culture. As a result the portrayals of horses in that culture tend to show the animal in almost 'God-like' terms.
>
> The illustration on sheet 3 shows what is meant by this, particularly when it is compared with the illustration on sheet 4, which is by an artist working in Victorian England in the latter half of the last century . . . .

How fully you do this is up to you and the *means of display* you intend for your work. It could be that the scale of your work is such that you decide to write an illustrated 'book'. Or it could be that you decide to use a 'concertina' display, and so on. The 'book' will accommodate more words than the 'concertina' display, which in turn will be more suitable to accommodate words than might be an exhibition display.

Narrative sequencing is probably more difficult than chronological sequencing, but it *is* a way to higher grades for the same work. This is not because it is necessarily better than 'chronological sequencing', but because it incorporates the widest demands of the examination syllabuses. The single disadvantage with it is that it does not necessarily show how much you *develop* through a study in Art and Design.

<table><tr><td>**12**〉</td><td>**SOURCES OF INFORMATION**</td></tr></table>

Your **information** will come from many **actual sources**, but they can all be divided into two types. These are:

- Primary Sources of Information;

and

- Secondary Sources of Information.

PRIMARY SOURCES OF INFORMATION

Primary sources of information are *real* events, places, and objects that *you* might work from. They are also the material which you originate yourself, perhaps by doing drawings, taking photographs, doing personal writing, or using questionnaires, and so on.

Primary sources of information do not necessarily have to be 'acknowledged', although you might, for instance, wish to 'label' a drawing with the name of the place it represents. It is taken for granted that the work which you originate in such circumstances is your own, taken from things which *you* have thought of, experienced, or observed.

SECONDARY SOURCES OF INFORMATION

Secondary sources of information are the works and materials which *others* have originated and you use in your own studies.

Sometimes you use this material in your work exactly as 'it stands'. For instance, in a study based upon 'Landscape' you might include a postcard reproduction of '**Salisbury Cathedral**', by **John Constable**.

You might also absorb some of the *influences* you get from the material you discover into your own creative and original work. If you do derive at least some of your inspiration from the work of others in this way, then you should always *acknowledge* this fact and credit the sources you have used. At the same time, in the best interests of your eventual GCSE grade, you should *document* your reasons for doing what you did and evaluate the outcomes.

For instance, it might be that you have just completed a study on the work of *John Constable*. Soon after this your teachers ask you to study the '*landscape*' theme. You might have been so struck by the work of Constable that you consciously, or even unconsciously, work in a way *similar* to his in order to produce your painting. You might choose a scene, or a particular view of a scene, which is similar to those that Constable chose to work from. Or you might apply your paint in the manner that Constable did. If you did so it would pay to *say* what you have done and to illustrate what you mean.

In your GCSE Art and Design you should always try to *explain* the influences upon you. To do so will indicate your breadth of knowledge of the subject and awareness of the factors influencing your decisions.

REFERENCING YOUR SOURCES OF INFORMATION

Artists, Designers and other Practitioners

It is easy to see how to acknowledge your source of information if it is a place, an event, an artist, a designer, and so on. You just put down the *name* concerned.

Books

You get your information about artists, designers and others from **books** on a number of occasions. If this is so, whilst you will mention the name of the person concerned, you must also acknowledge the book you have been using.

At the end of each chapter in this book you will have noticed that books that have been referred to have been listed in a particular way.

For instance, the book by Scharf has been listed,

SCHARF A. (1974). *Art and Photography*. London, Pelican Books.

This means that:

- A. Scharf wrote the book.
- The book was published in 1974.
- Its title is 'Art and Photography'.
- It was published in London.
- The publishers were 'Pelican Books'.

Each book referred to in this Guide is listed in this way and order.

The order is,

AUTHOR'S NAME, DATE OF PUBLICATION, TITLE OF BOOK, PLACE OF PUBLICATION, NAME OF PUBLISHER.

In referencing a book, the *title* of the book is usually in *italics*, or *underlined*.

Each time you use a book which affects your work, get into the *habit* of writing down a reference to it in this way. Always make a note of the book, and the page(s) you use from it, in a note-book of your own *as you pick up the book and use it*. Apart from the needs of your examination, if you do this you have an immediate 'retrieval system' at your finger tips if you should want to find the same thing again. This can save much valuable time later on, particularly at the time of your externally set examination.

Referring to a book when writing

If, when you are writing, you refer to the work of an author you have been using in your text, the usual way is to put the author's *surname*, followed by the *date* of the book *in brackets*. You will see that this was done earlier in this book in respect of Scharf. It shows your source of information and is a means to identify the book in the '**Bibliography**' at the end of your work.

If you *quote* from a book, put the words in *quotation marks*.

If you *absorb* the words of a book into your own words and argument, invent ways of *showing* that you have done this. You could say,

- as Scharf implies;

or

- Scharf appears to support the view that . . .

Referencing Magazines and other sources

Sometimes you gain your *secondary* sources of information from magazines, or newspapers. Again, if you use such sources of information, get into the *habit* of referencing them at the time that you find the material.

To do this it is usual to put,

NAME OF THE PUBLICATION, MONTH AND YEAR OF PUBLICATION, NUMBER OF EDITION, PAGE REFERENCE, NAME OF ARTICLE, NAME OF AUTHOR.

The methods of referencing given above are part of the methods usually used in research work. You can invent your *own* methods, but it is just as easy to use those that have been tried and tested. Whatever it is you do, use one method *consistently* in your work.

To reference your sources of information is *not a sign of weakness* on your part. It is not that you cannot think for yourself. It shows just how seriously and how deeply you study in your work. *Put your references into your work and you will gain more marks for it.*

13 > **COLLECTING AND COLLATING INFORMATION**

DRAWINGS FILE

It would pay you to make a **file** of different types of drawings done by other people for a variety of purposes and in a wide range of media. The purposes behind drawings are mentioned in the earlier section on 'drawing' in this chapter.

Sources of your drawings for your file might be:

- magazines such as the *Radio Times*, women's weeklies, and music magazines;
- record album covers;
- comics;
- art books;
- your brothers and sisters;
- your parents and relatives;
- leaflets from banks and other large businesses.

Collect your drawings wherever you see them. Try to *file* them so that you show how aware you are of their *differences* and their *similarities*.

Differences and **similarities** can be based upon things such as:

- materials used in the drawing;
- subject matter;
- purposes behind drawings;
- styles of drawing.

Photocopying

You cannot just tear pictures out of books, but it is possible to **photocopy** those parts of a book which are an essential part of *your individual study* without necessarily infringing copyright laws.

TO BE CERTAIN ABOUT COPYRIGHT, CONSULT WITH YOUR TEACHERS BEFORE YOU DO ANY PHOTOCOPYING. THEY WILL HAVE THE CURRENT REGULATIONS ABOUT PHOTOCOPYING IN YOUR AREA AND YOUR SCHOOL.

Scrapbook Collections

Part of your information will be in the form of **scrapbook material** which you cut out from magazines and newspapers, or find from other sources. Always be aware of suitable Art and Design scrapbook material, no matter whether you are doing Art and Design at the time or not.

When you get a new theme to study, start *another* scrapbook collection which is just about that theme. What you collect in this way is *not* 'scrap' material. Therefore:

- Cut it out tidily;
- Keep it in a book and not loose in a folder;
- When you use parts of it in a particular study include it in that study, by photocopying it, or re-mounting it;
- Remember to refer to your general scrapbook when starting a new problem, it could aid your contextual studies.

When you decide upon and collect scrapbook material, or anything else that you may 'cut out', always *trim* the material squarely on a guillotine before filing or mounting it. *Do not leave it 'torn out' or just 'snipped out' with a pair of scissors.*

SKETCH BOOKS

Sketch books are a familiar way of collecting and storing your information. Do not minimise their importance because of this. Try to get into the habit of recording in your sketch book, as a matter of course, whatever it is that interests you. Do not fall into the trap of thinking that your sketch book should *only* include 'finished' pieces of artwork.

Get into the habit of 'thinking' in your sketch book. It is one way of making sure that you provide 'traces of your thoughts' for your examination. *Your sketch book is a 'work-mate', not a book for your 'posh' work.*

Do not be afraid to use a *variety of materials* in your sketch book, provided the paper is of sufficiently high quality to receive some of the possible materials. This could include 'sticking things into it'. It should certainly include written work where it is appropriate to what you are doing. *Use your sketch book like a comfortable old friend to 'bounce your ideas around'.*

DIARIES

A **diary** can play an important role in your Art and Design studies.

In a diary you can put down:

- the things you *intend to do* for your homework, the next weekend, or in your Art and Design lesson;
- the things you *need to think of*;
- what it was you *actually did* at any time, for instance, during your homework, or in your Art and Design lesson.

A common-place book?

Some Victorian ladies kept a book which they called their 'Common-Place Book'. In it they recorded a variety of things in words, made drawings, stuck down scrapbook material, and pressed flowers.

Rather than having a *collection* of books, as has been suggested above, *you* might choose to have just one book, which you can use as a scrapbook, a sketch book *and* a diary.

If you decide to do this, you will have to select the book carefully. It will have to be:

- big enough in format for scrapbook material;
- fat enough to include all the work you want it to;
- handy enough to carry around for chance 'sketching';
- made of some sheets which are good enough to use for drawings;
- capable of allowing you to rule out some sheets as a 'work diary'.

You might think of this book as your '*Work Journal*'.

To serve all these purposes you might find it best to make the common-place book, or work journal, yourself! Or to find or make two books which divide the tasks suitably but match each other. Many stationers sell matching books of different sizes which might be suitable.

14 ▷ USEFUL RESEARCH METHODS

Some of the **methods** used in research transfer easily to studies in Art and Design. Be prepared to think about using them as a 'matter of course' in your work.

Perhaps the most useful methods are:

- conducting interviews;
- using questionnaires;
- constructing tests.

INTERVIEWS

It has been said already that *talking to people* who know something is a valuable source of information. The trouble with just 'having a chat' is that the conversation can get nowhere, and you can come away unable to recall the important features of what you have just heard.

If you have the opportunity, go to conduct an **interview** with:

- A definite understanding of what you want to find out.
- A discrete piece of paper, perhaps a postcard, with the points you wish to enquire about written clearly on it in the form of a few 'key words'.
- During the interview let it go the way the person you are talking to wants it to.
- Listen carefully for unexpected ideas which might come up.
- Keep an eye on your 'key words' and at different points put a direct question if necessary, to guide the conversation around to areas not yet covered by the conversation.

■ As soon as possible after the interview, make a note of some of the most valuable things you thought you heard.

Tape-Recorders

It is useful to use a **tape-recorder** in an interview.

If you do, you must:

■ get the person's permission to use it;

■ be adept at handling the machine, so that it does not 'get in the way' of the interview, making the situation false and inhibiting;

■ listen to the tape as soon as possible after the interview and edit it, picking out the important information so far as you are concerned;

■ store the unwanted material in case it 'comes in useful' later.

QUESTIONNAIRES

A **questionnaire** is a useful instrument to test your theories. Constructing a questionnaire which finds out what you really want to find out is a difficult task.

The things to remember in **constructing** a questionnaire are:

■ make each question as simple as possible;

■ try each question out on a variety of people, to find out if they understand what it is you are asking;

■ try to get direct answers from your questionnaires because it is difficult to 'score' abstract views and opinions;

■ consider who your 'sample' will be, and how you will select them;

■ consider how you will get your questionnaire reproduced.

Selecting your 'sample', or the people you will ask to fill in the questionnaire, is important. For instance, it is no use thinking that you will use a questionnaire to find out 'how much the toys designed for five-year-olds are liked by five-year-olds' if you do not have access to a number of five-year-olds!

Writing your questions and then 'testing' them on some guinea-pigs is vital if you are to stand a chance of getting answers to the questions you thought you were asking. Even when this is done, you often end up with replies to questions the person 'thought' you were asking!

You can either give each person you question a copy of your questionnaire, or you can have a copy, or copies, which you use to tick off the verbal replies you receive. *Which method* you use will obviously affect *how* you should produce your questionnaire. Whether you hand out copies or not, try to produce your questionnaire to a high technical standard. It is one of the occasions when it pays to use a typewriter and photocopier, or a word processor.

'Scoring' your replies

However you use your questionnaire, you need to have a means to '**score**' the replies you receive.

You could use the 'yes' and the 'no' replies to produce a *'percentage'* score. For instance, in the case of the five-year-olds, you might be able to say:

■ 59% liked their toys when they received them.

■ 46% still liked their toys after three months.

These two examples have been chosen because they also illustrate another important point in questionnaires and their use.

It is of little value to use a term such as 'like' without *qualifying* what is meant by it. In this case it might be that you thought that if five-year-olds *did not burst into tears* at the sight of a particular toy, you were going to say that they *'liked it'*. This is one qualification about the term 'like'.

The example above offers *another* qualification. In it the term 'like' is further qualified. It is suggested in the example that 59% of the five-year-olds you *asked* did not cry *at the first sight* of their toys. However, if 'liking a toy' was thought of as 'still playing with that toy after three months', only 46% of those five-year-olds 'liked their toys'.

There are other ways of scoring and presenting your findings. For instance, in the example of the five-year-olds and their toys, you could present the percentages as *bar graphs*, which would make them more visual and allow you to use colour if you wished.

You could use a sheet of *graph paper* to score replies of a more qualitative nature. For instance, you might ask people what they thought of a piece of your work in Art and Design. You could allow them to put their replies into their own words, or you could give them a questionnaire. In either case, if you sort out a few *headings* which describe the categories of information you have collected in the replies, you could put these headings along the top of your sheet of graph paper. Each time the replies you have gathered appear to refer to one of your headings, you *fill in a square* of the graph paper under that heading. When you have finished your 'scoring' of the replies in this way, you will have an indication of the values other people saw in your work.

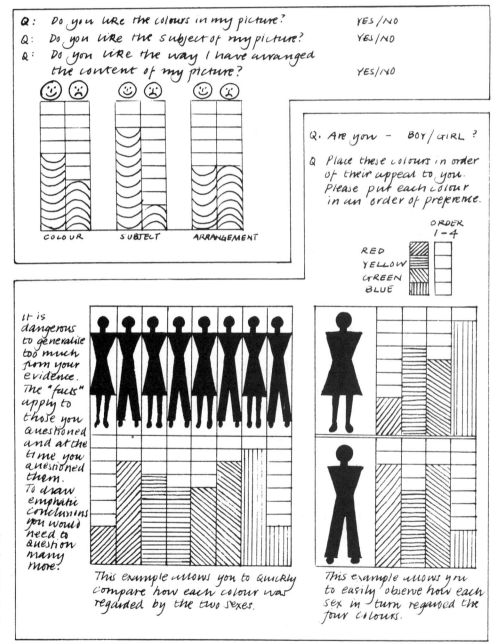

Fig. 4.8 The visual presentation of information. In this instance the 'Bar Graphs' have been made more visual by calling upon images and symbols which have already gained a high level of public understanding and credibility.

TESTS

In this instance '**Tests**' do *not* mean exercises which measure what it is that *you* do and *your* ability in doing it. Tests in Art and Design measure what it is that *Art and Design products do*, and how effectively *they* do it.

The methods of testing which are popularly associated with the consumer magazine, *Which*, can offer a lot to your studies in Art and Design. For instance, if you design and make something, an essential part of its evaluation might be 'how strong it is'. If this is so, then you might design a test to see:

■ how much weight the object will take;

■ how long it will hold an object before dropping it;

■ how long it will last when used constantly in the way intended.

However, in Art and Design there are *other* qualities in a piece of work which might need to be tested. For instance, in a piece of work in *Graphic Design* it could be essential that the result 'made people choose it' in preference to similar alternatives. If this were so, then it would be necessary to construct a test which measures its effectiveness in *this* respect.

This might mean setting up a small *display* of your product *and* similar products. Then, with the aid of a questionnaire, you could ask your classmates things such as, which product *looks*:

■ the most colourful;

■ the most enticing;

■ the most expensive;

■ the most useful;

■ the best value?

This represents a 'test' just as much as the more physical ones sometimes conducted by *Which* Magazine.

15 〉 PRESENTING YOUR FINDINGS

Each of these means of research, or enquiry, or investigation, or exploration, call them what you will, have their own distinctive qualities. Each one is suited to providing certain kinds of information. Once you have this information, and have 'scored' it, there are various means of **presenting** your results.

Scoring and presenting the results of your questionnaires can include the use of:

■ graphs;

■ bar graphs;

■ diagrams;

■ charts;

■ tables.

You will be familiar with some of these terms, and the method they represent, from your studies in other school subjects, such as Mathematics, Geography and Economics.

What they all do is provide the means to condense and present the most complex information effectively and in a *visual* form which is easier to read and digest than lengthy sentences and paragraphs would be.

You need to explore these methods and experiment with them in terms of your work (Fig 4.8). If you begin this early enough in your course, you will quickly become more proficient in selecting the best means for your purpose, and at being able to use that means.

SUMMARY

- All the information and material you gather from your contextual studies and your preparatory studies should be carefully noted and kept safely.
- To do this a variety of means and materials will be necessary.
- These might include, pencil, other graphic stick-media, wet and dry colour media, collage and constructional materials, and photography.
- Photography might be used by *you* to record your work, or as a creative medium in your work. Other people's photography might be incorporated into your work.
- Photocopying is a very useful tool in Art and Design studies. Photocopiers not only reproduce things, singly or in numbers, but can be used to enlarge or reduce original images.
- Your concept of drawing should be a broad one.
- Drawings serve various purposes, and are made by various means. This all creates a wide variety of *forms* of drawing.
- What is important, because drawings are so varied, is that each individual drawing should have its own consistent 'internal code'. This provides the means by which others can 'read' your drawings, an important aspect if they are to communicate information and ideas.
- It might help to compile a file of different 'types' of drawings.
- Writing is a historic form of drawing and is an authentic part of your Art and Design studies, particularly in the GCSE.
- There are many writing tools, in the same way as there are many drawing tools. You should explore their potential and match these to your needs at any time.
- Presenting your Art and Design work could take many forms. Some studies could be in 'book' form, others in a 'concertina' display, others in a file, others in a folder, and yet others in the form of an 'exhibition'.
- What you have done at any time will help decide which form of presentation you should choose to use.
- In presenting your work you should control its 'sequence'.
- There are two forms of sequencing suggested. One is 'chronological' and the other 'narrative'.
- Your information can come from either 'primary' or 'secondary' sources.
- Whatever your source of information, you need to get into the habit of 'referencing' its source. There are formal and accepted ways to do this. It is probably easier to learn and use these rather than invent ways of your own which might not be understood by other people.
- There are many ways to collect and collate the information and material you gather together. It might be in sketch books, diaries, scrapbooks, files, folders, or one 'common-place' book.
- There are some methods from professional 'research' which are useful in the study of Art and Design. Using 'interviews' and 'questionnaires', conducting 'tests', and presenting the evidence you come up with in the form of graphs, bar graphs, diagrams, charts and tables, as well as normal prose, all contribute to the depth and range of your studies.

GLOSSARY OF TERMS USED

Annotated drawing   A drawing which is made up of a *combination* of visual images and written notes which together register your responses to the subject.

Book   A collection of your work into a 'book' format. It will usually contain a reasonable proportion of written, or lettered work.

Concertina display   A method of gathering and presenting your work on hinged boards. For storage purposes these 'concertina' together, ending up the size of one board, but the depth of as many boards as there are in the concertina.

Documentation   The categorising of your information and material into various *storage* systems. It also includes the *retrieval* system designed to give you access to it in the future.

Dry media   That media in Art and Design which makes a mark, or constructs, *without* the need of fluids to release its properties.

Exhibition   The presentation of your work on a screen, or a wall-board, whereby the individual pieces are arranged together in the space available.

File   A means of keeping related collections of your studies together.

Graphic design   The design of forms and images most usually connected with communicating information, selling goods or ideas, protecting products, and so on.

Internal code   In drawings, the *consistency* within a particular piece of work which allows the information it condenses and contains to be 'read' and understood by others, or by you at a later date.

Interview   A research method used to gain information by talking to someone knowledgeable in the area being studied. Recording that information for future use in your own work.

Patina   The effect of time, atmosphere and use upon things.

Questionnaire   A research method whereby a set of questions is drawn up, designed to find out from others information which you require in your work.

Retrieval system   The means by which you can *find* information you have already discovered and put into an appropriate storage system.

Sample   In research, the people you might *select* to answer your questionnaire, etc.

Score   How you turn the information you might gather into a 'quantity' which enables you to measure and understand its meaning.

Stick-media   That Art and Design media which is in 'stick' form, such as, pencil, crayon, and so on.

Storage system   The various means you might use to 'categorise' your information and material, and the method you might use to keep each 'category' together.

Test   Any means you might use to evaluate and measure the worth of your material, ideas or work.

Wet media   That media in Art and Design which depends upon the addition of a fluid to release its properties.

PREPARATORY STUDIES

GETTING STARTED

Our discussions have so far looked at *preparatory studies* as a part of the *externally set examination*. In this chapter the emphasis changes.

Preparatory studies are first discussed as a fundamental aspect of *all* Art and Design practice throughout the history of the subject. The *essential* nature of preparatory studies in the production of all kinds of Art and Design work is considered. Then, a *case study* is worked through, using a specimen GCSE question, to give you an idea of preparatory studies in practice.

ESSENTIAL PRINCIPLES

Why do preparatory studies at all? First and foremost, because the GCSE in Art and Design says most emphatically that you should. You ignore this at your peril in the examination.

Every examination syllabus published by the Examining Groups for Art and Design shows that those responsible for art and design education and its examination at the age of 16+ believe that 'preparatory studies' are an important *operational* part of study in the subject.

The trouble with Art and Design in the real world is that you see only the *obvious outcomes* of all the work and knowledge artists and designers put into producing a piece of artwork, a design, or an object. You go to an Art Gallery and you see a number of fine pictures, framed in ornate gilt frames and hung without much explanation on a hessian covered wall. The pictures and the wall are usually in an impressive, old building, and a sense of awe is built up within you when you view the works displayed.

This sense of awe might be reinforced by your being vaguely conscious that people with a lot of knowledge about Art and Design probably selected the works which are to be found in the building. Because of this you are likely to think that each piece of work in the building was chosen because of its level of artistic excellence. All of this could make you think that Art and Design is all about producing such apparently highly acclaimed pieces of work!

This is of course *part* of what Art and Design is about. But the pieces of work you see, and maybe admire in Art Galleries, represent only the tip of a very large iceberg so far as the individual artist or designer is concerned.

- The artist, or designer, draws upon *knowledge* and *experience* accumulated over a long period of time.
- The artist, or designer, usually does a lot of *exploratory* and *supportive* work in order *to be able* to produce the work which you see on the wall in an Art Gallery.

This exploratory and supportive work is most often contained in *sketch books* and conducted in *trials and experiments*, which include, perhaps, many false starts in the early stages of a particular piece of work. Gradually the artist selects and narrows down the alternatives and opportunities which exist in any piece of work in Art and Design, until one 'outcome' emerges.

The *single* piece of work which you see on the wall of the Art Gallery is usually the *result* of all this exploratory and supportive work. If you could see the exploratory and supportive work, you would probably see just how much the artist's first idea has been *developed* and *expanded* as the work progressed.

Of course there are occasions when an artist *does* 'just do' the work which you see without any *apparent* exploratory or supportive work to surround it. For instance, if artists are well known as portrait painters, it is probably because they are very experienced and highly proficient at painting portraits. In this case it *might* be that there is not much, or even *any*, exploratory and supportive work behind the particular portrait which is painted. Even so, there may have been some preliminary sketches of the sitter and of the sitter's belongings and usual surroundings. There is also probably many years of experience as an artist and a number of previously successful portraits behind the particular work you might see. So the individual portrait is drawing on a wealth of previous exploratory and supportive work, which is now built into the artist's 'experience'. We can hardly then say that the portrait is 'out of the blue'!

At the age of 16+ you cannot have done too many pieces of work in Art and Design so far in your life! This is not a criticism of you. It is just a simple fact. As someone who is comparatively inexperienced in Art and Design, in order to 'succeed' in your work, you will have to 'work out' *your* ideas in considerable detail *before* and *during* the actual production of the final piece of work in a project.

This will apply just as much to you if you are an artist, a designer, or a craftsman or craftswoman. All this 'working out' that is part of the process of getting around to, and producing, your final piece of work in a project, is what will constitute your **preparatory studies**.

The process of 'working out' in Art and Design builds up *within you* the knowledge and experience necessary to go on and produce better and better pieces of Art and Design work. Part of this development is bound up in the fact that if you *do* enough pieces of Art and Design work, you *will* get better. After all, *Practice makes Perfect*.

By engaging in a thorough exploration of your theme you are more likely to produce good, or better, *pieces of Art and Design work*. At the same time you are more likely to get *better marks* for what you do for your GCSE Art and Design assessment.

<table>
<tr><td>

2 ▷ EXPLORATORY AND SUPPORTING STUDIES

</td><td>

The term 'preparatory studies' can give you a false idea of what is really involved in producing Art and Design work. Already in this chapter it has become necessary, when explaining things to you, to use the terms '**exploratory**' and '**supportive**'. Perhaps these two terms, *together with* '**preparatory**', more accurately describe what actually goes on. For instance, if you are set the task of doing some work based upon the *human form in action*, it might be a good idea if you find out how *others* have treated this subject in the history of Art and Design. You might also write down some *places* such as, the gymnasium, the swimming pool, staircases, and gardens, where it is probable that you will be able to *see* figures in action. If you do, what you have done is not just 'preparatory', it is also 'exploratory', and it will be 'supportive' at a later date so far as your work is concerned.

</td></tr>
</table>

Your next step in this task might be to make some *drawings* and take some *photographs* of people jumping, swimming, going up and down stairs and digging. At the same time, you could begin a *scrapbook* of cuttings showing people doing a *much wider range* of activities, in case your ideas *change direction* later.

Again, this work is as much 'exploratory' as it is 'preparatory'. So far you do not know exactly what it is you will *end up* doing, so it is not strictly 'preparatory' work. At the same time it *is* 'supportive' work, no matter whether you use any of the particular pieces of work or not. *All* that you are doing so far will 'support' you *in making your final decision* about proceeding with the problem before you.

Imagine that you have got as far as deciding that you are going to produce a *statue in clay of a swimmer just leaving a diving board*. You might then find that, despite all your 'preparatory' work, you do not have enough information about the way 'one thing follows on after another' as a person dives off a diving board. So, you have to *return* to the swimming pool armed with a camera and the intention of taking a number of photographs of people as they dive from the diving board.

If you take the necessary trouble to do this, what you are doing cannot be described accurately as 'preparatory studies'. In the *strictest sense*, if you have already *started* to carry out your idea for the sculpture, your 'preparatory studies' have finished. Taking photographs in this way is not just an aspect of *coursework*. It is vital to understand that you *can* go and do this *even during your externally set examination, with most Examining Groups!* This will be explained more fully in the next chapter.

To sum up so far, the word 'preparatory' suggests:

- something done at the beginning;
- something done before you start work on your idea in its final form;
- your planning.

Whereas *in practice*, at *all* stages of their work, professional artists and designers:

- **continue** gathering information;
- **re-direct** their ideas;
- **change** their mind altogether.

Therefore it would pay you to regard your 'preparatory studies' as being:

- preparatory;
- exploratory;
- supportive.

In the SEG Art and Design syllabus there is actually a reference to *'preliminary/ supportive'* studies. These are explained as:

> studies carried out before and during the production of work. They may take many forms, e.g. notes, sketches, the exploration of different ideas.

(SEG (1985). *Draft Syllabus in Art & Design for the 1988 Examination*. Aldershot, AEB, page 3)

This provides you with a good, *working definition* of the term, 'preparatory studies', no matter *which* examination syllabus you are using. It emphasises that such studies can be carried out as *preparation* for the production of your work, but that they can also be carried out *during* the production of your work. Whenever we use the term *preparatory studies* in this book, we will mean *all* these things.

3 > USING OTHER PEOPLE'S FINDINGS

In scientific research, you may wish to say for instance that 'summers in Great Britain are colder and wetter now than they were ten years ago'. This may be in order to proceed with your proposal that 'everyone should receive plastic coating injections into their skin'. However, you will have to *prove* that summers are colder and wetter nowadays. If *someone else* has *already* done this, then you need only *quote* that person's findings in order to go ahead with your proposal. The same principle applies just as much to Art and Design.

Suppose you are working on a picture based upon 'landscape' and you want to paint the features of the landscape in your picture in colours which you consider to be '**symbolic**'. It might be that in the course of your studies you discovered the work of artists such as the Frenchman, **Paul Gauguin (1848 – 1903)**, and the Russian, **Wassily Kandinsky (1866 – 1944)**. Your enquiries might have led you to understand that both these artists used some form of 'Symbolism' in their work. In fact, it might have been that discovery that inspired *you* to paint your landscape in the way you intend.

SYMBOLISM

Plate 11 Paul Gauguin, 'Haystacks'. *The Courtauld Institute Galleries, London.* You can see in this work that Gauguin has 'organised' natural objects and environments into a 'pattern of shapes', probably regardless of their actual 'reality' of existence.

'Symbolism' in Art and Design was part of a broader set of activities which involved poetry and music at the end of the nineteenth century. Its roots may be traced back to the 'Arts and Crafts Movement' of William Morris and also to the 'Pre-Raphaelite' painters. Amongst the major artists associated with Symbolism Gauguin is probably one of the best known.

Gauguin expressed the thought that artists should not slavishly copy nature, but should harmonise all the accidental forms and colours of nature into one 'design'. He thought that artists should make judgements and change the relationship of objects to each other, if necessary, in a way that created a greater truth than naturalism.

An approach like this meant that the pictorial results were related more to the *emotional effect* of what was observed rather than its *objective reality*. Shape and colour became much more important in the picture than the strict adherence to an exact likeness (see Plate 11).

In Gauguin's work this led to the flattening of shapes with his use of colour organised and ordered to complete the visual pattern of his pictures. As a result, not only did the *colours* get modified in Symbolist pictures but also the *shapes*. Then, gradually, these shapes departed from the natural outlines of the objects they stood for. This had significance for a movement called '*Art Nouveau*', which can be seen to have a relationship with Symbolism. This point is raised in a later chapter in this book.

In these circumstances, to quote the work of Gauguin and Kandinsky could be adequate justification for you to proceed with your intention for your landscape. The concept of 'Symbolism' is *known* to exist, and you do not have to 'prove' its existence beyond *referring* to its accepted presence in the work of Gauguin and Kandinsky.

What will now happen, is that your work will be partly assessed on the basis of *how well* you know, understand, and can use the principles of Symbolism. For instance, it will not be enough for you to paint the hills 'pink', the sky 'green' and the earth 'white', simply 'because it is meant to be symbolic'! You will have to *show* that you know and understand more than that about the concept of Symbolism and that you have *interpreted* your knowledge and understanding into your work in a coherent and satisfactory way.

To help with this, you may have found out something about the *nature* of 'Colour Symbolism'. You might be aware that in the culture represented by the United Kingdom, it is customary to wear 'black' at the time of a death. Yet you may have discovered that in Imperial Rome it was the custom to wear 'white' at the time of death!

Just to confuse you, you might then have found out that the Cherokee Indians associated 'white' with happiness! Yet at the same time they used 'white' to signify South on the compass; but the Pueblo Indians used 'red' to signify South!

From all this you would have discovered that colour *is* associated with 'Symbolism' but that 'Symbolism' has a strong *cultural* basis to it.

It *might* have been knowledge like this which led artists such as Gauguin and Kandinsky to their *own* understanding and theories about Symbolism. But whether it was or not, *their* theory and practice can be adopted by *you* as justification for your own work in this connection.

What you would need to do for your GCSE assessment is to show that you were not merely 'copying' their work into your own, but that you had:

- genuine interest,
- genuine knowledge,

and

- genuine understanding,

of the concept of Symbolism.

LEONARDO DA VINCI

The negative feelings which many people seem to have towards the notion of the presence of preparatory studies in Art and Design work is based upon the argument that much of the work done in Art and Design is 'inspirational'; it 'comes out of the blue'!

But does it? **Leonardo da Vinci (1452 – 1519)** is widely regarded as a 'genius'. The popular interpretation of the word 'genius', particularly in the case of Art and Design, is that it is a natural attribute that exists *within* someone *without training or development*.

In fact, Leonardo was apprenticed to a leading Florentine Workshop, that of the Italian painter and sculptor, **Andrea del Verrochio (1435 – 88)**, where he learnt '*many things*', according to Gombrich (1984).

Leonardo lived at the time of great discoveries. From **Mathematics** came the '*Science of Perspective*'. From the **Study of Anatomy** came deeper insights into the *structure* and *operational methods* of the human body.

Not only did Leonardo contribute towards the growth of knowledge surrounding these discoveries, but he also *studied* perspective in Verrochio's workshop, as well as plants, animals and the technical procedures of foundry-work (Gombrich 1984).

This hardly suggests someone whose ability was *so natural*, so internally complete, that he had *no need* to study, to explore things, to test and to evaluate!

Even if he *could* produce his masterpieces without reference to other things and other areas of knowledge, it appears that he actually *did* make such studies and references.

Much of the material of his which still exists abounds in material which could be labelled as preparatory studies, in the full sense that the term is intended here. He had a preoccupation about flight and flying machines. His *sketch books* show that he did not just 'inspirationally' invent flying machines, but that he *studied* the flight of insects and birds, *analysing* their movements and methods. If this does not represent preparatory studies, what does?

The whole notion of preparatory, preliminary, or supportive studies, call them what you will, is well within the *normal* tradition for working in Art and Design. This applies as much to professional work in the subject as it does to its study at the level of the GCSE. To be *involved* in these studies puts *you* in the *mainstream* of Art and Design.

4 > PREPARATORY STUDY-SKILLS

Always remember that *contextual studies* are not a subject in themselves, but are the backbone of your **preparatory studies**. As we saw in Chapter 3, the skills essential to your contextual studies are all associated with:

- RESEARCHING;
- RECORDING;
- ANALYSING;
- SELECTING;
- EVALUATING.

PRACTICAL STUDIES

Again, your *practical studies* are not an end in themselves, but involve further skills essential for your preparatory studies. You cannot carry out your practical studies successfully without using and developing the skills associated with:

- CONDUCTING OBSERVATIONAL STUDIES;
- MAKING AND DOING.

> " You must learn to work out your *own* Preparatory Studies. "

'Independence' is a quality which the GCSE aims to encourage and develop. In the National Criteria for Art and Design there is specific mention of this quality with regard to the Controlled Test. In working on your preparatory studies you will invariably develop a measure of independence, because *you* are taking decisions on *what* to follow up.

PREPARATORY STUDIES – A CASE STUDY

What is said in this section will apply *equally* to your coursework as much as it does to your externally set examination. However, the *example* and discussion will centre on your externally set examination.

5 > CHOOSING A QUESTION

In your externally set examination the first task you have is to *choose the question* you are going to answer.

In the case of the LEAG examination, you do not appear to have a choice of questions. That examination sets just *one theme* for the examination each year. Even so, because you can choose *to do* what you like *within* that theme, you still have a choice.

With *all* the examination papers from the various Examining Groups, the first thing you should do is *read your examination paper most carefully*. Do not form an opinion of which question you *will* answer by just 'scanning' the paper.

If you are in full-time education it might be that your teachers will introduce the examination paper to you, discussing its 'pros and cons'. In the GCSE this is perfectly in order.

- First of all, strike out those questions which you *know* from experience that you will be *unable* to deal with adequately.
- THEN WRITE DOWN EVERYTHING YOU CAN THINK OF ABOUT THE REMAINING QUESTIONS.

    Put down things such as:

    - materials you might use;
    - places you could conduct 'observational studies';
    - types of information you might find;
    - possible sources of information;
    - probable 'contextual' references.

- At this stage *do not* 'sketch out' what your finished work will look like.

    If you do as instructed above you will probably see that two or three of the questions seem to provide a lot more opportunity so far as *you* are concerned. Concentrate on these questions which are emerging.

    Now begin to go to the *places* where you thought you might conduct some observational studies. Or *collect* the things together which you might use to work from if you are planning some 'studio-based' work. You might take a camera with you and get some suitable photographs which would allow you to evaluate the possibilities at a later date. To do so it would help if your school had its own darkroom where you could quickly develop and print your work. Even if you are working from objects in a studio, it could still be a good idea to use a camera to help evaluate their possibilities.

- Begin to collect the information which is readily available to you in respect of *each* question.
- Try to assess its *actual worth* to your intentions. Do not judge it 'by the kilogramme'!
- Visit a library to see what historical and other contextual references are relevant to what you want to do.

It has been pointed out to you already that the Examining Groups allow you *differing* amounts of time to carry out your preparatory studies during the externally set examination. *You* will have to judge how much of the time available you allocate to going along this 'optional' path. There will have to come a time when you select *one* question and concentrate on that.

Insofar as it is possible to say 'how long' you *can* afford to follow up a number of options, perhaps about '**two-thirds**' of the time available to you for your preparatory studies might be a sensible guide. Don't panic at this proposition! Think about it rationally. If you have *six* weeks to carry out your preparatory studies, and you spend *four* of those in this way, you still have a fortnight to concentrate on one question. If, at the other extreme, you have only a fortnight to do your preparatory studies, and spend two-thirds of *that* working in this way, it will divide your time into approximately '**ten**' and '**five**' days.

In both extreme cases quoted above, the examiners know *how long you have had to spend at your preparatory studies*. They will therefore know how much *work* you can be expected to do.

In any case, when you are exploring the possibilities which might be present in a *number* of questions, you are actually spending part of that time on the question *you finally choose to do*. Therefore, you are *not* restricting yourself to just 'one-third' of your available time to work on that question.

Perhaps most important of all, *everything you do* during your preparatory studies, based upon the Examination paper you have had given you, *IS* YOUR PREPARATORY STUDIES. Even exploratory work on questions you do *not* eventually answer, you will give in, and it will be assessed for your examination.

All that is necessary is that you put your preparatory studies together in such a way that it *explains how you worked* and *why you made the decisions you did*. By this means you will make everything you do during your Preparatory Studies available for assessment.

When the time comes for you to decide which question to continue with and to carry out in your *controlled test*, make sure that you apply some suitable *reasons* in order to come to your decision. We've considered possible reasons earlier in the chapter. Try to *avoid* choosing something which you cannot resource adequately on the basis 'It's what I *fancy* doing'. Your 'fancies' should take second-place to your examination prospects at this time.

PROCESS AND PRODUCT

All the Art and Design examination syllabuses emphasise the need for attending to PROCESS as well as PRODUCT.

The **PROCESS** embraces:

- Preparatory Studies;
- Contextual Studies;
- Skills Knowledge and Ability;
- Technical Knowledge and Ability;
- Subject Knowledge;
- Critical Evaluation.

The **PRODUCT** embraces *all* these things, in varying mixtures and quantities, expressed in the form of a satisfactory Art and Design '*outcome*'.

The PRODUCT might be a drawing, a painting, a print, a poster, a pot, a cushion cover, a sculpture, a construction, an environmental design, a photograph, a video clip, a critical appreciation of an artist or an Art and Design Product, and so on.

THE QUESTION

With this in mind, consider the following question.

IGCSE ART AND DESIGN SYLLABUS, 1988. PAPERS 3/4.
'INTERPRETATIVE AND CREATIVE RESPONSE.'

Q6. Self-Portrait.
Using preparatory drawings made by using a mirror, interpret this theme in any way you wish.

Imagine that you have considered one or two alternative questions from that paper and have decided on *this* question for your externally set examination. What follows will not all have been done *after you came to your final decision*. Some of it will have been done whilst you were *still exploring* a number of questions.

6 ⟩ ANALYSING THE QUESTION

First of all, the question **instructs** you to conduct preparatory studies. It states, '*using preparatory drawings*'.

The next few words in the question suggest that your work is going to be very restricted. It seems to tell you exactly what you should do, and consequently, what your work will look like.

'*Using a mirror*' is apparently a command which you should follow – or else! But is it? Amongst other things, the 'Aims' in the IGCSE syllabus specify that:

The aims of Art and Design Education are to stimulate, encourage and develop:

- an interest in, and a critical awareness of, environments and cultures;
- knowledge of a working vocabulary relevant to the subject;
- intuitive and imaginative responses showing critical and analytical faculties.

In the section of the IGCSE Syllabus entitled 'Domains', references are made such as,

Interpretative and Creative Response Domain

- Demonstrate quality of idea as seen by interpretation rather than literal description of a theme.

Personal Investigation and Development Domain

- Impress with personal vision and commitment, and make purposeful movement towards maturity.

- Research appropriate resources.
- Assess a design problem and arrive at an appropriate solution.
- Show the development of ideas in a series of rough layouts or experiments which lead to a final solution.

You can see from this why it is important that you should *know the contents of the syllabus you are using*.

Whereas it might have appeared on reading the question that you *were* being restricted as to what you should do, the Aims and Domains quoted above show that you are also told to do 'many other things' in your work.

This is *one important reason* why *you* should read your syllabus yourself. Your teachers may tell you to pay attention in your work to those various and many 'other things' which are contained in the syllabus. But you are only likely to really remember this and to act upon it *if* you have *read them for yourself*!

If you did *not* pay attention to these 'many other things', you *might lose* marks in your examination. If you *did* pay attention to them you *should gain* marks for your work in your examination. In addition to this 'bonus' as it were, the 'many other things' provide you with a key to 'unlock' the question and to begin to be a little more original in your response to it.

BRAINSTORMING

Under 'Choosing a Question', we said that you should write down *all* that you can think of that might be relevant to the question. There is a good way of doing this. Tony Buzan (1974) writes about this and calls it making 'Pattern Notes'. In this book the system will be called '**Brainstorming**'.

'Brainstorming' is a term which comes from the work of Edward de Bono (1970). Begin by sorting out a few major *headings* which will enable you to think about the problem and to categorise your thoughts as they come.

In the case of this question, your major headings might be,

MIRROR   SELF-PORTRAIT   INTERPRETATION

Get a sheet of paper.

Head the sheet with the number of the question, and write the question out in brief, to act as a constant reminder.

Pick a coloured felt-tip and, using these headings as '*key words*', write them on the sheet in *capital letters* and put a box or a ring around them. It need not be done 'neatly'.

Space them out on your sheet so that there is plenty of room around each.

Now, using *antennae*, or *legs*, start writing notes to yourself, as they come into your head when you consider each 'key word'. DO NOT STOP TO 'WEIGH-UP' WHETHER EACH THOUGHT YOU HAVE IS WORTHWHILE, OR INTELLECTUAL ENOUGH. JUST WRITE THEM ALL DOWN.

Perhaps as your 'diagram' develops you begin to see *connections* between some of your thoughts. If this is so, link them with arrows. THIS DIAGRAM IS A PERSONAL MESSAGE TO YOURSELF. DO NOT WASTE TIME MAKING IT LOOK 'ARTY'.

- It is a 'trace' of your thoughts.
- It will develop its own appearance which will arise naturally out of its 'method' and 'content'.
- Retain this appearance and do not 'tart it up' for your examination.
- Your teachers and the examiner will know what the diagram is and will assess it entirely on its '*credibility*', and not its '*artiness*'.

You should keep this diagram by you at all times. If you think of *other* things later on, *add* them to it. It could be a good idea if you use a different coloured felt-tip each time you do so, and perhaps put in a 'key' to show *when* you used these different colours. If you do this, the diagram will also become a 'time-chart' of your thoughts and your progress in your work.

Fig 5.1 Brainstorming diagram for the 'self-portrait' work.

SELF-PORTRAIT BRAINSTORMING DIAGRAM

For this particular 'Case Study', the 'Brainstorming Diagram' which was used is shown in Fig 5.1. In this book it is not possible to use colours to show you the 'time-sequence' in the thoughts. Instead this is represented by using different 'type faces' for later brainstorming diagrams. A key explains their use.

The following describes the *thoughts* behind the diagram. They were made at a speed faster than it takes you to read them. Whilst each thought came to mind, a word, or a few words, were written down to summarise it.

Mirror

A mirror is a reflective surface. Everyone doing a self-portrait starts by picking up a mirror. What other reflective surfaces are there? Some will not make a very clear image. What possibilities does that open up? Broken images? How about catching sight of yourself unexpectedly in a shop window? Dressing-table mirrors allow you to see yourself from the front and from each side at the same time. This is a bit like 'Cubism', isn't it? You don't just see yourself in a mirror; what about the backgrounds?

Self Portrait

Self-portraits are a popular thing in art. Plenty of artists through the ages have done them. Why? Is it possible to know why? It might be possible to sort out the differences in approach that each artist has made, rather than trying to read a dead person's mind. Could compare some self-portraits by some of the great artists and sketch and write about them.

Not all portraits are self-portraits. Some artists make a living from painting pictures of other people. Did photography knock all this on the head? Do portraits 'look like' the sitters? It might be dangerous to make them too much so! Does every artist make a portrait of someone else look like themselves, to a degree? Do the subjects always like the result? Graham Sutherland's portrait of Winston Churchill was not liked by the family. Didn't they burn it?

Interpretation

Interpretation could be 'style'. If the so-called 'photographic likeness' portraits of, say, Velazquez and Rembrandt, appear different in ways other than their subject-matter, what is it that makes this difference? 'Cubism' and 'Pointillism' would certainly make the same thing 'look different'! Are there other Movements in Art which would help to build up knowledge of this kind?

It is said that Rembrandt painted 'the character' of his sitters. What does this mean? Character might be shown by including the belongings of the subject in the picture. Perhaps some of those Kings shown on rearing horses were trying to have something said about their characters. If you painted a picture of a 'Yuppie' reflected in the hub-caps of his Porsche, would it say something about his 'character'?

The *words* in the brainstorming act as a *future aid to your memory* of the *thoughts* such as those above. They prompt you when your interest begins to flag or your work appears to be losing direction.

The unrestricted thoughts listed above offer plenty of avenues for practical, experimental work, as well as posing serious contextual questions which should be answered.

The next step is to decide how to begin to **follow up** some of your ideas. In the IGCSE examination you have only two weeks for your preparatory studies. It will be necessary to bear this in mind.

First, begin to sort out your unrestricted and random thoughts into some sort of **order of priority**. Be careful about concentrating only on what you know already. At the age of 16+ you are likely to be a little stuck in knowing quite where your ideas might lead you, so keep some of the 'unknown' options open.

If you show your diagram to your teachers they will be able to give you some 'short-cuts' towards the information you will need. Their knowledge of Art and Design will be considerable, and not restricted to the technical and the productive alone. *Use your teachers' advice to follow up some of your thoughts more fully.*

PRIMARY SOURCE MATERIAL

Apart from this it might be best to begin from some '**primary source**' material. You could start to do some 'preparatory drawings', as the question demands that you should. Rather than thinking of drawings to do which will lead you to a definite 'end' which you already have in mind, set up a 'comparative' experiment.

In the brainstorming diagram the idea of using *different reflective surfaces* came to mind. *Collect* a variety of these surfaces, such as, foil, stainless steel utensils, broken mirrors, water, and so on, which will reflect your image, and *do a drawing* from each of them. *Write your responses* to each of these drawings.

Because you know that the medium you use to 'draw' with affects the way that the drawing 'looks', you might use just one reflective surface which gives you a result you like and do a number of 'drawings' of yourself, using a *different medium* each time. You could collect together pencils, pen and ink, pastels, crayons, water-colours, collage material, and so on, to do this. Again, you should *write down* your opinion of the effect of each drawing.

SECONDARY SOURCE MATERIAL

When you receive your examination paper you will probably be in an Art and Design lesson. Once you are free to go where you like, you could make straight for the school library, or your Art and Design Department's 'Resource Area', if there is one. Armed with the advice your teachers gave you when you showed them your *brainstorming diagram*, you will be in a position to follow up on some *historical references*.

Books, slides, reproductions, articles on art and design, scrapbook material, useful photographic references are *all* valuable '**secondary source**' material for your needs. How you select from them, and how you use them, will make them personal to your studies.

If you just collect mountains of material in this way and force it all into your folder, what you have will be largely meaningless. Worse than this, it will be very difficult to *retrieve* anything really useful from amongst it all. You must use 'secondary source' material so that it provides you with *relevant* information, helps to *develop* your knowledge and understanding, and to improve your own *creative work* and *products*.

Of course, you might demonstrate part of your level of understanding by finding and saving one or more things which 'connect' with your studies, although you do not actually use them in your work. What you might do then is try to explain the 'connection' you saw between the material you have found and your own work.

If you cannot find what you need at the school library, your next port of call is the local library, then the local Museum and Art Gallery, if you have these in your area. If there is no Art Gallery near you, steal a march and see if your parents will 'have a day out' at one next weekend!

You might suggest to your teachers that it would be worthwhile arranging a school-trip to your nearest Art Gallery as quickly as possible. Of course, the likelihood is that your teachers have already planned for this, and you are already booked on the trip. *It is immensely beneficial to see Art and Design work in its original form instead of in books and other reproductive forms.*

As you only have two weeks for your preparatory studies in the IGCSE examination, it might be best if you concentrate on the best source of supportive information you were able to find on one of your 'early' visits during that period to a library or art gallery. Once you do this, be sensitive to *anything and everything* you might come across which supports your line of investigation.

Remember to put the fresh avenues of exploration and information which crop up *into* your brainstorming diagram, using a different coloured felt-tip to represent *when* they occurred in your preparatory studies.

7 > CONTEXTUAL STUDIES

In the case of the 'self portrait' your discoveries might proceed along the following lines, based on a study of five reproductions. The five reproductions which follow offer you examples of the **differences of appearance** when artists paint the *same subject matter* for *different reasons*, at *different times*, and in *different societies and cultures*.

Velazquez (1599 – 1660), in his earlier work, owed a lot to an Italian artist, **Caravaggio (1573 – 1610)**. Carravagio believed that Art should be concerned with 'truth' and not 'beauty'. His work caused him to be called a 'Naturalist', meaning that he painted what he saw. He painted it in such a way as to try to make the figures and objects in his paintings look 'solid' and 'tangible'. One of the ways that he did this was to use 'light' and 'shade' to '*model*' his originally three-dimensional subjects on his two-dimensional canvas.

Velazquez, who was only about eleven when Caravaggio died, actually did an early painting which seems to almost 'copy' Caravaggio's **'Doubting Thomas'**, only 'transposing' it to a different situation and surroundings. This Velazquez work is called **'The Water-Seller of Seville'** and was painted twenty years later.

In the light of this it seems odd that Velazquez later worked as the 'Court Painter' to Philip IV of Spain. In a position such as this, particularly when you consider that he also painted a portrait of Pope Innocent X during that time, it seems that he might have been unwise to paint in his former 'Naturalistic' way. His subjects would be likely to expect to see themselves as they would wish that others would see them, and it could well be that it was in Velazquez' interest to make sure that he produced pictures of them which fulfilled this desire!

Whether this was so, or not, Velazquez can be seen to have changed his style as his life went on. He became much 'freer' in his brushwork and lost the stark contrasts of light and dark which characterised Caravaggio's work.

One of the things which Velazquez did so well was to show in his work what the environment of the Court of Philip IV was like, although this is not evident in this particular painting (Plate 12).

Rembrandt painted portraits of himself from his youth to his old age. He is often said to show the 'character' of his subjects. In this (Plate 13) and other self-portraits done in his later years, Gombrich says, 'his face reflected the tragedy of bankruptcy and the unbroken will of a truly great man'.

Do you think this self-portrait by Rembrandt does this? Is it possible to show 'the tragedy of bankruptcy', or is this something people read into the work only when they know that Rembrandt was bankrupted?

Whatever your answers are, there is something undeniably great in Rembrandt's work and most people can sense it, even if they have no knowledge about Art and the History of Art.

What is it that is 'great' in Rembrandt's work so far as you are concerned? You might be able to explain and justify it by comparing his work with that of some of the other artists in this section.

Gainsborough (1727 – 88) was a 'country-man', of whom it is said he would have

Plate 12 Diego Velazquez, 'Philip IV of Spain'. *Reproduced by courtesy of the Trustees, The National Gallery, London.*

rather painted 'Landscapes' than the commissioned portraits which gave him his living. In the painting of a country squire and his lady (Plate 14), Gainsborough seems to have been able to introduce his love of the landscape into one of his commissioned portraits.

Why do you think he was able to do this? Was it that his subjects had a 'pride of ownership' in the landscape in which they are depicted and so wished Gainsborough to show what it was they 'owned'? Or does the whole picture just reflect an image of 'social elegance' which might have been indicative of the age?

Plate 13 Rembrandt, 'Self Portrait Aged 63'. *Reproduced by courtesy of the Trustees, The National Gallery, London.*

Plate 14 Thomas Gainsborough, 'Mr and Mrs Andrews'. Reproduced by courtesy of the Trustees, The National Gallery, London.

Whatever it was, Gainsborough's painting can be seen to be 'different' for some reason from either the Velazquez or the Rembrandt, and as they are all 'Portraits', it seems reasonable to assume that you might find that the differences might be in the 'reasons' why the pictures were painted.

The British artist, **Joshua Reynolds (1723–92)**, was a contemporary of Gainsborough. In the same way that Gainsborough's wish was to paint landscapes rather than portraits, Reynolds was more interested in things in his work other than just creating 'likenesses' of his sitters.

In the picture (Plate 15) he has placed the young girl in an 'invented' setting, all of which is designed to create an internal 'harmony' in his work. This attitude reflects, in turn, *one* aspect of the society in which he lived. Reynolds was an intellectual and in his own circle of acquaintances it was natural at that time that he should set out to create his picture according to a set of 'intellectual theories'.

What do you think of the result?

The work as a work of art has definite similarities with the Velazquez and the Gainsborough, yet it is different from both. Miss Bowles certainly looks 'sweet and charming' in this picture, but does the whole picture look any more 'real' than any of the others in this section?

Is 'reality' more about the beliefs the artist holds rather than the 'photographic likeness' of the picture? There can be no doubt that there is a sense of acute 'reality' in this picture by Reynolds, but is it about the 'attitude' of some young people towards their pets rather than the 'photographic representation' of both? Who is to say that this sort of 'character' reality is less significant than a 'photographic likeness'? After all, it is the 'character' which Rembrandt gets into his portraits which is so praised by critics and public alike.

Which 'portrait' do you like most so far, and why?

The next picture (Plate 16) is by the Netherlands artist, **Jan van Eyck (1390 – 1441)**. You were introduced to him when it was suggested in an earlier chapter that he was associated with the invention of 'oil paint' as a painting medium.

Van Eyck certainly moved the style of pictorial representation forward into one of accurate and 'naturalistic' reality. This work pre-dates the others so far in this section, and in a way they are all dependent upon it in part for their own style and sense of 'reality'.

Oil as a painting medium allows the artist to achieve a 'blending' of one colour edge into another in a smooth and gentle manner. Prior to the invention of oil painting, colours were mixed mainly with 'eggs'. This provided the means for the colour to be 'suspended' in a medium and to adhere to the surface it was put upon. But 'egg' paintings did not allow this careful 'blending' and as a result each thing in a picture is painted within its own carefully delineated 'boundary'. This does tend to deny 'visual' realism; human beings tend not to see with such carefully delineated clarity when they take in a whole scene.

'The Marriage of Arnolfini' shows a little piece of both the fifteenth century and the world of a Merchant of that time. In many ways it is like a 'marriage certificate'. It is

Plate 15 Joshua Reynolds, 'Portrait of Miss Bowles with her Dog'. *Reproduced by permission of the Trustees of the Wallace Collection, London.*

Plate 16   Jan van Eyck, 'The Marriage of Arnolfini'. *Reproduced by courtesy of the Trustees, The National Gallery, London.*

signed, 'Jan van Eyck was present' and includes the reflection of the painter and a 'witness' in the mirror on the wall.

In this sense, not only is van Eyck involved in a new painting medium and a new form of realism, but also in a new form of 'documentation', one which is wound up with 'contracts', 'events' and 'possessions'.

A useful exercise would be to use these five reproductions as a basis for an illustrated comparison of the works. It might even form the basis for a unit of coursework.

PHOTOGRAPHY

What was attempted by each of these artists so far has provided a model for **photography**.

Fig 5.2 is a photograph of a wedding scene, taken in the 1930s. Once again, the picture provides a 'social document' of the time. Although the content is largely a matter of 'costume', the photograph does tell you of a change in the social order of things since the van Eyck picture. In this photograph the Bride and Groom are surrounded by their parents, the Bridesmaids and the Best Man. In a way, the Bride and Groom emerge as the 'possessions' of all the other characters in the picture! They certainly look the most ill-at-ease!

The next photograph (Fig 5.3) shows you how the professional 'High Street' photographer could create a feeling of 'grandeur' and splendour for their clients. This lady comes from a humble background and a family who worked on market stalls. Yet, in this picture, she is shown not only in her 'Sunday best', but against a heavy tapestry drape and sitting on a quality chair, with padded arm-rests, which is placed on a rich 'Axminster' carpet. It is unlikely that any of these 'furnishings' featured in the lady's home life!

This photograph appears to have many similarities with the Velazquez portrait above. Try to write a comparison between the two, pointing out the similarities and the differences between them; the nature of the two mediums used, that is to say, paint and photographic film; and the differences which their respective historical, scientific, and cultural times contribute towards the two images.

The 'seaside' portrait (Fig 5.4) represents a 'fun' approach to portraiture but it also reflects, in turn, a social and cultural attitude of a particular time. It is rare to go to the seaside today and to see the set-ups for this type of photography.

It is essentially a 'fair-ground' culture. It is not unlike the 'Hall of Mirrors', whereby people are happy to see themselves distorted, grotesque and figures of fun, whereas they might usually look in a mirror to see themselves as they would like most to be seen.

Fig. 5.2 A 1930s wedding photograph.

Fig. 5.3 A 'High Street' photographic portrait at the turn of the century.

Fig. 5.4 Comic 'seaside' portrait. You would stick your head through the 'hole' represented by the black oval.

Plate 17 Paul Cézanne, 'Self Portrait'. *Reproduced by courtesy of the Trustees, The National Gallery, London.*

Plate 18 Georges Seurat, 'Young Woman Powdering Herself'. *The Courtauld Institute Galleries, London.*

In the same way, whereas most portraits, either painted or photographed, are concerned to show people as they would wish to be seen, in this type of photograph, the subjects put themselves up as 'figures of fun'.

Finally, we look at two pictures which deal more with the 'Theory of Painting' which each artist holds, rather than with striving towards 'likenesses', be it of people or landscapes.

In this work (Plate 17) Cézanne has 'constructed' realism by using his paint like a set of small, various coloured, 'building' bricks. Each colour is the result of careful and close observation of nature. Each dab, 'brick', or brush-stroke of colour is carefully placed in relationship to what is before Cézanne's eyes, *and each other on his canvas*.

In the next example (Plate 18), Seurat, who largely painted Landscape, constructed his pictures by means of a series of small dots of different coloured 'spots' of paint. His theory was to do with the scientific theory of colour vision (Gombrich, 1984). He believed that the human eye and mind would blend dots of pure colour into intense and luminous shapes of colour. Working in such a way led Seurat to simplify shapes and forms within a picture. As a result, although he might achieve such effects of 'pure' colour as his theory led him to believe he would, the end result was further away from the natural and realistic appearance of things than he may have originally intended.

Cézanne was striving for a feeling of solidity and depth, whereas Seurat was concerned with the way that colour is 'seen', striving towards a means to re-create in paint this visual reality of colour. Nevertheless, the appearance of the work of both artists is governed as much, if not more, by the 'theory' behind the *painting method* as it is by the subject matter and the attempt to make the picture 'look like' that subject matter. In their different ways, both Cézanne and Seurat were involved with creating 'order' in their work, order in each case being concerned with 'realism'.

You might use the work of Cézanne, Seurat and the various photographs, to write about 'realism' in art and design.

CONCLUSIONS AND THE NEXT MOVE

At this point you have explored all that your original *brainstorming diagram* brought to mind. This has meant that you have:

- increased your levels of knowledge and understanding;
- added to your original diagram;
- made some very useful drawings;
- collected a number of reflective surfaces;
- experimented with materials;
- used Primary Sources of information;
- used Secondary Sources of information;
- made some drawings from 'direct observation'.

YOU ARE NOW IN AN EXCELLENT POSITION TO BEGIN TO DECIDE ABOUT YOUR 'CONTROLLED TEST'.

8 > PLANNING FOR THE CONTROLLED TEST

DO NOT get together all the materials for your controlled test, including a piece of paper the size you intend to use, and then have a *'dummy run'* at what you intend to do in the controlled test. IF YOU DO THIS, THE OVERWHELMING LIKELIHOOD IS THAT YOU WILL PRODUCE A 'STALE' AND 'UNINSPIRING' PIECE OF WORK IN YOUR CONTROLLED TEST.

Consider where you are at this stage.

If you *have* worked in the way suggested above, you will not only have a pile of 'preparatory studies', but you will also have a number of *alternative* ways in which to proceed. Just weigh-up these alternative ways. If necessary, do one or two quick *experimental sketches* of the possibilities. This will test the credibility of each of them. The results will also be an important part of your preparatory studies.

The likelihood is that you will be in a position to:

1 Do a 'straight' **self-portrait** by setting up a large mirror, sitting in front of it, and making a picture of what you see.

- Will you '*see*' the *background* which is the reflection of your surroundings?
- Will this be a carefully arranged, neutral-coloured, *piece of cloth*?
- Will it be an equally carefully arranged *collection* of the things which interest you and help to build up an image of you?
- Will it just be the *chance surroundings* of the room you happen to be working in?

All these choices are yours. How will you *convey* your thinking and your decisions on these matters to your teachers and the examiner?

In Art and Design the best way is to do a quick study of each of the above scenarios. What materials will you choose to work in? What scale should your work be? Again, all these choices are yours. If you made some experiments earlier on in your preparatory studies, these will help you now in explaining to your teachers and the examiner *why* you worked in the materials you did and to the size you did.

2 You could choose to do a **self-portrait** from a reflective surface other than a mirror.

- You will already have made some drawings of this kind. Are they enough?
- Have you made enough experiments with different media to be able to understand their individual qualities, decide between them, and justify your decision to use one in preference to another?
- Is your decision really suitable for your final idea and intention?

3 You could choose to make your **self-portrait** in the *style* of a Movement in Art and Design, or of an individual artist.

- Have you got enough information to *really understand* the Movement or the work of the artist in question?
- If you have *not*, then all that you are likely to do is a 'pastiche' of the original.

This means that your work is likely to be no more than an 'imitation' of something else and will probably be a mere 'copy' of the style and appearance of the other work. If you think back to the discussion about 'Symbolism', you will understand what is meant here.

4 You could decide to be influenced by the effect of photography on the appearance of 'portraits'. You might choose to *reflect* some of the settings used in formal photographic portraits, or the settings used in the 'fun' portraits of the seaside.

- Have you been able to collect or study such photographs?
- Have you bothered to try to find out why they came about? For example, what were the *social conditions* which influenced the way that people lived and thought of themselves at the time? Why *do* people like to have 'records' of themselves?
- Have *you* had your 'portrait' taken in a way which is influenced by social values, rather than your personal values. For instance, have you ever been photographed in a class, or a team photograph. In such circumstances you do not make many personal decisions, but are swept along to do 'the right thing'.

Making your choice you might find that you have to do one or two more things to get ready for you examination. Whether this is so or not, you can see that you have more than enough to do in your preparatory studies without having a 'dummy run' at the work as you intend to do it during the controlled test.

9 USE AND PRESENTATION OF PREPARATORY STUDIES

You will need to make your preparatory studies freely available to yourself at the time of the controlled test. Therefore, do not waste time 'trimming' your work and 'mounting' it during the time given for your preparatory studies.

After you have finished your controlled test you will need to order and present your preparatory studies in support of the work you did for your controlled test. This will be dealt with in the next chapter.

For now you should sort out your preparatory studies so that they will help you *during* your controlled test and make it easier for you to work at that time. Your preparatory studies should provide work which falls into at least one of the following categories:

Contextual Studies are part of Preparatory Studies.

1 Work done in the investigation of at least one other question from your examination paper.

2 Work which is 'contextual'. This might be the results of your investigation into the way that *other people* have worked on similar ideas, or into the way that people lived at *other times*, and so on.

3 Work which considers the properties and qualities of materials.

4 Work which is the result of direct observation and recording on your part.

5 Work which outlines and develops your ideas in preparation for starting work in your controlled test.

If you have got a collection of work which represents *each* of the categories above you have worked *extremely well* during the time of your preparatory studies.

To get ready for your controlled test you can carefully wrap-up the work you did for Category 1. You are *not* likely to need this *during* your controlled test; but just in case you do, put it into the folder of work you take into your test.

The same applies to any work which represents Category 2; but again still take it into your controlled test with you.

All the work which represents Categories 3, 4 and 5 is *essential to you as you carry out your controlled test*. Therefore it should be readily available for you to use and refer to *during* your controlled test.

According to *what* this work actually is, *how much* there is of it and *what form* it all takes, you should devise the most suitable way to make it readily available to yourself during the conduct of your controlled test.

■ *If* this means sticking some of it onto single, larger sheets with something like 'Blue Tack', then do so.

■ *If* this means sorting it out and putting it into separate files, then do so.

■ *If* this means putting it into a certain order and then clipping it together in that order, then do so.

In the end it might be that you think your work from categories 3, 4 and 5 is best taken into your controlled test in *loose form*, but in a *folder* to keep it together with your work from Categories 1 and 2.

Part of your decision on these matters will rest with the *amount of space* you will have available for carrying out your controlled test. For instance, it is clearly a bad decision to stick your work onto large sheets, if you only have a small work-space to work in.

But, whatever you do, do remember that you may need to re-order it *after* your controlled test, so that it is *presented* in such a way that it 'supports' *what it is you actually did for your controlled test*.

S U M M A R Y

■ Preparatory studies are an essential part of your work in your course of studies, as much as they are an essential and sometimes compulsory part of your externally set examination.

■ Preparatory studies can be seen to be a fundamental part of Art and Design work throughout history.

■ In the expert and professional work carried out by artists and designers, preparatory studies can be seen to be 'Exploratory' and 'Supporting' studies, rather than 'preparatory' studies alone.

■ Apart from their historical significance and pedigree, you have to do preparatory studies in your work because your examination syllabus either instructs you to do so, or implies that you should.

- In studying the work of professional artists and designers you can be led to believe that their work is 'inspirational'. However, even in such work it can be seen that 'preparatory studies' are present in the sum total of their previous experience and knowledge, rather than a specific set of 'drawings'.

- In your preparatory studies you should be alert to *new* information as you come across it, even if you believe you know already what it is you are going to do. You should be ready to allow this new information to re-direct your ideas and intentions. You should be particularly willing to change or modify your work when you discover new material which is relevant to your intended work.

- In your preparatory studies you can use the 'findings' of other people without having to set out to 'prove' their validity. If someone else has 'proved' something, or shown something by their work, you can *adopt* this 'proof' and proceed from there with your own work. This is so as long as you *acknowledge and explain* what it is you have found out and are doing.

- Preparatory studies enable you to use and show your ability in a *wide range of skills*. You can show how well you Research, Record, Analyse, Select, and Evaluate. You can show how well you work from 'direct observation'. You can show your level of 'independence', whereby you might make your studies personal and even original. You can demonstrate your 'practical' skills and knowledge.

- In the *externally set examination*, part of the necessary skill will be in your ability to *select* your 'question' from the examination paper. This will cause you to analyse the question, and to 'weigh up' the information you need, and would expect to find, relevant to that question.

- In beginning to sort out your responses to a question and its investigation, it helps if you '*brainstorm*' your thoughts down onto paper without worrying how valid and important each thought is.

- In your preparatory studies you will use 'primary' and 'secondary' source material. Make sure that you do provide evidence of *both*, and that all your work in either respect is valid and of a good quality.

- At the *end* of your preparatory studies you need to make some *conclusions* from what you have done and found out, so that you might begin to plan for what you intend to do in your controlled test.

- Do *not* have a dummy run at your controlled test during your preparatory studies.

GLOSSARY OF TERMS USED

Brainstorming	A system of committing your thoughts to paper without pre-judging their worth or validity.
Exploratory studies	Part of preparatory studies, whereby you 'tease out' all the possibilities in a problem or idea, and 'find out' relevant information in support of that problem or idea. This might be drawn, photographed, written, cut out, and so on.
Pastiche	A mere 'copy' of something which neither *explains* nor *develops* your understanding of it.
Supporting studies	This might be considered an *alternative* name for preparatory studies. It does away with the suggestion that 'preparatory' means *beforehand*.

BIBLIOGRAPHY

de BONO, E. (1970). *Lateral Thinking: a textbook of creativity*. London, Ward Lock Educational.

CONTROLLED TEST

GETTING STARTED

At the *end* of your preparatory studies for the Case Study on self-portraits in Chapter 5, you were left with *more than one* possible direction to take. This is an excellent position to be in at the *start* of your **controlled test**. It means that your work will continue to develop *during* your controlled test, and not degenerate into a bored repetition of the 'big' piece of work you had practised originally in your preparatory studies.

The *National Criteria* for Art and Design stipulates.

6 **Techniques of Assessment**
    6.3 (ii) **Controlled Test**
        A test in which candidates are able to show their ability to work independently. The unaided work should also demonstrate the candidate's ability to work to a brief within a specified time limit. One form might be a written examination. Where the controlled test is practical work, preparatory studies must be included where appropriate.

In this stipulation two things emerge:

1 'Independently' in the controlled test means 'Unaided'. As a result of this, the controlled test is often referred to as the 'Unaided Test'.

2 The Controlled Test and the Preparatory Studies *together* make up the *Externally Set Examination* for the GCSE.

E S S E N T I A L   P R I N C I P L E S

Think of *the controlled test* as your opportunity *to work unaided* on your *own* ideas.

If you remember, each Examining Group allows slightly varying periods of time for you to do the controlled test. These amounts of time vary from the minimum of three hours allowed in the IGCSE, to the twelve hours allowed for both the NEA and the NISEC examinations. Table 2.3 on pages 22–23 shows these details. The result of all this is, once again, that you will have to 'cut your cloth' accordingly.

As Table 2.3 will have reminded you, IGCSE allows a *minimum* of *three hours* to a *maximum* of *six hours* for their controlled test. This means that even if you use the full six hours allowed by IGCSE, you will only be able to plan to do *half* as much as you would if you were taking your examination with NEA, who allow up to twelve hours. Once more, however, this does not matter. Whichever examination syllabus you are using, the examiners *will not expect* more of you than the time allocated for the controlled test will allow.

In the case being dealt with here, the first thing you *must* do is be determined to use the *full six hours* IGCSE will allow for the question on the self-portrait. Having only six hours in which to do your work will help you to decide *which* of the alternatives to carry out in your controlled test. But do *not* decide to limit your ambitions unduly. Set yourself a task which *will* stretch you to your limits in the time concerned.

1 > POINTS TO CONSIDER

In the circumstances you need to consider:

- the *scale* of your work for the controlled test;
- the *medium,* or media you choose to work with;
- the *method* you choose to work in;
- the *content* of your work.

SCALE

Suppose you decided your work should measure 75 cm × 50 cm. You would be unwise to set out to paint a picture of this *scale* in the way used by an artist such as Constable. In fact unless you painted part of the picture as a series of large 'flat' areas of colour, in the way that an artist such as **Matisse (1869 – 1954)** might, you would be unlikely to finish it in the time. If you chose to do this, that is to say mix two styles which contrasted as much as those of Constable and Matisse do, your work would probably lack any **'internal consistency'.** You would have to consider this very seriously.

MEDIUM

You could work on such a large scale as 75 cm × 50 cm if you chose a more suitable **medium** than paint.

- If you chose to use **Collage** materials you could probably manage work of this scale in the time available.
- If you chose to use something like **Silk-Screen Printing** to carry out your work, you would also be likely to finish in the time available.

So you can see that the *medium* you intend to use will help to decide the *scale* of your work.

METHOD

You could use paint as your *medium* for the *scale* mentioned if you chose a suitable **method** of working.

- For instance, if you chose to 'paint' large areas of your work with printing rollers and then to work into these with smaller paint brushes, putting in more and more detail, you could cope with the task in the time.

So you can see that the *method* you choose to work with can influence your choice of *medium* and, indeed, *scale*.

CONTENT

Plate 19   Richard Dadd, 'The Fairy Feller's Master Stroke'. *The Tate Gallery, London.*

The picture (Plate 19) by the British artist, **Richard Dadd**, is full of the most intricate 'fairy-like' detail. To attempt to paint it during your controlled test would be folly, unless you can conceive of a 'short-cut' to achieve a *similar* effect.

This could be done in ways such as those suggested in the text of this book.

The thing is not to lower your level of ambition by 'playing safe', or thinking that you would like very much to do something but do not believe that you will have time to do so.

2 > MAKING DISCOVERIES

In this book great pains have been taken to stress to you that there is not a 'right' and 'wrong' way to do something in Art and Design, but an *appropriate* way. Therefore, if you have an idea and you are constrained by time, as in the circumstances of your controlled test, then *search around* and try to discover an alternative way of carrying out that idea. This is what is meant by 'appropriate'. It does not matter how something has been done before, look for another means to do what it is you want to do. After all, this is what van Eyck did, and discovered Oil Painting!

The following diagrams (Figs 6.1, 6.2 and 6.3) show how 'searching around' can lead to discoveries and to a developing piece of work.

To use a 'concept', such as Gluttony or Fear is a good idea. Rather than beginning a portrait with the often ill-defined, and consequently not fully understood, objective of 'getting a likeness', in this case the 'concept' provides you with a closely defined objective to work to.

This work shows how changes of 'focus' and changes of medium can affect and alter the nature of a set of studies. It is exploratory and its effect is quite powerful and even disquieting.

These three examples of student work are good examples of how a task such as painting a portrait can be expanded and made much more personal in this way.

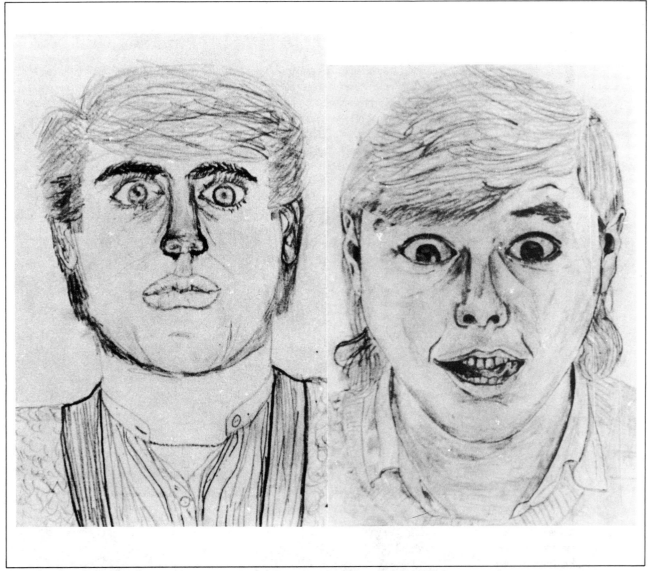

Fig 6.1 Alternative studies: self portraits. These two self-portraits by different candidates, although very sincere, illustrate how a restricted approach to your work can limit your levels of achievement, no matter what your level of ability might be. In fact, one of these pieces of work is quite accomplished in the 'traditional' art examination manner, and would still be likely to achieve a reasonably good grade in the GCSE. But 'all the eggs are in one basket'; the success of the work depends upon its use of material, efficiency in terms of its composition, and, perhaps, whether it is a 'good likeness'.

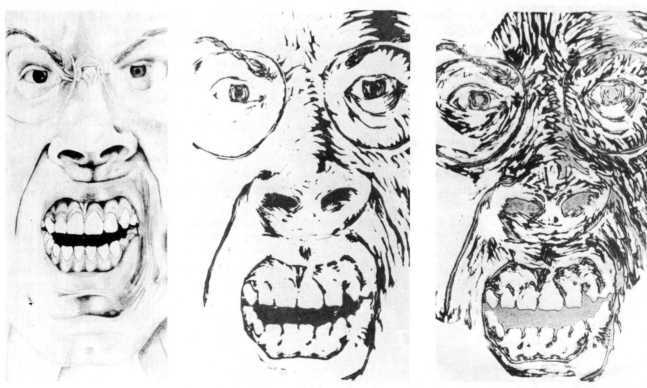

Fig. 6.2 Alternative studies: terrifying. Here the work depends upon its effectiveness in dealing with the concept of being 'terrifying', as well as the qualities spelt out for the works in the preceding diagram. The candidate seems to be more concerned about expressing the terrifying nature of his face than just getting a 'good likeness'. He is also experimenting with a range of materials as each drawing progresses. As he does so, his face seems to be almost 'falling apart', like something from a Sci-Fi Film. Altogether the work looks more relaxed than those in the preceding diagram and this fact alone has probably allowed the candidate to achieve a very high standard of achievement. The candidate seems to be preoccupied with working out the idea to the best of his ability and the results have just followed this, although it must be said that he looks to be an accomplished artist anyway!

Fig 6.3 Alternative studies: fear. Here again, the idea behind the work has been a strong contributing factor behind the success of this work. The whole thing takes on a vitality when compared with other work and this enriches the result as a consequence.

3 > INTERACTION

In an effort to show you how 'scale', 'medium', 'method' and 'content' all **interact** and affect your decision making, imagine you were going to do a painting similar to '**The Fairy Feller's Master-Stroke**'.

You could decide that, using the **medium** of paint, the **method** to deal with the problem of putting in so many flowers is to find a way to 'reproduce' the flowers on a fast repetitive basis.

- You might decide to quickly paint in the background to each area which has many flowers in it by using a roller or a very large brush and then to 'print' the flowers on this by using '**Printing Sticks**'.

- You would need to *have prepared* these printing sticks during your preparatory studies.

- This shows you the necessity to '*experiment*' during your preparatory studies.

- You could, perhaps, use a *similar device* to 'print' in the trees and all their leaves.

- If you study '**The Fairy Feller's Master-Stroke**' carefully, you will see that by this means, or 'method', you could quite quickly fill in most of the picture. It might take you about two hours to do so satisfactorily, even if you were working to the **large scale** suggested above.

- This would allow you about a further four hours to deal with the detail of the **content**. In this you could easily afford to use fine paint brushes to paint in the figures and to put more colour and fine detail on the flowers, and so on.

> *Choosing what to do requires you to* balance *decisions about scale, medium, method, content against* time.

4 > PHYSICAL PREPARATIONS

Because you are working to a *specified time limit* during your controlled test it is *important* that you prepare things well for your test *beforehand*. If you are going to use anything such as printing sticks, you should *make these* and *experiment with them* during the time allowed for your preparatory studies.

If you know that you will need a *facility* which is restricted in its availability, such as a screen-printing frame, or the darkroom, then book your use of that facility with your teachers well in advance of the day of your controlled test. If something happens during your controlled test to stop you using the facility you have booked at the time you booked it, tell the teacher-in-charge *at once* and well in advance of the time concerned. The teacher-in-charge may then be able to allow someone else to use the facility and even to book its use for you at a later time.

If you wish to paint on 'stretched-paper', then stretch *two* pieces of paper of the size you need a few days in advance of your controlled test. This will ensure that it is dry and ready for use, and that it has not split in drying. Also, having two sheets means that you can either work on *two versions* of your work at the same time in the controlled test, or you can *start again* if things 'go wrong' on your first attempt.

If you discover that you will need a 'specialist material' which neither you nor your teacher has, then go and buy it yourself well in advance of the time of your controlled test. Whilst your teachers might repay you the money you spend in this way, remember it is *your* examination which is at stake. Your teachers will do all that they can for you to help you succeed, but you are not the *only* candidate your teachers have to look after! So if, for instance, your teachers have helped you to realise that you should use some *Transfer Lettering* in your work, and it is not available in your art department, then volunteer to get it for yourself.

See if your teachers will allow you to put your things into your work-space *the night before* your controlled test. It is much more 'comfortable' to do this than to struggle in with everything on the morning of your test. It might mean that you have to wait until the room is prepared and cleaned after school finishes, but for the 'calmness' it gives you the next day it is well worth this little bother.

So, **plan ahead** for your controlled test in the following ways:

- Know what you are going to do from your preparatory studies.

- Prepare and collect your material well in advance of the day of your controlled test.

- Install *all* your preparatory studies and your materials in your work-space the night before your controlled test.

The first thing to find out is how the **time** for your examination will be *arranged*. Even with only the six hours IGCSE allows, it should be clear to you that it will be most unlikely that your examination will be *carried out* and *completed* in *one* day. The likelihood is that you will be allocated *two* sessions of three hours each, and these two sessions will probably be on different days. It might be that they are on consecutive days, or that the second session occurs on the same day of the week as the first, but a week later.

What *you* must do is to find out *how* the time for your examination will be broken up, and *which days* on the calendar each session is to be. Once you know this you can begin to plan *exactly* how you *intend* to use the parcels of time for your examination *and the time in between them.*

Of course you cannot, and should not, specify *precisely* what will happen in each period of time. But if you *have* been using a **Diary/Work Journal** approach throughout your studies, you will understand:

- how to plan your time in advance and on paper;
- how to evaluate your progress both during and at the end of each session;
- how to re-direct your intentions and activities both during a session and for the next session.

If you do *plan, evaluate,* and *develop* your activities and your work in this way throughout your controlled test, then your work *during* the controlled test will be alive and exciting to you.

Do not fall into the trap of working out how long it will take you to 'finish' your work, and then 'pacing' yourself throughout the time allowed for your controlled test in order to achieve the finish as the test draws to a close.

If all that you are going to do during your controlled test is to 'fill-in' the outlines of your work, whether this be working in paint, clay, lino-printing, or whatever, then you might as well finish this as fast as you can, and get it over with.

On the other hand, if you see your controlled test as an extension of the *active development* of your work, then you will want to work at as fast a pace as you can, in order to give yourself the time to *take up* the new opportunities that might occur as you work in this way.

In the GCSE *more than one* piece of work from the controlled test will be accepted by the Examining Groups, so do *not* be afraid to retain an early piece of work done in the test. Also, be ready to follow up any exciting idea which might unexpectedly develop from it.

A C A S E S T U D Y –
T H E C O N T R O L L E D T E S T

Let us now return to where you were at the *end* of the preparatory studies for the self-portrait in the previous chapter. If you remember, at that point you were confronted with a number of *alternative* possibilities for your work during the controlled test.
They were:

1 You could do a 'straight' self-portrait, using a plain mirror.

2 You could include as the background to your work, what already exists in the room in which your are working and is reflected in the mirror.

3 You could arrange a neutral-coloured cloth behind you, perhaps in folds, and use the reflection of this as the background to your self-portrait.

4 You could arrange around you a collection of personal things which show your interests and character, and use the reflection of these as your background.

5 You could choose to use a reflective surface other than a mirror for your self-portrait.

6 You could choose to carry out your self-portrait in the 'style' of an artist you discovered in your contextual studies, perhaps using the media, techniques, and manners of composition of that artist.

7 You could choose to carry out your self-portrait in the 'style' of a Movement in Art and Design, whereby you try to 'see' yourself in the way established by the particular Movement.

Take into account the time you have for your controlled test, the fact that you should not be too 'modest' in what you set out to do, your interests and enthusiasms, and the range of your ability and knowledge. You then have to *choose* between these alternatives *before the start* of your *controlled test,* but *at the conclusion* of your *preparatory studies*.

For the purposes of this exercise, suppose that your teachers arranged your controlled test in two 'three-hour' sessions. The second one to be *exactly one week* after the first.

The information about the timing of your controlled test tells you a few things:

- Having two separate sessions will mean that you will have to 'switch in' to your work at the beginning of the second session.
- You will not want to waste any time doing this.
- It also tells you that you have one week between the two sessions.

Knowing that you have a week between the two sessions you should plan to take full advantage of this situation. This means that you could seek out *further information* in support of your work during that time. You could also plan how you intend to 'start up' at the beginning of the second session.

Now your teachers, or the Examining Group, might *forbid* you to take any extra 'preparatory studies' of this nature *into* the examination room with you at the time of your second session. This does not matter unduly. None of them can stop you *thinking* about your work during that week. Your 'thinking' could include both practical and theoretical research. This research will equip you with the knowledge of the *possible direction* your work will take in its final stages and how to get started quickly at the beginning of the second session.

You will want to use the three hours available for the *first* session to the full, but at some point *near the end* of the first session you should become increasingly aware of the problems which confront you in seeking to complete your work, as well as the new possibilities which are beginning to develop as a result of your work during the session. So, near the end of the first session you should begin to *organise* your thoughts on these lines.

You could *write* your thoughts, ideas and decisions down on paper. By doing this you will *know* the essential things you must do *before* you return for the second session. *Notes* such as these would become an important part of your work for the Controlled Test and should be *saved* and *given in* at the end of the test.

6 > PLANNING IN ADVANCE

So far then, you have decided to use *all* six hours available to you and you know that you will have a further week between the two sessions when you could follow up important leads in your work from the first session. Which of the alternative ideas you have for your controlled test should you choose to work on?

There was never any reason for you to accept the normal **background** of the room in which you do your controlled test. It is easier to work from *some* visual stimulus. Therefore you might as well organise the background to your work in the first place. You have lost nothing if you do.

Even if you do not include the background in your final work, you could always photograph it to show your teachers and the examiner what it was you *thought* of doing at one stage in your work. This means that you *could* perhaps collect and arrange your own 'background' to your work and install it in your examination room, preferably the night before the controlled test. You would not then lose any time on your work.

The question you must now resolve is whether this background is to be a collection of some of your personal possessions, or a neutral cloth.

- If it is to be your **possessions**, how *many* should you select; what *size* should they be; what *colours* should they be; how should you *arrange* them?
- If it is to be a **piece of neutral cloth**, what *colour* will it need to be; how *big* should it be; will it *hang* in folds?

Suppose things go wrong with your work and you begin to run out of time, having started to include a *collection of your possessions* as background. You could always *change* to a neutral cloth as the background to your work. With the gap of a week between the two sessions, you could easily obtain a cloth and arrange it in the examination room just prior to the *second session* of your controlled test.

In exactly the same way you could use either a *plain mirror* or an *alternative* reflective surface, and still change from one to the other between sessions if anything goes wrong.

7 〉 THE DECISION

For the purposes of this case study imagine that you discovered the work of Picasso in your preparatory studies and that you conducted a number of *contextual studies* on him and his work.

Perhaps your immediate reaction would have been to say 'anyone can do what he does!' You may have said as much to your teacher. Your teacher may then have asked that you take a *particular* book home to look at. This book may not be specifically about Picasso, but may be about the art movement known as 'Cubism'. Whilst art historians might argue about the absolute origins of 'Cubism', it is popularly accepted that Picasso was the driving force behind the Movement. Your teacher may have thought that if you read about 'Cubism,' and looked at 'Cubist' pictures, you would begin to see Picasso and his work in a new light.

Imagine that this was so and that it interested you. You then began to make a small *study* of 'Cubism' and of Picasso's role in the Movement. You might have compiled a little *booklet* of your work.

In such a booklet you would probably have *written down* your findings *and* your *reactions* to these. You would probably have copied some of the paintings representing the Movement into your booklet, or collected some postcards of them from Art Galleries. If you were unable to visit a Gallery where you could see some original 'Cubist' paintings, it is always possible to get such postcards by writing to the major Art Galleries in the United Kingdom.

It might have been that you compiled a booklet such as this *during* your course of study and it is, therefore, not strictly, 'preparatory studies' insofar as the *externally set examination* is concerned. If so, do not worry. It does not matter. You can *still* use it in your preparatory studies as 'secondary source material', which has the advantage of being originated by you!

One of the qualities which will demonstrate your skills and abilities in the widest requirements of the GCSE is your ability to *make connections* between different things and situations and to *transfer* your knowledge and experience in one situation to another situation. As a consequence you would be foolish not to take advantage of opportunities to show your ability to do this. Using some material from a previous set of studies in your externally set examination would be a fine example of this.

CUBISM

Having completed your study of **Cubism**, you might have decided to include some aspect of it in your work for the controlled test.

It was mentioned earlier that one way of seeing yourself was in a 'dressing-table mirror'. With only six hours in which to do your work you may decide that using such a mirror is as far along the road to 'Cubism' as you want to go.

A 'dressing-table mirror', remember, is *three* mirrors arranged in relationship to each other so that you can see the front of your face *and* each of your profiles through the angles the mirrors form. Suppose you intend to draw yourself as you are reflected in such a dressing-table mirror. You are going to try to draw yourself showing yourself in 'full face', but overlapping this drawing with the two profiles of yourself which you can see in the arrangement of mirrors.

By this means you are going to show yourself in the three ways that other people know and recognise you, but *all in one drawing*.

8 〉 PHYSICAL PREPARATION

So, for your controlled test you collect *either* a 'dressing-table mirror' or three mirrors (Fig 6.4). If you have to do the latter, experiment *beforehand* with them to see *how* they need to be related to each other *and how you will keep them safely in this position*.

You now *arrange* your mirrors in the way that you want in your *examination work-space* the night before the controlled test if your teachers will allow you to do so. At the same time you put all your preparatory studies into your work-space.

Of course you must have sorted these out so that you begin work *immediately* your teacher says that you can start your controlled test the next day. At the *top* of your folder of preparatory studies work, put the studies you have made which will be important to you at the *beginning* of your work in the controlled test.

You may have decided that you will *start* work in *pencil* and then use some water-colour in your drawing. Your idea will be to explore the possibilities in your work more fully, before arriving at a definite decision on how to proceed. To help in this you might need a *sketch* you did in your preparatory studies which is in pencil. You particularly liked the 'effect' of the pencil work in it, and your teachers may have remarked how impressed they were with the drawing.

The outcome is that you want it *before you* as you work the next day, to remind you of what you *can achieve*. So you put it at the *top* of your folder of preparatory studies.

You have also planned that you can afford to spend about an hour and a half on this exploratory work. As a consequence you have decided the *size* you should work to and you have already stretched two pieces of paper to the size you require.

You go home, go to bed at a sensible hour, and get a good night's rest.

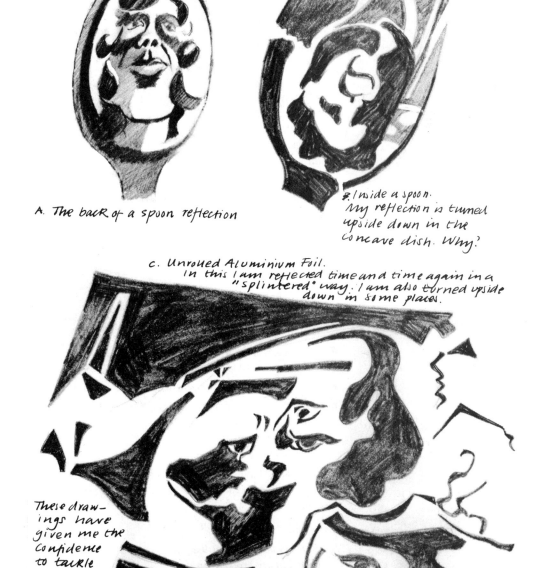

A. *The back of a spoon reflection*

B. *Inside a spoon.*
My reflection is turned
upside down in the
concave dish. Why?

c. *Unrolled Aluminium Foil.*
In this I am reflected time and time again in a
"splintered" way. I am also turned upside
down in some places.

These draw-
ings have
given me the
confidence
to tackle
the "three-
way"
portrait.

Fig. 6.4 Preparatory studies. Use of alternative reflective surfaces other than a mirror.

❝❝ Start each *session* of
your *controlled test* with
something *specific* to do
which will allow you to *relax
and work naturally.* ❞❞

Without breaking the normal rhythm of your early day, you turn up at school ready to sit your controlled test. If you have planned for it in this way there is every chance that you are excited at the prospect before you. This excitement is not worry, but *anticipation*. You know that you are well prepared for your controlled test.

- Without pause, once you are told you can start, you begin work.

- You work in the confidence that you are only doing an 'exploratory' study and that you can redeem any shortcomings in your early work in the second half of the first session of your test (Fig 6.5).

- As you work you realise what a good decision you made in *starting* your work in this way. Because the work is likely to be only a preliminary study in your controlled test, you see that you are beginning to 'get your hand in' without any strain or worry. You are relaxing and thinking of what you are going to do *next* as you are doing one piece of the work.

- The drawing by your side, which you did during your preparatory studies, and which you liked, is a *good reminder* of your previous successes and you refer to it occasionally.

- As your work *proceeds* you are beginning to go back to earlier pieces in it, amending them to fit in with your idea and with the *direction* it is now taking.

- Your *initial* idea was to try to 'superimpose' a drawing of each of your profiles on the top of a full-face view of yourself. As you are *doing this* you are wrestling with the problem of getting bits of each separate drawing to *coincide* with each other in the 'overlay' you are producing. This preoccupation is stopping you from worrying whether your drawing looks 'good' or 'arty'. The problem, and its solution, is giving your drawing its own *form* and sense of identity. The sheer task of putting down on paper what it *is* you intend, so that it '*communicates*' your intentions, is outweighing *all* your other concerns.

- It may even be that the problem and the pleasure you are getting from what you are doing, is totally absorbing you. Because you are engrossed with getting the spatial and the dimensional relationship between the three overlapping drawings right, you are not worrying about what the drawing 'looks like'.

ANALYSING

- After about an hour you notice the time. You stand up, turn your chair round, and put your work upright on it.

- Now you step back from it, looking at it; weighing it up; deciding whether to proceed any further with it; deciding how to proceed with it.

- You could do this with *any* work you were doing, not just this self-portrait.

- Imagine that you decide that the drawing is 'not bad', and that you think it would be worth spending about another twenty minutes on it (Fig 6.6). In this time you might decide that it was necessary to 'lose' some shading you had put in at one stage, and to keep the whole drawing as an overlapping network of 'outlines'.

- You might have thought that the shading, applied to *one view* of your face, was interfering with the way the *other two views* looked and was making the whole drawing confusing.

- You sit down and get on with your work.

If what has been said in the paragraphs directly above does not describe the way that you work, then you are probably in danger of becoming too 'tight' in your controlled test. If you do 'tighten-up', no matter how good you are at Art and Design, you will not do yourself full justice.

Try to enjoy what you are doing. Of course, like a good athlete, you should be 'keyed up'. But this means that your mind and muscles are relaxed, fully receptive to what is going on in your work, and working in complete harmony with one another. Always remember that Art and Design is a 'physical' and an intellectual activity combined.

Fig 6.5 '3-way' self portrait; early stages.

Fig 6.6 '3-way' self portrait: with initial shading.

Fig 6.7 '3-way' self portrait: with shading amended and 'new' shapes coloured in.

Fig. 6.8 '3-way' self portrait: final result.

- Returning to your work. Having got to the point you decided upon when you first stood up and reviewed your work, you might find that your original time limit of an hour and a half has also been reached.

- Now you need to stand your work up again and study it closely, *analysing* once more its strengths and weaknesses.

- Once this is done, sit down and *write down* the results of your mental analysis. Remember, to do this provides 'traces' of your thoughts.

- Keep this written analysis. It will help you in the rest of your work in the controlled test. It will also add to the reward you get for your work if your teachers and the examiner can see and read it.

- Your analysis might help you decide:
  - if you should leave your work in its present state;
  - if your work should be developed further in a particular direction;
  - if you should move on to *another* piece of work at once;
  - if such a piece of work should be an obvious 'major' product.

DECISION-MAKING

Do not decide to start a 'major' piece of work because you believe your controlled test has to be of a particular size to be successful in your examination. Always remember, your teachers and the examiner will *not* mark your work by the kilogramme! They will instead search out the level of ability and achievement you show in your work, note its quality, and reward those things. Size is a matter of suitability to *your* intentions, the medium you are using, and the time you have for your work.

- It is worth bearing in mind that your drawing so far has been a matter of enquiry and of 'getting your hand in' for your controlled test.

- Perhaps you very deliberately left yourself with this particular drawing to do at the end of your preparatory studies. You could easily have done such a drawing in your preparatory studies, but you knew you wanted to have an 'inroad' into your controlled test.

- As such, the drawing is 'finished' *as soon as* you decide from your analysis that it has served its purpose and that you *know* what it is you need to do next.

- In this case, suppose that you decided that you were going to *carry on* with your original drawing, perhaps using up the time you have remaining in your first session. You need to know:
  - that you can work on it for another hour, or more, so that it 'develops', and does not just become a matter of 'filling-it-in' fairly mindlessly;
  - that there is something positive and very direct that you can start to do at once.

- Always remember that 'something positive' to do means you need to have the knowledge and resources to hand to *enable* you to do it. If you have a good *idea* for your work, but need to get some *more information*, it may be better to postpone your work on it until the next session, and to start another piece of work in the time left in the first session.

- In the question of the 'self-portrait', suppose that you thought that now you have 'rubbed out all the shading', it is clear that the three overlapping drawings have created shapes which you did not intend, but which surprise and interest you. This would be very possible, as the line used in one drawing crossed and re-crossed the lines used in the other two drawings.

- It might be that you decide to get your water-colour box out and to *paint in* some of these 'unexpected' shapes, to draw attention to them.

- You wonder whether to use 'flesh' colours for this purpose. But remembering that Picasso went through his 'Blue Period', you decide to use shades and tints of blue for your work at this stage. What you are doing is almost 'in homage' to Picasso!

- Thinking further, you decide to show that some of the new shapes would occur 'further forward' or 'further back', if your drawing were an actual three-dimensional head.

- Looking in the mirror, you notice that the parts of your *own* head which are *furthest forward* catch *more light* than other parts of your head. Your forehead, your cheekbones, the tip of your nose, are almost shining in a creamy looking colour. You decide that this gives you the criteria, or your 'reasons', for choosing, mixing, and applying your shades and tints of blue to various of the new and unexpected shapes which have appeared in your drawing so far. You get on with your idea (Fig 6.7).

THE END OF THE SESSION

To your surprise, the teacher-in-charge warns you that it is nearly time to 'clear up'. *Don't panic! The teacher-in-charge will have left you with a few minutes in hand.*

- Finish the part you are doing. Pause, and sit back and look at your work.
- Get up and clear your things away whilst your work dries.
- Now go back to your work, set it up on your chair again, and step back to 'review' your progress and achievements so far. Make some mental notes of this.
- At the same time, think about what you will do in the *next* session and, again, make some mental notes of the things you will need to find out in order to carry out your plans.
- Put your work carefully and safely where your teacher-in-charge tells you, and leave.
- Write your 'mental notes' down on paper at once!

10 › THE GAP BETWEEN THE TWO SESSIONS ❝ *Do not waste the opportunities given you by a break between your working sessions in the controlled test.* ❞	- During the week you now have, *find out* the things you wanted to know. - Use this information, and your knowledge and assessment of your work so far, to decide *how* to continue with and finish your work in the next session. - There is no sense in 'forgetting' your work during this week. You have *not yet completed* your controlled test, so you cannot afford to 'switch-off'. Least of all can you risk ruining your good work so far. - It might be that you have not really done anything to the *background* during the first session of your controlled test. You might therefore feel the need to look again at the work of the Cubists during this week, to see just what it was *they* did as regards background. - So you return to a Library, or look at the slides in your Art and Design Department, to study the Cubist paintings further. - This might show you that your work has moved a long way *away* from your intention to make it in the 'style' of a Cubist study. If so, you need to weigh-up if this is necessarily a bad thing. Do you *want* to 'bring it back' into a Cubist style? - Imagine that as you start to look at the work of the Cubists, again, you are still not sure. Then you are reminded that Picasso did not only *do* Cubist paintings, and go through his 'Blue Period', but that he also used 'collaged' materials in his works. You might come across his use of a 'caned' tray in one of his paintings (Fig 6.9). - As was remarked above, your work could already be taking on the shape of a 'homage' to Picasso. Assume that you decide to *increase* this aspect of it, and to collect a piece of 'caning' and take it into your controlled test in the next session. - Now that you know *where* you are with your work, you *can* afford to forget it for a while.
11 › THE CONTROLLED TEST – SECOND SESSION	- The likelihood is that you will have had to *take down your mirrors* and *take away your preparatory studies* at the end of the first session. This means that, once more, you need to *set up* your work-space the night before, if your teachers will allow you to do so. - At the start of the second session of your controlled test, your teacher-in-charge will give you your work from the previous session. Whilst you want to refresh your memory of your work so far, you need to *begin* the session with something *specific* and purposeful to do *If you do not, you can easily waste valuable time, or start to make your work so far look 'pretty', rather than 'develop it further'.*

Fig 6.9 An impression of 'Still Life with Chair Caning', by Pablo Picasso. In the original painting Picasso stuck a piece of patterned oil-cloth into the picture. The pattern on the oil-cloth imitated chair caning. A modern parallel of this type of imitation might be 'wood grain' Formica.

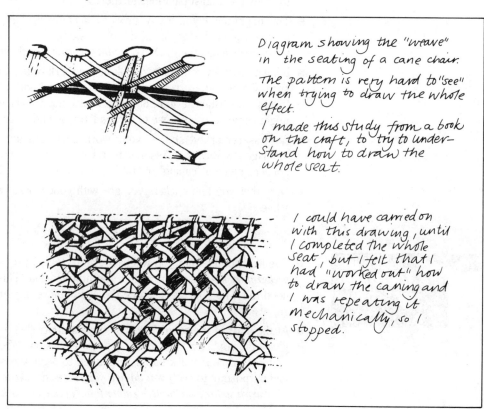

Diagram showing the "weave" in the seating of a cane chair.

The pattern is very hard to "see" when trying to draw the whole effect.

I made this study from a book on the craft, to try to under-stand how to draw the whole seat.

I could have carried on with this drawing, until I completed the whole seat, but I felt that I had "worked out" how to draw the caning and I was repeating it mechanically, so I stopped.

Fig. 6.10 Chair caning studies.

BEGINNING AGAIN

- You have turned up with your piece of 'caning'. It might have been hard to find, but you persevered. It is *your* examination, after all! You might have eventually found the seat of an old caned chair.

- You put this against your drawing so far, 'trying it for size'. You decide that, because your drawing is in pencil and water-colour it is fairly delicate, and that to use the *actual* piece of caning in your work would be a mistake. So you decide not to 'collage' it onto your work.

- Instead you decide to make a pencil drawing of part of the piece of caning, using a separate sheet of paper and working from just part of the piece (Fig 6.10).

- You now have a clear idea of how to start your second session. Once again, it involves you doing something which may, or may not, be part of your 'major' piece of work.

CONTINUING

- After about *ten minutes* you realise that this *was* a very good idea. No matter what else your new drawing might lead to, you are once again 'getting your hand in' at the beginning of a session of your examination.

- Your new drawing, whilst it is highly relevant to your work, is not seen by you at this stage as an essential part of your finished work. You are able to draw in a relaxed way, just 'exploring the possibilities'.

- After a while you are relaxed. You have the confidence back which you had at the end of the last session. You are 'warmed-up' and looking forward now to getting on with your examination work from the previous session.

- From your drawing of the piece of caning you are studying, you now know that you are going to make a *background* to your self-portrait which consists of a pattern of the caning, but a pattern which *you will draw* into your work.

- You begin to draw this into your work from last week.

- It is likely that half of the second session has gone when this is completed. You get up, stand your work on your chair and step back to analyse it.

ANALYSIS

- Suppose you think that the colour you used last week is alright, but it looks 'flat'. This might be because in your drawing of the caning you began to introduce the *effect of light* on the material. You might have begun to put into your drawing the shadows you could see between the criss-crosses of the strips of cane. You can now see that this new 'type' of drawing contrasts too much with the work from the first session of your controlled test.

- You remember from your study of the Cubist works that it looked as if, in some of them, the artists had 'shaded' areas by using a series of close, parallel lines, done in what looked like pencil, or using dark paint and a very thin brush.

- You decide to *go back* to putting 'shading' in your work, even though in the first session you decided to remove some shading you had done!

- But, you write down a note of this 'change of mind', trying to explain *how* it came about. If you do this you will increase the overall value of your work in the eyes of your teachers and the examiner.

- Knowing the time you have left, you decide to use a *pencil* for speed. You then intend to *paint* on top of the shading you produce in this way.

- Having started with *blue* the session before, you decide to carry it on throughout the work, perhaps knowing that you could move towards purple and green if necessary, without destroying the 'blueness' of the effect.

PROCEEDING

- You sit down, pick up your soft pencil and begin.
- You decide where and how to put the 'shading marks' by studying your reflections in the mirrors most carefully.
- After a while you begin to use your colours.
- Some time later, if your time does not run out, you feel that you have gone about as far as you can with your work. Again, stand it up and look at it (Fig 6.8).
- You might decide that there is still *something* you need to do. Or you might feel that you were right, your work is 'finished'.
- If you *still* have something to do, *get on with it* straight away. If you think that you *have finished*, there is still *plenty for you to do*.
- Because you have studied your examination syllabus closely, you know that you have to give in *all* the work you have done in your controlled test.
- You have, in this example:
  - your 'finished' piece of work;
  - a couple of studies you made of the caning;
  - the caning itself;
  - perhaps a sheet of paper with dabs of your colours where you 'tested' them;
  - some written notes.
- Everything listed here is your 'controlled test'. It must *all* be given in.
- Quietly, you guillotine your drawings of the caning and your sheet of 'colour dabs'. Then you mount these on to a suitable card or paper.
- You collect your written notes together, read them and decide if you wish to add to them.
- If you remembered to write on *one side* of a sheet of paper only, you can mount your sheets on to a suitable piece of card or paper.
- Otherwise you have to decide how you will present them in your work. You could, perhaps, put them in a small sugar-paper 'folder'. If you do so, have you got time to 'illustrate' the cover of this, so that it fits in with the 'subject' of your overall work?
- What you have been doing in all this is getting your work into a condition where you can submit it to your teachers and the examiner with confidence.

THE NEXT MOVE

What you need to do next is decide 'how' it will be collated, so that you *explain* to your teachers and the examiner not only 'what' it is you have done, but also 'why' you made the various decisions you did. This, if you remember, was dealt with earlier under the headings:

- chronological sequencing;

and

- narrative sequencing.

Having done, or considered, all this you find that your time is up.

THE END OF YOUR CONTROLLED TEST

- You have all your work for the controlled test sorted out, ready for assessment.
- You know that you have done your best.
- You might even feel that you have done better than you could have hoped for.
- You are able to go home confident and happy.

AFTERWARDS

If you worked in your controlled test right up to the end, you may not have been able to mount various pieces of your work and to consider how you will present it to your teachers and the examiner. IF THIS IS SO, IT DOES NOT MATTER. At the first opportunity *after* your controlled test, ask your teachers if you may have your work to do the tasks described above.

At this point you have to make *selections* from your *coursework* and display these, together with a selection from your *preparatory studies*, as well as your work done during the *controlled test*.

What this means, and how to go about doing it, is described in Chapter 7.

SUMMARY

- The controlled test is only part of your externally set examination.
- It represents the opportunity for you to do unaided work on your ideas which arose during your preparatory studies.
- If your preparatory studies were carried out well, you will have a *choice of directions* to take in your controlled test. Deciding between these possibilities requires you to *balance* the scale and content of your work, the medium and method you work in, and the time that you have available for your controlled test.
- There are many things which you can prepare *in advance* of your controlled test. These might include specialist equipment requirements, but should certainly involve 'setting up' your examination work-space the night before your controlled test, if this is possible within your school.
- Your 'forward planning' for your controlled test should set out to ensure that you use *each session* you may have to the full, and that you take advantage of the *time between* sessions, if there is any.
- Your forward planning should also try to ensure that you *start* each session with a piece of work which you are not afraid to 'fail' at.
- At the *end* of your controlled test you *must* submit *all* the work that you do during it.
- It is worthwhile *sorting this work out* and '*mounting*' it so that it helps to explain *what* it was you did during your controlled test, and *why* you did it.

GLOSSARY OF TERMS USED

Printing sticks	Really, *anything* which will make a mark if coated with paint, or ink, and pressed onto paper or any other suitable surface. Printing sticks can be bought ready-made, made by yourself, or just 'found'.
Rollers	Usually print-making rollers which are coated with paint or ink and used to 'paint' on paper or any other suitable surface. When tilted onto their edge, they can produce a thin line which can be used to 'draw' with.

CHAPTER

7

PRESENTATION
AND
ASSESSMENT

EXHIBITIONS

FOLDERS

PREPARATORY STUDIES

LEAG

**THE ALTERNATIVE
EXAMINING GROUPS**

EXTERNAL CANDIDATES

GETTING STARTED

In the case of Art and Design there are two compulsory components in the examination: coursework and the externally set examination.

What this all means to you is that for *all* the Examining Groups:

■ how you order and select from the work you have done in the externally set examination;

and

■ how you organise and present that selection,

is of vital importance.

In the case of the LEAG examination this matter is slightly more complicated and so it will be dealt with separately as this chapter unfolds.

At the time of 'External Assessment' you will be asked by your teachers to present your work in a particular form. The term 'External Assessment' means the time when the Examining Group's Visiting Examiner comes to your school in order to help to assess your work.

Before this date, your teachers will have already marked your work and given it the grade *they* believe it should have received. Depending on which Examining Group's Art and Design Syllabus is being used, your teachers will have had to opt for either;

■ 'In-School' Assessment and Moderation;

or,

■ 'Postal' Assessment and Moderation.

In the first, your work is held in your school and the examiner visits it in order to help decide which grade it is worth. In the second, your teachers parcel up your work and deliver it to the office of the Examining Group, where the Group's examiner will look at it for the same purpose as before.

Only some of the Examining Groups allow for 'Postal' assessment and moderation. You have no need to know whether your Examining Group does this as the decision to use this method of assessment rests entirely with your *teachers*. If your teachers decide to keep your work for 'In-School' assessment and moderation, then they have two *further* choices of how your work should be presented for this purpose. It will be in the form of either:

■ an Exhibition;

or contained in

■ Folders.

E S S E N T I A L   P R I N C I P L E S

1 ⟩ EXHIBITIONS

If there is enough space, and there are sufficient display boards, your teachers could ask you to put your work up in the form of an '**Exhibition**'. Even if they do so, there is unlikely to be enough space for you to put *all* your work up in this way. Some of it will have to be presented in a '**Folder**'.

Selecting what should go up in the exhibition, and what should be contained in a folder, is a difficult decision to make.

The tendency might be to put into the *exhibition*:

- the work you liked doing most;
- the work you consider to be your 'best' artwork and design work;
- the work which shows the range of materials you used in your GCSE;
- the work which 'stands out' most in competition with the other exhibitions.

You would however be better advised to select your work on the basis of:

- what you have *achieved* during your course of study and the externally set examination;

and

- what helps to explain *what it is you have done* in your GCSE and *why you have done it*.

2 ⟩ FOLDERS

When you present your work entirely in a folder, you do *not* have the problem of *selecting* a restricted amount of it in order to show what you have achieved and to explain why you did what you did. However, you still need to *sort* and *present* your work so that it shows what you have achieved and why you did what you did.

This might be done so that the work:

- demonstrates the extent of your *development* during the course of study and the externally set examination;
- is in a *sequence* which shows *how* you have worked, and explains *why* you made certain decisions and took one direction in a particular project rather than another;
- shows how the *direction your work actually took* as it unfolded modified or even changed your intentions.

In the case of GCSE Art and Design assessment it is necessary for a number of *different people* to look through your folder. As each successive person does this, the 'order' of your work within your folder may be destroyed. Therefore you need to devise a system of presentation which takes this problem into account:

- You might *identify* each project more clearly within your folder. *Perhaps* through the use of *different coloured mounting paper*, or the addition of *stick-on coloured shapes* to your work.
- You might *separate* your work more distinctively. For instance, you might *place* your work in different '*wallets*' within your folder.
- You might *present* each project on a '*concertina*' *display* within your folder. This, probably above all else, will ensure that *within a single project* your work *remains* as you want it to be seen.
- You might make each 'concertina' '*colour-coded*' in some way, either by the colour of the mounting board, or by using a 'stick-on' coloured shape in each corner of the folds of the concertina. This will help ensure that it is understood in which order you intend the work to be seen.
- You could stick a '*chart*' on the cover of your folder to explain the *sequence of colours* you intend the work to be in.

If your teachers decide to send your work away for 'postal' assessment, you will not have the chance to put up an exhibition. *All* your work will necessarily be in a folder, so the above points become still more important.

All these factors have been dealt with fully at various points in this book. At this point it is sufficient only to repeat and emphasise that to attend to all the factors listed above will *increase the value of your work for assessment*.

3 〉 PREPARATORY STUDIES

You should use your **preparatory studies** to:

- help explain what thoughts led you to arrive at the work you did in your controlled test;
- indicate the range and extent of your exploratory investigations into the problem;
- show how you investigated some of the alternative questions in the examination paper.

If you are putting up an *exhibition* of your work, because of the possible limitations on space, it will probably mean that you need to *select* from your preparatory studies those pieces of work which between them best show all of the above factors.

If you are presenting your work in a *folder*, without the need for a selection in this way, you will find it easier to incorporate *all the work you did* in your preparatory studies for your controlled test.

If your syllabus is set by the London and East Anglian Examining Group (LEAG), read the next section. If not, move on to the next section.

4 〉 LEAG

The LEAG Art and Design syllabus suggests that your work is better displayed in the form of an 'Exhibition' for the purposes of assessment.

COURSEWORK

Remember that *what* you are asked to do for your externally set examination, and the way that you are asked to do it, illustrates what is expected of you *throughout* your course of study. In this respect, the externally set examination both guides and influences your coursework. Therefore, it is vital that from a very early date in your course of study you find out and understand what will be required of you in your externally set examination.

Of course, during your course of study you are expected to *progress* from the stage at which you were at the beginning of the course, *over and beyond that which can be put down to maturation, or 'growing older', alone*. This will mean that your teachers will *plan* your work so that it steadily becomes more complex in the demands it puts upon you, and steadily allows you to make more and more 'independent' judgements and decisions in your work.

Your teachers will also make sure that you are asked to work in the way either specified or implied in the externally set examination. To arrive at the stage where you *do* work in the way intended by the externally set examination, it is likely that your teachers will use a 'brick-by brick' method in the way that they teach you. That is to say, they will be unlikely to ask you to do 'everything at once' and from the very beginning.

The point in explaining all this to you is to emphasise that *what is said about the presentation for assessment of your work from the externally set examination, applies equally to the presentation for assessment of your work from your course of study*.

At the end of each project in your *coursework*, you should fall into the habit of finishing and presenting your work in *the way described for the externally set examination*. This applies equally for the syllabuses of *all* the examining groups.

EXTERNALLY SET EXAMINATION

Controlled Test

For the purposes of assessment the work that you do for your **controlled test** should be:

- presented in its entirety;
- trimmed square on a guillotine;
- mounted appropriately;
- organised so that it explains what it is you have done and why you have done it.

The syllabus also suggests that the work is better displayed if it sets out to:

explain the degree of learning and the working habit, as well as exhibit the degree of achievement.

Referring to the assessment of your work earlier in the syllabus, it is stated that:

For each (of the Syllabus Assessment Objectives) the evidence afforded by the Timed Test (Controlled Test), the Preparatory Studies, and the five pieces of coursework, should be considered in turn with the awareness of the reinforcement each may give to the others. Finally, there should be consideration of the extent to which evidence of outstanding work in respect of some syllabus objectives may well compensate for lack of evidence in respect of other objectives.

This appears to mean that:

- You do not have to fulfil the requirements of each of the assessment objectives in every piece of work you do.
- You may show your ability to fulfil the assessment objectives of the syllabus in any portion of your work, whether this comes from your coursework, your preparatory studies, or your controlled test.
- The ability you display in *any* section of your work will contribute equally and posivitely towards your final grade.
- Outstanding ability in a restricted area represented by the assessment objectives will make up for weaknesses in other areas.

Because of this it is necessary that you display your work in such a way that it enables you to direct your teachers' and the examiner's attention to what it is you have done best.

At the same time, however, you should try to ensure that, in your work, you do cover *all* the assessment objectives in the syllabus, even if your performance in some is weak.

Therefore, if you are putting up an 'exhibition' of your work:

- You *must* include **all** the work you did in your controlled test;
- You *should* include a **selection** of your preparatory studies which will help to explain your controlled test;
- You *should* include a **selection** from your coursework which helps to 'fill-in' any of the assessment objectives which may be missing, or not dealt with very well in your exhibition so far.

Everything else that you do over the duration of your course of study, plus any of your preparatory studies which have not been used in your exhibition, *must* then be put into an accompanying folder of work. This accompanying folder of work should be presented so that it achieves all that was specified above in the section entitled 'Folders'.

If you do not present your work in this way you will lose some of the advantages which the particular examination appears to offer you in its method of assessment.

5 ⟩ THE ALTERNATIVE EXAMINING GROUPS

Because *all* the other Examining Groups have a 'weighting' between the work done as coursework, and the work done in response to the externally set examination, you have a slightly different problem in gaining the best possible mark for your work in those examinations.

COURSEWORK

For the remaining Examining Groups' examinations you should order and present your coursework so that it shows:

- how well you have attended to each of the assessment objectives which are contained in each separate syllabus;
- what the range and extent of your investigations and work was in each project you tackled;
- why you took certain decisions;

- how you thought your decisions helped you to fulfil your original intentions;
- in what ways your work, as it unfolded, modified and altered your intentions.

If you can do this, and present your work in the manner your teachers want it presented, that is to say as either an exhibition or in folders, then you will get the best possible mark for the work you have done.

If your teachers want you to put your coursework up in the form of an 'exhibition', then you should pay particular attention to *all* the references to 'exhibitions' which we have considered in this chapter.

If, on the other hand, your teachers want your coursework presented in a 'folder', then all the earlier references to 'folders' will apply most strongly in deciding *how* you should order and present your coursework.

EXTERNALLY SET EXAMINATION

Again, all that has been said about presenting your work in either the form of an exhibition, or the form of a folder, will apply to your work from the **externally set examinations**.

What you must make certain is, that during your externally set examination, that is to say, your preparatory studies and your controlled test, you should try to ensure that you are covering *all the assessment objectives contained in the syllabus you are using*. Unlike the situation with LEAG, you cannot guarantee to have allowances made for the assessment objectives which are *missing* in your work from your externally set examination, on the basis that they are contained in your coursework.

Of course, in practice any achievement you reach in this respect in your coursework will be *positively* rewarded. This positive reward *will* contribute towards your final grade, when it is added to the mark given on your work from the externally set examination. But with most Examining Groups it will not contribute to the mark you actually get from the externally set examination.

| 6 > **EXTERNAL CANDIDATES** |

If you are an **external** candidate, you will find that all the above will apply to you as it stands. For instance, if you are doing your GCSE with NEA, you will have to produce coursework and work from an externally *approved* examination.

If you refer to Table 2.4, on page 14, you will see whether the syllabus you are using allows, or requires you to submit coursework for the examination.

On the other hand it might be that your GCSE is conducted on the basis that you do not do coursework which is assessed for your examination.

If this is the case, then you need to follow every reference to ordering and presenting your work from the externally set examination most closely.

All of your eggs are 'in one basket' in such cases. You do not even have a coursework mark to add to that you receive for your externally set examination work!

How you will have to show your work for assessment will depend entirely upon the regulations contained in your examination syllabus.

You must study your examination syllabus closely in order to find out what is required of you in this connection. If you are in any doubt, contact either your Examining Group, or the Centre where you are taking the examination, immediately.

It is necessary that you know what you will have to do in this respect because it might be that you have your work *taken away from you* at the completion of your controlled test. If this is so, you will need to order and present your work *somewhere near the end* of your controlled test. This will not necessarily be a waste of valuable time if it is so. As our earlier advice suggests, it is to your ultimate advantage to *present* your work so that all that is contained within it can be understood by the examiner.

S U M M A R Y

- To get a mark for your work which could be in advance of the 'face-value' of that work, you need to 'order' and 'present' your work so that it shows up in its 'best light'.

- You need to 'order' and 'present' your coursework as much as the work you do in your externally set examination.

- The way that you 'order' and 'present' your work will differ according to whether you are to present some of it in the form of an exhibition, or whether it is all to be contained in a folder.

- External candidates need to attend to the 'order' and 'presentation' of their work as much as candidates who are in full-time education.

- External candidates should make certain that they check with either the Centre where they are taking their examination, or the Examining Group concerned, about the arrangements for the assessment of their work. If it is to be sent for 'postal' assessment and or moderation, this might mean that they will need to consider 'ordering' and 'presenting' their work during the time allowed for their controlled test, or tests.

G L O S S A R Y   O F   T E R M S   U S E D

Exhibition display	The display of some of your work on boards, tables, stands, and so on.
Face-value	The merit, or worth, your work has on the basis of what it looks like, or how well you have done it.
Folder display	Whereby your work is gathered together in its entirety and contained in some form of package.
In-school assessment	The system whereby your work is marked by your teachers and kept on display *within* your school for moderation by a visiting examiner.
Postal assessment	The system whereby your work is marked by your teachers but then *sent* to the Examining Group for their examiner to moderate it.

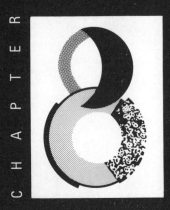

CHAPTER

8

THE UNENDORSED CERTIFICATE

ASSESSMENT

THE AWARD OF GRADES

THE EXTERNALLY SET EXAMINATION

ANALYSIS

BEGINNING WORK

THE PAINTING

CONCLUSIONS

GETTING STARTED

In the remainder of this book the way it is written will change. You will no longer have everything explained so fully, drawing your attention to what is being done, why it is being done, and the advantages it would give you if you did it in the same way. Neither will each chapter end with a 'Summary' and a 'Glossary of Terms Used'. The nature of the remaining chapters makes that approach less relevant.

Instead, the following chapters will be in the form of 'Outline Answers' to a small selection of actual GCSE Art and Design examination questions. These questions have been drawn from the seven Examining Groups' examination papers, with each chapter involving just one Examining Group and one of its examination questions. The principles involved in tackling that question are of course relevant to you *whatever* syllabus you are following.

In this chapter we concentrate on the Unendorsed Certificate in GCSE Art and Design, and concentrate on the Southern Examining Group Syllabus (SEG) for our case study. We first look at the relevant examination regulations, before turning to an actual question to show how these regulations can be applied.

The specimen question is answered in both an *illustrated* and a *written* series of notes which reflect the thoughts and actions of the person compiling the answer. Again, these 'outline answers' are not models for you to follow slavishly but they are examples of how you should operate in dealing with your GCSE in Art and Design.

ESSENTIAL PRINCIPLES

Remember, what is said about the unendorsed certificate and presented in the Outline Answer in this chapter also relates to Examining Groups other than the SEG. Also remember that much of what we say about the *unendorsed* certificate will also be relevant to the five *endorsed* certificate titles.

The question to be answered in this chapter is taken from,

ART AND DESIGN SYLLABUS (AD/1), GENERAL CERTIFICATE OF SECONDARY EDUCATION ART AND DESIGN (1988 EXAMINATION), SOUTHERN EXAMINING GROUP

This syllabus is for the *unendorsed* Certificate and is described by the SEG as:

A syllabus with a broadly based open-ended approach referred to in the National Criteria as the Art and Design (Unendorsed) Syllabus.

SEG also publish *separate* syllabuses for each of the five endorsed titles in the GCSE Art and Design.

1 > ASSESSMENT

Each of these separate endorsed title syllabuses have assessment objectives which are *common* to each other, and to the unendorsed certificate. But each *also* includes assessment objectives which are *specific* to the particular endorsed title syllabus only.

In the Art and Design syllabus (AD/1), the unendorsed certificate, the SEG states that the content of the candidate's work and course of study should:

- be flexible and open-ended;
- develop according to individual circumstances and resources;
- enable candidates to develop their personal ideas and skills;
- be approached either through the exploration of a broad range of work, or by studying a narrower field in greater depth;
- allow work in a variety of media which may be two- or three-dimensional or a mixture of both;
- encourage an open-ended approach to the use and type of materials and form of expression;
- demonstrate a clear response to the assessment objectives.

There is also a *cautionary* note in the syllabus which says,

Whilst photographs and magazine or similar reproductions may be used as initial stimuli, slavish copying of such material will be penalised.

All of this so far appears to mean that:

- You must know the assessment objectives and be certain that your work contains evidence which shows your ability in each of them.
- You can carry out the externally set examination in any media you choose.
- You may have studied a very restricted area of Art and Design during your course of study and that you may, nevertheless, carry out your externally set examination in the same restricted area, without penalty.
- If you use any reproductions as secondary source material, you should make sure that you translate it into original work.

2 > THE AWARD OF GRADES

It is difficult to discern from the present SEG Art and Design syllabuses, both for the unendorsed and the endorsed certificate titles, how your work and the published assessment objectives will be translated into grades in the examination. So far the published syllabuses do not contain either a 'mark scheme' or any 'assessment criteria'. Without either of these types of information it is unclear how *levels of achievement* in each of the assessment objectives will be decided and how distinctions will be made between them. It is these 'levels of achievement' which will result in the *grade* you are awarded for your GCSE Art and Design.

However, your teachers *do know* what standards are expected of you in the various grades. They have *grade descriptions* for each of the seven 'pass' grades, as well as one for 'unclassified' work. *If your work is 'unclassified' in any of the Examining Groups' examinations, you will not receive the award of a grade for your GCSE Art and Design.*

Condensing the SEG grade descriptions for what have been identified as the 'trigger' Grades F and C, the SEG grade descriptions range from:

- **GRADE F**: Candidates will produce work of a personal nature which reflects signs of interest and effort, as well as unity and organisation. The work will show levels of independent judgement and activity; some ability to research and select relevant information; limited success in selecting and manipulating materials and processes:

via,

- **GRADE C**: Candidates will make sensitive, imaginative and self-aware responses in their work; be able to sustain independent work from conception to realisation; show clear evidence of acquired skills and technical competency; be able to record from direct observation and personal experience; recognise and use the visual elements sensitively and appropriately; show clear evidence of the ability to investigate, analyse, and interpret:

to,

- **GRADE A**: Candidates will demonstrate the ability to produce work of excellence. The work will display qualities of personal perception and imagination; reveal considerable independence and maturity; be coherent, showing the ability to research, analyse and resolve complex problems; demonstrate an understanding of the purpose and function of Art and Design.

Remember, although only three grade descriptions used by SEG are included here, the Examining Group has published grade descriptions for *all* seven GCSE grades.

3 ❭ THE EXTERNALLY SET EXAMINATION

- The SEG allows you *six weeks* to carry out both your 'preparatory studies' and your 'controlled test'.
- Everything you do during this period must be given in with your 'final work.'
- There is no specified time for the controlled test.
- You are advised to spend *at least eighteen hours* on both parts of your externally set examination, and that you should use the first two weeks of the six weeks on your preliminary/supporting studies.

With the SEG, the *externally set examination* is allocated 40% of the total marks for the whole of your GCSE. In the syllabus it states that this section of your GCSE will test particular assessment objectives: namely that a candidate should show the ability to:

- sustain a chosen study from conception to realisation;
- work independently in realising his or her intentions;
- analyse an idea, theme, subject or concept and to select, research, and communicate relevant information and to make and evaluate in a continuum.

Apart from these *three* assessment objectives there are a further *five* objectives contained in this particular syllabus. Each, or any of these might well come into your work in the externally set examination, but they must obviously be covered during your course of study and the evidence of them contained in your coursework. Nevertheless, there is one of these five which is likely to be as important for your externally set examination, as it is for your coursework. Objective 8 in the syllabus states that you should show the ability to:

use and compose visual elements, e.g. line, tone, colour, pattern, texture, shape, form, space.

The reason for making this point is to emphasise to you that there is really no 'minimum requirement' upon you at any time in your work in the GCSE. You should know and understand *all* that is expected of you in the syllabus you are using, and then set out to fulfil *all* that, and more if you possibly can.

THE   QUESTION

In the SEG specimen paper there are *ten* separate questions listed, from which you choose one. One of these has three alternative sub-sections within it, whilst other questions imply that you can create your own 'options' within the question. As a consequence, you have plenty to choose from. At the same time it might be that the paper does not contain the question you would most like to answer!

For instance, there is no question which deals with 'Space Travel'. If you wanted to do something based upon the imagery associated with this it would appear that you would be unlucky. But one of the questions, whilst it gives you a poem to work from, does invite you to provide your own poem. It is highly likely that by now some poet has written about space travel, and you could work from that. If there are no such examples, or you cannot find one, then write your own poem and include it in your work for the externally set examination!

The questions, apart from the poem, cover between them a variety of subjects and ideas:

- Some of the questions concern *specific objects* or *reference materials* which are to be used as 'starting points' for your work, e.g. 'plants and people – animals and people'.
- Other questions deal more with 'concepts' or 'ideas' as 'starting points'. These are references such as, 'delicate, light, fine, sensitive, tender'.

For the purposes of this chapter the following question from the SEG specimen paper will be used:

Collect, select, arrange.

OUTLINE   ANSWER

Here the outline 'answer' is in the form of the *student's* thought processes at various stages. The *examiner's* comments are shown in italics.

1 ANALYSIS

'This question appeals to me. It allows me to work from things that I like to work from, and not what the examiner thinks I *should* work from!

I thought at first of a still life, but the more I look at the question, the more I think of doing a collage, or a print, or a photo-montage.

I am going to resist the idea that these things might be easier than doing a still life, because I know that they are not necessarily so. To arrange "real" things and to make a "work of art" takes a lot of skill and knowledge to do it originally and well. My skill, so my teacher tells me, is my ability to "draw" from real objects. If I do a collage it will not let me do any drawing.

No. I am going to stick with my original intention, to do a still life. I came into the examination hoping that I could do a still life and this question gives me a golden opportunity.

I *am* going to do a still life.

I will start my "brainstorming diagram", and I will include in it the other ideas the question gave me.

But first, are there any *other* questions which would let me do what I *want* to, that is to say, a still life?

There is one entitled "Scrap" and another which tells you to "gather and work from three different collections of objects". But this last question, whilst it is good, emphasises "decay" and "destruction". I do not want to do that kind of work.

I will do my brainstorming, and if my choice does not seem to be turning out too well, I will consider some of the other options, such as the question on "decay" and "destruction".

Here goes.'

BRAINSTORMING DIAGRAM

3.D Collage
3.D Collage (real objects, sprayed/wood)

Kurt Schwitters (Collage)   Matthew Smith
Willem Kalfe   SLIDES   WINE BOTTLES
                             LIBRARY   CLOTH
WILLIAM SCOTT   GOMBRICH   FLOWERS
VERMEER   PLACES TO LOOK   FRUIT
PAUL CEZANNE   POTTERY
OTHER ARTISTS   GOOD OBJECTS

STILL LIFE

                                                  TROMPE-L'OEIL
         MATERIALS   OTHER THINGS
PAINT   WATER-COLOUR   SIZE?
         POWDER COLOUR   VIEWPOINT
         ACRYLIC   TECHNIQUE?
PENCIL
CRAYON   HOW MANY STUDIES?
FELT TIPS?   PRELIMINARY STUDIES & FINAL PIECE?
COLLAGE

Just 'work' and see 'what happens'

KEY: CAPITAL LETTERS = FIRST THOUGHTS
         Capitals and small letters = Further Thoughts

THOUGHTS

'I have been doing Still Life towards the end of my coursework. Will it be wrong to do another one in the controlled test?

My teachers seem to think it is alright. They say that it is sensible of me to do something I can do reasonably well.

I liked those "Trompe-L'oeil" paintings my teachers have on slides. Painting so "real" like that, so that it fooled you into believing that you could knock a drop of water off the petals and leaves of the flowers was marvellous.

I cannot do that myself, but I am interested in trying to show how things "look" and how they are arranged in interesting groupings.

In my last piece of coursework I worked from a painting by Cézanne, trying to copy what he did so that I might understand how, and why, he did it. This was my teacher's idea, but I enjoyed it.'

DECISIONS

'After looking at some more slides and books, and reading Gombrich, all of which gave me some more information and ideas, I think I shall try to paint a still life like those by Cézanne.

I shall try to collect some objects which are similar to those he used to work from.

I think I shall use acrylic colours. Cézanne worked in water-colours and oil-colours. Acrylics will allow me to work in a way that is similar to oil-painting.

Instead of doing "preliminary" and "supporting" studies as such, I think I will set up my still life in a corner of the art room, leave it there for six weeks, and just work from it whenever I can. My teacher says it will be alright for me to do this.'

2 > **BEGINNING WORK**

'Now that I have managed to collect together a number of objects I like and which remind me of the Cézanne still lifes, and have selected from them an old jug, a plate, a wine glass, a chequered cloth, and some fruit, because I think that their shapes and colours go well together, I shall arrange them on a board, so that they look like the still lifes which Cézanne used to paint.

My teachers recommended me to "draw" round each object, where it stood on my board, in case they get moved. If they do I can easily replace them on the "marks". I can see the sense in this. It is what my Drama teacher does with the furniture which is used on the stage in a play. It lets the "scene-shifters" put the furniture in the right place each time.

In addition to this, I shall borrow a camera from the Art Department and photograph the group from a number of angles so that I can easily get it all back into position if it is necessary to do so.

My teachers also told me that my fruit will "rot" over the six weeks, and that, anyway, I should put it away each time I finish work as it is a temptation to other people! I will have it locked in the store cupboard.

As I decided to "just work" at my still life, I shall begin by doing three drawings. One will be from the front, and then one towards the left, followed by one towards the right. This will let me see what the group looks like from different angles.'

I arranged the group from the front and I like the way that the objects look in relationship to each other in this view.
But the general view is rather "parallel", and slightly boring.

"HEAD ON" VIEW

I think that this is the worst view.
The composition is very boring and the objects look too jumbled together.

"FROM THE RIGHT" VIEW

This is the most exciting view.
I like the way that the cloth changes direction.
I also stood up to draw it and I am looking down into the objects more.

"FROM THE LEFT" VIEW

Fig. 8.1 Still life: preparatory/ supporting studies.

Plate 20 Paul Cézanne, 'Still Life
with Plaster Cast'. *The Courtauld
Institute Galleries, London.*

LATER

'After I had completed my first three drawings, I was upset that I could not see very much
of the cloth and the plate in them. Cézanne was able to make it look as if you were almost
"looking down" on things.

Perhaps if I sit up on a table it will let me "look down" on things.

I tried that, and it worked! The only thing is I have now lost the best view of the jug and the
glass. They do not look so good from this new position as they did in my first three
drawings.

I remember my teacher telling me that Cézanne used to "prop-up" some things so that he
could see them better. I might try this.

Thinking of that reminds me, the Ancient Egyptians used to draw people so that they were
in profile and full-on, all in the same drawing. So, I am in good company if I do what I intend
with my still life!

Arranging things, I decided to put a "block" in my group, to stand the wineglass on. It was
getting lost as I propped-up the plate and the cloth.

My latest drawing now seems to be fine. The only thing I do not like now is the colour of
the wall behind my group. It looks out of place.

Plate 21 Paul Cézanne, 'Still Life with Water Jug'. *The Tate Gallery, London.*

As my teachers felt that I was still doing my "Preliminary/Supporting Studies", they could help me here. They suggested I brought in a piece of wallpaper that matched my group, and they gave me permission to put it on the wall.'

Examiner: *In the GCSE it is usual to see your 'Preparatory' studies as a 'taught' situation. This means that it is perfectly in order for your teachers to advise you on matters, provided you are doing something positive yourself which is relevant to your work.*

This work by Cézanne (Plate 20) shows how he would 'prop' up items in his still life paintings, and also how he would use more than one eye-level in the same work in order to get the results he wanted.

The next work, also by Cézanne (Plate 21), shows how the artist would 'sketch-in' the outlines, main masses and even shadows of a still life group, using a brush and very liquid paint rather than a pencil or charcoal.

This is an excellent way to start your work. In the first place it speeds you up, which is a vital consideration in a 'timed test'. Secondly, it stops you first doing a drawing and then just 'filling-it-in' with colour for the remainder of your available time. One of the problems with doing this is that if you run out of time, it makes your work look very incomplete and sometimes very difficult to 'read' and understand. Often, you do not have enough of the work 'finished' to explain the relationships between the objects in your painting. Here you can see how Cézanne is working 'all over' the work at the same time, exploring those 'relationships' as he goes and from the beginning.

Student (cont.): 'Now that that is done I feel much happier about my group. The colours have become integrated and interesting now.

I think I will start a painting, from the position I feel the group looks its best.

I do not know if this will be my "final" piece of work, but I shall make it fairly large, and use an easel to work from.

As I have been working with the fruit for a couple of weeks now, I shall change it for this new painting.'

3 > THE PAINTING   'I decided to only "draw in" the main outlines, as my teachers taught me.

When I did my previous study on the work of Cézanne, I noticed that he "drew" with a paint brush and very "fluid" paint. With this he put in the outlines and shapes of things and began to show shadows and the colours in his subject.

I quickly got onto doing this.

One of the results of this was that I could easily "correct" things as they went on. It was very easy to paint things "out" and move them this way and that. I was pleased to be working this way.

Another advantage the method gave me was the speed at which my "painting" grew. In no time at all I was able to see the whole subject on my paper.

I was left with plenty of time to get down to "tightening-up" the drawing and adding detail and more and more colour. The painting was becoming enjoyable.'

THE FINAL COMPOSITION
In this I tried to keep the original visual relationship between the objects, as in the "Head On" View.
I propped the plate up, so that I could 'see' into it and stood the wine glass on a block underneath the cloth.
I also angled the table, so that I could get "changes of direction" at the front of my composition.

Fig. 8.2 Still life: final composition.

4 ⟩ CONCLUSIONS

'Working in this way I was able to:

- "collect" a number of objects for my still life;
- "select" from them, until I had the things I thought best for my work;
- "arrange", and "re-arrange" the objects until I was satisfied with things;
- do a number of "supporting" studies as I analysed and researched my subject;
- change my mind and modify my ideas as the work went on, evaluating my progress as I did so;
- produce a "final" piece of work, which was my painting.

As a result I felt that I had fulfilled all the requirements of me in this examination question, and my GCSE.

I felt that I had particularly paid attention to the three assessment objectives specified for the externally set examination.

I had:

- *started* and *finished* my ideas and work;
- carried out my work *unaided*, apart from some permitted advice from my teachers;
- *analysed* and *researched* my idea, put down all the information I had found out and the decisions I had made, and *weighed-up* what I was doing as I did it.'

5 ⟩ EXAMINER COMMENTS

In this work, as the candidate claims, all the broadest requirements of the syllabus and its aims and objectives had been dealt with.

All the assessment objectives in the syllabus had been dealt with in the work.

There was a critical and contextual content in the work.

The work was in the best traditions of its kind in the history of Art and Design.

This candidate arranged the objects into a group and studied their relationship to one another.

Many candidates study each object which they collect for a still life one by one, in complete isolation from each other. They tend to make a separate drawing of each object in turn. Then they re-draw each object, from the first drawing they made of it, constructing a new drawing of all the objects together.

This is not a good way to make a still life study, as it does not allow you to see and record the actual way they relate to each other. This relationship is one of the vital aspects of still life studies, one that has preoccupied professional artists throughout the history of Art and Design.

There is a value in drawing each object separately and then constructing, perhaps a formal pattern, or a new design from the objects, but this is a different matter to painting a 'still life' as it has become known historically.

As the written notes above show, a clear understanding was evident in the whole work. It would have been more re-assuring to know that the candidate had actually recorded the written notes above, and included them with the practical work.

The candidate chose to ignore the alternatives, but the way that the question was worded it would have been perfectly in order to carry out the work in a collage or assemblage form.

Although this candidate was concerned to show 'drawing' ability, the question specified the qualities of 'selection' and 'arrangement'. In doing collage or assemblage, these qualities could be admirably displayed.

Their satisfactory deployment would have adequately compensated for a display of drawing skills.

However, if a collage or assemblage had been done it would have been vital that some evidence of good drawing from 'direct observation' was present in the candidate's coursework. This aspect of Art and Design work is specified in all GCSE examination syllabuses.

Provided the quality of this candidate's artistic skills was considered good enough, the way that the work was carried out, and what was done, should have resulted in a high mark for the externally set examination.

The method and the outcomes should have increased the 'face-value' of the candidate's work.

The work certainly attended to Assessment Objective 5, of the syllabus. This requires that the candidate should, briefly, analyse, select, research, communicate relevant information and evaluate in a continuum. Attending to this should enhance the 'face-value' of the work.

The final grade the candidate received would depend heavily on the standard achieved in the coursework. This syllabus, remember, weights the two compulsory sections of the GCSE Art and Design Examination, and only 40% of the overall marks available are given to the externally set examination.

Nevertheless, assuming that the candidate worked in the same way, and to the same general standards, during the course of study concerned, it is reasonable to expect that at least a Grade C should be achieved for this, or similar work. If you refer back to the condensed account of the grade description for Grade C (page 4), you will begin to see why this should be so.

S O M E   O T H E R   A L T E R N A T I V E S

Still life groups do not need to be 'arty' or pretentious.

The work (Plate 22) by Van Gogh (1853 – 90), shows how the most humble objects can become worthy of a serious artist's attention. In this work, not only do the objects appear to be 'everyday', they seem to have been come across 'by chance', as if the pipe had been left on the chair at some other time and then 're-discovered'.

The next illustrations (Fig 8.3) are done by another candidate as a response to still life. They show the tendency to study 'isolated' objects which might be included in the eventual still life composition. To do this avoids relating *all the objects in space*, and as a result the final composition can suffer.

Plate 22 Vincent Van Gogh, 'The Chair and The Pipe'. *Reproduced by courtesy of the Trustees, The National Gallery, London.*

Fig. 8.3 Alternative studies: still life. This work illustrates the mistaken approach to still life, whereby the objects which are to make up the composition are studied in isolation. The individual drawings are sincerely carried out but would be unlikely to lead to a 'traditional' type of still life work. Using this approach could lead to a still life 'design', perhaps, but it would require further intermediary drawings, exploring the shapes more carefully not only of the items, but of the shapes evident within each item.

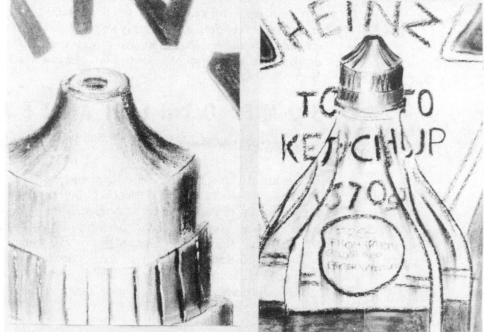

DRAWING AND PAINTING – ENDORSED

GETTING STARTED

Again in this chapter we take a *particular* syllabus and question to illustrate some *general* principles relevant to your work. Remember that although this chapter deals with the 'Drawing and Painting' endorsed certificate title, it also explains how LEAG covers the alternative endorsed certificate titles and the unendorsed certificate. Also remember that what is said about the 'Drawing and Painting' endorsed certificate title here, and about the 'Outline Answer', apply equally to *all* the other Examining Groups and their GCSE Art and Design examination syllabuses.

ESSENTIAL PRINCIPLES

The question to be answered in this chapter is taken from

GCSE, ART AND DESIGN, LONDON AND EAST ANGLIAN GROUP

The LEAG examination syllabus does *not* publish separate syllabuses for the GCSE Art and Design endorsed Titles. One syllabus covers the unendorsed *and* the endorsed certificates.

In the syllabus it states

This syllabus has been devised to provide two forms of certification, 'unendorsed' and 'endorsed'. The 'undendorsed' form aims to give pupils a broad understanding of art and design but, provided that an appropriate breadth of study has been experienced during the course, candidates will be able to offer specialised options for the examination.

The 'endorsed' form is restricted to the five categories listed in the National Criteria for Art and Design . . .

1 ▷ PROCESSES AND PROCEDURES

It goes on to state in the syllabus that, whatever specialisation may take place, for either the unendorsed certificate, or for any of the endorsed titles,

. . . specialisation should not exclude processes such as 'sequential development of ideas', visual research, analysis, observation and recording, or 'structured discussion and critical appraisal'.

These 'processes' occur in a list of 'Processes and Procedures' in the syllabus. This list is published as a guide to you and your teachers. It specifies different 'ways of operating' in your practical work in Art and Design, in the expectation that you will know and understand *how you are working* and *why you are working in the way that you are*.

For instance, one of the processes and procedures is

Project-based thematic enquiry and response.

Later in the syllabus this is described as

An approach or methodology which is designed to allow maximum opportunity for exploration of a given topic, constrained by the established theme.

This appears to mean that, whilst you might be studying the theme of 'Architecture', at one time you might be studying architecture using the topic of *'Appearance'*. If this were so, you might be making drawings and paintings, or photographs, or models of, perhaps, small panoramas of your environment.

Using the same theme, if the topic were to be the *'History of Architecture'*, you might be identifying and explaining different architectural styles to be found in your environment.

And so on.

Another process and procedure listed is

Problem solving and restricted exploration.

This is described later in the syllabus as

Closely related to design theory and practice.

Here you might be studying your environment with the intention of re-planning parts of it, or developing barren parts of it in order to propose your designs for a 'Leisure Centre'. Or you might be designing and producing a pamphlet which is intended to encourage 'Tourism' in your area.

2 ▷ CONTEXTUAL STUDIES

But, no matter what your process and procedure, or 'way of working', might be, *you are expected to include in your work*:

■ visual research;
■ analysis;
■ observation and recording.

At the same time you are expected to *show*:

- a sequential development of your ideas.

As you prepare for and carry out your work you are also expected to *take part in and produce*:

- structured discussion and critical appraisal.

What all this does is begin to spell out to you how you should approach your work, no matter what the content of your work might be at any time.

Briefly, this approach appears that it might be explained as:

- looking and seeing;
- understanding and explaining;
- criticising and justifying.

If this is so, it means that the LEAG syllabus requires 'contextual studies', and their associated skills *as much as* it does products and the skills necessary to produce them.

3 ▷ ASSESSMENT

The assessment objectives and the assessment criteria are *exactly the same for any version of the examination you may wish to take*. The LEAG examination does not have a 'mark scheme'. Your work is measured against 'criteria' only.

The assessment criteria in the LEAG syllabus is published in three 'groups'. Each 'group' describes a performance which is suitable for the award of certain grades. As your work measures up to the next group, and the next group, so it rises in terms of *levels of achievement* and, consequently, reward. The three groups are as follows.

The examination will assess the extent to which candidates are able to:

Group 1
- show in the work produced a successful inter-relationship between the 'basic elements', 'processes and procedures' and 'practices', as reflected in the course which has been followed;
- produce a personal response to an idea, theme, subject or other stimuli;
- show some evidence of their ability to work independently in realising their intentions.

Group 2
- show ability to work from direct experiences by finding, using and developing source material where appropriate;
- demonstrate the breadth and/or depth of study followed in this course, either through evidence of work in a variety of media (unendorsed form) or an understanding of the relevance of studies in media other than those of the main area of practice (endorsed form);
- reflect in their work some ability to see the activity in its widest cross curricular, cultural, environmental and historical context;
- select and control materials and processes in a systematic way, taking account of considerations of costs as appropriate.

Group 3
- understand the concepts involved in the 'basic elements' and 'processes and procedures' as listed in the syllabus aims and framework;
- have command of a critical vocabulary applicable to the subject, particularly in respect of the critical and historical studies included in the course.

The 'Basic Elements' are things such as line, tone, colour, pattern, and so on. You should be familiar with these by now. They are common to all the GCSE Art and Design examination syllabuses.

Understanding the 'concepts' involved in the 'basic elements' and the 'processes and procedures', is really a matter of making and doing *successful art*, or *successful designs*.

This means that those of you who are better at Art and Design will get better rewards for your work. This is only to be expected in an Art and Design examination, after all!

The assessment criteria does suggest, however, that to get the best grades you need to show that you can, *and do*, conduct *critical* and *historical* appraisal.

4 > CRITICAL STUDIES

You can conduct '**critical appraisal**' visually as much as verbally. So, just by drawing and painting, you can show your ability in this respect, *provided you set out to make some kind of critical statement in your work.*

This might mean no more than selecting the 'correct materials for the job'. Or it might be that you draw a slum in order to make a critical point about the environment as you see it. Or you might paint a picture, or design a poster to make people think about the need to conserve trees. And so on.

An excellent example of 'criticism' in works of art are the etchings by the Spanish artist, **Francisco Goya (1746 – 1828)**, called '**The Horrors of War**'. These etchings are each a 'work of art', but they also express Goya's indignation at the atrocities performed under the guise of war. A modern-day counterpart of this might be the photographs of the *Vietnam War* taken by the British photographer, **Don McCullin**.

Whatever you do in respect of critical studies, it would certainly pay you in this Examining Group's examination to keep a *notebook*, in which you log your *decisions* from time to time, *as well as the reasons for them*. But this would apply equally to any of the other Examining Groups' examinations if you wanted to *enhance the mark your work gets*.

5 > THE AWARD OF GRADES

Returning to the assessment criteria quoted above.

■ It should be obvious to you that **Group 1** standards should be fulfilled by most candidates taking the examination. This means that to fulfil this level of the assessment criteria will probably reward you with one of the lower grades in the examination, perhaps Grades E, F or G.

■ Therefore, if you fulfil the assessment criteria in **Group 2**, you will get a result worth a *higher* grade in the examination, perhaps Grades C or D.

■ The award of Grades A and B are likely to be for work which fulfils the very demanding assessment criteria in **Group 3**.

6 > THE EXTERNALLY SET EXAMINATION

LEAG allows twenty school working days for your preparatory studies. This means that you have a *minimum* of four weeks to carry them out. It could mean that you have about six weeks in all, because the likelihood is that your Easter Holidays will fall into this time span and 'holidays' do not count as 'school working days'!

After this you have **ten hours** to carry out your controlled test. The actual timing of your controlled test will be decided by your teachers and this timing will also affect when you begin your preparatory studies and whether you end up with more than 'four weeks' for them. Your teachers will also decide how many sessions you will have to do the ten hours' work, and how long and when each of these sessions will be.

All of this should indicate to you that, because plenty of time is available for the LEAG examination, you will be expected to carry out some *in depth* and *worthwhile* preparatory studies.

THE QUESTION

For their GCSE Examination LEAG publish what they call a **Candidates' Paper** for each year's examination. The candidates' paper is your 'examination paper' with this Examining Group and is common to the Unendorsed Certificate *and* all the Endorsed Certificates.

In the candidates' paper there is **ONE THEME** only. There are **NO QUESTIONS SET** IN THE CANDIDATES' PAPER. Instead, in the candidates' paper you are introduced to the theme and then the theme is discussed for you. *From this discussion* you are expected either:

■ to follow up some of the points raised in the discussion;

or

■ to decide upon a point, or points of interest of your own within the Theme.

This means that if you wanted to do '*Drawing and Painting*', you would get your idea, based upon the theme, and then carry it out in 'drawn and painted' form. On the other hand, if you wanted to do '*Photography*', you would get your idea from the theme and then carry it out in 'photographic' form. And so on.

If you wanted to do the *unendorsed* certificate you would use the theme in *any* medium or combination of media you wished.

So, from the one, *common theme*, you work out your ideas for *either* an unendorsed certificate, or any of the endorsed certificate titles, and then carry out your work accordingly and appropriately.

Let us take either the theme:

- TOWNSCAPE;

or

- LEISURE

You will see that you have an almost unlimited choice to follow up in your externally set examination, whichever of these themes was set in your paper. For instance, if you like drawing *modern buildings*, you could draw a 'Leisure Centre' for either theme. On the other hand, if you like drawing *people* you could draw them on the staircase of a building, or in a gymnasium, and you would still satisfy each theme in turn!

In the candidates' paper each year you are reminded of the work requirements you *must* fulfil in order to be awarded a certificate in your GCSE. These are:

- the stipulated amount of coursework;
- your preparatory studies for the externally set examination;
- the work from your controlled test.

It is emphasised in the candidates' paper that if you fail to produce *any* of these work requirements, YOU WILL NOT RECEIVE A CERTIFICATE.

Apart from this, the candidates' paper points out various things to you and gives you some tips on how to conduct your preparatory studies and then how to proceed into your controlled test.

It is obvious with the LEAG examination that you cannot afford to fail to produce some *preparatory studies*. Because they are stipulated in this way, it would pay you to work hard at your preparatory studies.

At the same time, apart from doing the best Art and Design work that you are capable of, you should make sure that you introduce some *critical* and *historical* aspect into your work. Of course, the critical and historical aspect in your externally set examination might be minimal if you wish, *provided you have attended adequately to this side of Art and Design in your coursework*.

For the purposes of this chapter the following "question" is considered:

TOWNSCAPE

OUTLINE ANSWER

Again the outline 'answer' is in the form of the *student's* thought processes. The *examiners'* comments are shown in italics.

1 **ANALYSIS**   'I do not like this question.

First of all, I live in the countryside, in the Yorkshire Dales, and I like painting the countryside, not towns.

My teachers have pointed out to me that a "village" can be regarded as a "town", for the purposes of the examination, but I am not interested in houses.

I like the "natural way" that the landscape around my home looks. It is nice, with people farming, and the moors to walk over. The buildings around where I live are old and they seem to merge in with the countryside.

The trouble with this examination paper is that there is only one question and you have to answer that!

But still, I am going to make a start. First of all I am going to do some drawings of my school and then, later, I am going to do a drawing of some buildings around where I live.

I will see what I think of these before I decide how I shall continue.'

Examiner: *The advice given by the teachers was good. It took into account the 'spirit' of the candidates' paper.*

Your teachers are helped to understand the 'spirit' in the theme and the candidates' paper each year by means of a Teachers' Paper which the Examining Group publishes to accompany the candidates' paper.

This teachers' paper discusses the theme and assists your teachers to understand what the examiners who wrote the candidates' paper were thinking about.

In the candidates' paper for this question it went to great length to say that the theme, 'Townscape', could be interpreted widely.

Apart from admitting 'villages' into the theme, it went even further when it quoted from Cullen (1961) that,

'. . . a townscape could be two or more buildings in juxtaposition.'

This means that in the outline answer in this chapter the candidate could actually do a 'Landscape!'

All that would be required would be that it included two barns somewhere in it, and close together!

THOUGHTS

'Now that I know that it is alright for me to work from the countryside, as long as I include buildings, the question seems to have plenty of possibilities.

If "two barns in juxtaposition" add up to "Townscape", I wonder if the beautiful stone walls in the Dales also add up to "Townscape"?

They would certainly feature in my "Landscape-Townscape".

I know a spot near where I live where a cluster of old barns are in a hollow where walls and hills meet. I shall concentrate my work on those during my preparatory studies.

It is possible to see these from a variety of viewpoints and distances.

I did a sketch of my school, but I do not want to work any more on this, or that subject-matter.'

BRAINSTORMING DIAGRAM

FROM HEADHIGH   FROM CLOSE UP
FROM LOW   FROM MIDDLE DISTANCE
FROM HIGH   FROM AFAR

DIFFERENT VIEWPOINTS   DIFFERENT DISTANCES

TOWNSCAPE

DIFFERENT MEDIA   DIFFERENT SCALE

PENCIL   MEDIUM
INK   LARGE
PAINT   VERY SMALL
COLLAGE   Nicholas de Staël
PHOTOGRAPHY

KEY: CAPITAL LETTERS = FIRST THOUGHTS
        Small letters = Second Thoughts

DECISIONS

'Where I am thinking of, the ground falls away in the front of the barns. I can try drawing them from down this slight hill. If need be I could squat, to get a lower eye-level.

In the same way I can get up the hill and see the barns from afar and from above.

It is a good idea to do a "drawing" of a subject which has got a series of large, simple shapes in it by using "collage" to represent those shapes. It helps you to understand how they all merge together in a pattern.

This helps later when you are painting. It is a good idea to work from drawings, paintings *and* your collage when doing a final piece of work. Each different type of "drawing" and the type of information each can contain contributes to how your final piece of work looks.

If I am doing collage, drawing and painting, it is sensible to change the scale of my work in each case, because the scale represented by the medium in each case differs.

Using a camera to "look at" the subject always helps me.

Seeing the subject framed in the camera viewfinder lets me explore its possibilities. I begin to understand something about the possible composition present in a scene.'

2 > BEGINNING WORK

'I started my first drawing (Fig 9.1) in pencil, looking at the scene from up a little hill and from a distance.

The drawing seemed to go quite well. It was interesting to see how the roofs looked from this angle. I was looking down on them and I could see their shapes clearly. They began to make an interesting pattern amongst themselves.

Fig. 9.1 The view, from afar and above.

Fig 9.2 The hill lit from behind.

Fig 9.3 The view, from close-up.

Fig. 9.4 The 'close-up' view re-worked.

Fig. 9.5 Painting in the manner of de Staël. Despite the candidate's enthusiasm this does not appear to be a very satisfactory piece of work. It is no good slavishly copying what you believe to be the 'technique' of an artist based upon the apparent appearance of a piece of work. Tied up in your understanding of how an artist works must be your ability to select an appropriate subject to work from yourself which will show, amongst other things, that you have analysed the original artist's work and that you appreciate the significance of the composition, and not that you know how to copy the artist's style alone.

The old trees growing around the barns broke up the harsh lines of the buildings and I liked that. I must put a lot of the trees in my final work.

From this viewpoint it was also good to be able to see "into" the fields. They were laid out below me like a "patchwork quilt". I had often seen this effect in films and television programmes, where the camera was in an aeroplane or a helicopter.

My position also meant that I could see and put in the line of the top of the hill in the background. Because of my raised position, the outline of the hill "looked" quite low in my picture.

As the evening came, the hill was interestingly lit from behind by the sun (Fig 9.2). It made the whole scene look dark and powerful. I might do something with this effect.

Starting my work with the camera the next time I went back was a good idea. It enabled me to get around the whole subject quickly, framing "pictures" of it in my viewfinder. I think that I learnt a lot about the subject by this means.

It was my own camera and I had a few colour shots left in it. After I used these up I put in a small cassette of black and white film which my teachers had prepared for me at my earlier request, and used this.

On this second visit to my subject I got a lot closer to the barns (Fig 9.3). After I had drawn in the major outlines of the scene lightly, using a soft pencil, I began to try to show the mass of the walls of the buildings by using washes of ink.

From this distance it was difficult to see the top of the hill if I kept everything in scale and "perspective" in my drawing.

Thinking of how the hill looked against the sky the last time I was here, I decided to "cheat" and to put the outline of the hill into my picture, with some sky showing above it (Fig 9.4)!

This time the sky was not light above the hill. It was quite stormy looking. I was struck by how "leaden" and grey everything looked.

I wondered if the scene really looked so, or if my choice of medium was influencing the way that I "saw" things. I decided I would be interested to see how the scene looked in my photographs. As I had colour photographs and black and white ones, it would be interesting to compare the effect the two different films had upon the way the scene "looked".

So far, since receiving my candidates' paper I had worked away from school on my ideas.

When I returned to school I told my teachers that I had been noticing and thinking of different "effects" in the scene and my work. They suggested I made a list of my thoughts at once, in case I forgot them.

My list looked like this:

1 The pattern of roofs and fields.
2 The pattern and texture of buildings contrasted with the pattern and texture of trees.
3 The silhouette caused by the light sky.
4 The grey, solid and heavy feel of the whole scene when I was close enough for it to seem to envelop me.

My teachers thought that I had got a long way with a subject I "did not like"!

They let me develop my black and white film and were interested to see the colour prints when I got them back.

They felt that I might have something amongst my photographs to turn into a "critical study". They suggested that I could work on this at school during my preparatory studies, and do my drawings at home at weekends.'

LATER

'When I looked at my ink wash drawing later I did not like it.

I ran it under a tap for a while, trying to lose some of the "harshness" of it.

It made the work look "blurred", but not much better. I decided to work on it using white poster paint to draw into it.

Returning to the scene I tried to do a water-colour. This was not very successful, either.

Before I left I made some close-up studies in pencil of the stone walls around the fields and the grasses and plants which grew at their feet and on them.

At home I worked on my ink wash drawing with white paint, as I intended. It began to look better.

Later, at school, I made a collage from my water-colour failure.

I began by working from it, using torn paper to make up the shapes. I used coloured sugar paper and coloured sticky paper. Little pieces of colours I did not have I tore from colour magazine photographs.

I still did not like the water-colour, so I painted over it with a glue which would dry transparent.

I cut and pressed pieces of coloured tissue onto the gluey water-colour. Suddenly it became much more interesting.

I felt good. I had made two bad drawings look a lot better. At the same time, I was working in response to my subject, but "interpreting" it, moving it away from a literal copy.

One of my teachers suggested I took home a book on an artist called Nicholas de Staël, and that I looked at his paintings with my collages in mind.

Nicholas de Staël seemed to work in large "slabs" of colour. I think I could see what my teacher meant me to realise.

My collages were like "jig-saw puzzles", with all the shapes interlocking and fitting together. If I painted them including the detail of the walls, the fields, the trees, the buildings, I would lose this simple effect.

De Staël's paintings were colourful, but simple.

I decided to do one or two little paintings from my collages next time I was at school, working like de Staël did.

When my colour photographs returned I compared them with my black and white photographs.

They did make the scene look different to the black and white photographs.

The black and white photographs seemed to make the scene look very forboding, rather like the actual scene appeared on that stormy day.

I used the colour schemes from my colour photographs to do my "de Staël" paintings (Fig 9.5).'

3 〉 SELECTION

'I was getting near the end of the time I had for my preparatory studies. I had a number of alternatives which I could do for my controlled test.

I decided that as I had done my collages and made two paintings from them, I would not do anything more in this way.

The pencil drawing from a distance, and a few photographs, looked like the thing I usually did in my Art and Design studies, and looked like I liked things to look. But I decided against doing this sort of picture.

Instead I decided to "take a chance" and to work from closer to the buildings, so that they were larger in my picture, and to try to get the effect of the hill silhouetted against the sky, *as well as* the effect of the "leaden greyness" into my work.

This whole thing was a change from what I usually did, but I was pleased about this. I felt that my coursework showed plenty of examples of the way I usually worked and the scenes I usually did.

In a way I was grateful for the question I had had to answer. It made me look again, and think again.

I decided that whilst I did my controlled test, I would work at home also, and pull some of my other preparatory studies ideas together.'

4 ⟩ CONCLUSIONS

'At the end of my controlled test I had a largish painting which was different to anything I had done before.

I was interested in it, *but not certain it was as good as I usually did.*

I also had a small study put together on Nicholas de Staël.

This included my collages, my paintings from them, and a colour slide of "**Landscape Study**" by Nicholas de Staël, which I got by post from the Tate Gallery, London.

I had also written up some historical notes on this artist and my own appreciation of his work.

In addition to this I had my photographs, the ink wash and white paint study, (from which I had largely worked in my controlled test), and one or two pencil studies I had done in my preparatory studies.

I felt that I had used my time well.

I had taken a risk with my work in the controlled test but the result, whilst I did not think it to be up to my usual standard, did expand the type of work I had in my coursework.

My other preparatory studies did show that I was working up to my usual standard when I did the things I was used to doing.'

5 ⟩ EXAMINER COMMENTS

The content of the Outline Answer here is such as might have come from a candidate's 'work journal'.

The idea of a work journal was discussed earlier in this book, in Chapter 4.

If it was to be documented in a work journal as it stands above, it would go a long way towards fulfilling the second part of the assessment criteria in Group 3 (see page 133). This is the criteria which refers to having command of a 'critical vocabulary applicable to the subject'.

Each study the candidate did was a 'critical appraisal and appreciation' not only of the subject itself, but of the work that was being done, as it was being done.

The little study which materialised on the Russian artist, Nicholas de Staël, was a 'critical and historical study' in its own right. This would have further fulfilled the requirements of the assessment criteria in the second half of Group 3, referred to above.

'Risking' everything in the controlled test is a rational thing to do in the LEAG examination.

Remember, the syllabus does not have any 'weighting' between your coursework and the externally set examination.

This means that an 'explained failure', such as the candidate believes this to be, need not detract from your final grade.

In this instance the work was evaluated and appraised as it was going on and once it was all completed. This means that it could not only be that poorer work in the externally set examination could be compensated for by more successful coursework, but that the 'failure' itself could also earn credit for its critical content!

So, all-in-all, doing what the candidate did was a rational and calculated risk well worth taking.

It was one which would possibly result in a higher grade than would otherwise be achieved by repeating previous successes.

The work done during the externally set examination, as described above, represents a very good model of how your work should continue to develop over your preparatory studies and throughout your controlled test.

Nothing in the work was 'repeated'. Instead it was modified and/or developed at each stage of its production.

The candidate did not carry out everything listed in the brainstorming diagram.

This does not matter.

The brainstorming diagram is a 'flowing forth' of everything that you can think of in response to, in this case, the 'Theme'.

In fact this particular brainstorming diagram is not a good example of its kind. It seems very restricted and pre-meditated. It seems like a 'calculated' recipe of what the candidate intended to do.

This may be understandable when you consider that, to begin with at least, the candidate did not 'like the question'.

Even so, not doing all that was listed does not matter.

The candidate seems not to have made a sketch from 'lower down'.

Starting from 'higher up' and then moving to 'close-up', which would presumably also be 'head high', the candidate discovered and recognised enough 'sub-problems' to maintain the work at a high investigative and developmental level throughout the preparatory studies and into the controlled test.

A number of problems exist in Fig 9.3. The choice about the direction of the light makes it difficult to create an interesting and contrasting composition in the work. The dark sky does not add a sense of 'drama' to the scene, which the photograph above did appear to. The 'marks' so far in the drawing make the work look 'repetitive' and very 'subdued', even 'boring'!

In all, the drawing does not reflect a very high level of personal excitement and involvement on the part of the artist.

Now that the drawing has been 're-worked' in a studio (Fig 9.4), the result is much more satisfactory.

It is possible to sense that the artist has become much more involved and excited with the work, and is likely to develop it in a worthwhile way at the next stage.

If the coursework of this candidate, and the general 'artistic' standard of the work done during the externally set examination, was of a high enough standard, then there seems every reason to believe that the candidate should receive a grade at least as high as a Grade C, but probably higher.

Even if the 'artistic' standard of the work done in the externally set examination was not of the best quality, if the coursework 'artistic' standards were good, then the same level of grade could result in the LEAG examinaiton.

If the general 'artistic' standard of the candidate's work was lower than the standards necessary for the absolutely top grades of A or B, even then, if the way that the candidate worked during the externally set examination was the way that he worked throughout the course of study, it would still be reasonable to assume that a Grade C, or thereabouts, could still result.

STUDENT'S ANSWER – SOME FURTHER ASPECTS

The water-colour by the British artist, **Henry Bright (1810–73)**, of the 'Norwich School' (Plate 23), shows that the 'countryside' can easily answer the theme of 'Townscape' if it is 'Buildings' which are paramount in that theme rather than the concept of towns as, perhaps, arteries of communication and conglomerations of people and buildings alone.

In the same way, the following photograph (Fig 9.6) taken in the Yorkshire Dales, shows that there is a relationship between one small 'man-made' structure and another, the parts of a building one to another, and buildings and people's effect upon nature. To be 'buildings', or 'architecture', does not demand that the constructions that human beings erect around themselves to live and work in, must be 'grand' and large-scale edifices.

Fig 9.7 shows another candidate's response to the sub-theme of the 'barn'.

In Figures 9.8 and 9.9 the candidates have had the opportunity to work in what is obviously a genuine 'town' situation. The question is, is the work better for being done in an actual 'Town'?

The point you can learn here is that it is not necessary to feel that you are restricted to 'answer' what the 'question' *appears* to be asking. If you work well, showing that you can handle the 'qualities' represented by the *practice of Art and Design* efficiently, it should not matter that your 'answer' appears to deviate so far as the 'question' is *strictly* concerned.

It has been stressed in this book that there are no 'right' and 'wrong' answers in Art and Design, only the 'appropriate' and the 'inappropriate'. What is at stake is your ability to fulfil the objectives which are peculiar to Art and Design. These objectives are about your ability to research, analyse, select and use your information and your practical materials and techniques in the most fruitful way.

For instance, if you study the following work by Vincent Van Gogh (Plate 24), do you think that it would have been awarded a poor grade in a GCSE Examination because it does not appear to actually answer the theme of 'Townscape'?

The answer must be 'No'. It is so obviously a first-rate piece of Art and Design work that its genuine 'Art and Design' qualities must be recognised and rewarded handsomely.

Plate 23 Henry Bright, 'Old Barn, Kent'. *The Castle Museum, Norwich.*

Plate 24 Vincent Van Gogh, 'Farms Near Auvers'. *The Tate Gallery, London.*

Fig. 9.6 The Yorkshire Dales.

Fig. 9.7 Alternative studies: barn lino-cut. In this work another candidate has produced an alternative solution to the theme, still using the 'countryside' rather than the 'town' as a source of imagery. In the lino-cut the candidate has achieved a rich textural effect, which is often part and parcel of the process of the craft of lino-cutting. This effect is very evocative of the countryside and its appearance. If the candidate was able to comment verbally and/or visually upon aspects like this and develop them into some critical/contextual accompaniment, then an already good piece of work would be even more highly rewarded.

Fig. 9.8 Alternative studies: street scene. This work is very interesting. The raised eye-level, the perspective, and the use of pattern and texture makes it a very successful response to the problem. There are drawing mistakes, particularly in respect of some of the perspective, which does detract slightly from its level of achievement. Even if the drawing is consequently of limited success so far as the accuracy of the perspective is concerned, as a drawing it has much 'character' and a strong internal 'consistency' and 'completeness'. Hopefully the work would be viewed and rewarded on the basis of these qualities. They are, after all, qualities which enhance many famous works of art!

Fig. 9.9 Alternative studies: town views. This candidate has made a series of very promising studies of particular buildings in a town. They have the air of preparatory/supporting studies and would benefit through the development of one or more of them during the controlled test.

BIBLIOGRAPHY

CULLEN, G. (1961). *Townscape.* London, The Architectural Press.

GETTING STARTED

The various Examining Groups, where they have specific examination syllabuses and specific examination papers for 'Graphics', contain a variety of activities under this 'umbrella' title. These can be seen to range from rather formal 'Lettering' practices, through what used to be called 'Commercial Art', products such as posters and book Illustrations. In fact the term 'Graphic Design' is now widely used to cover this range of activities.

E S S E N T I A L   P R I N C I P L E S

1 GENERAL USAGE

The term 'graphic' has a very definite meaning. In everyday language it is often used to describe something which is '*very striking*', or '*vividly descriptive*'.

2 ART AND DESIGN

In *Art and Design* the term 'graphic' has a *specialised* meaning. This meaning is usually associated with 'drawing'. It is fairly common to refer to artists' 'drawn work' as their 'graphic work.' Because of this the 'drawing materials' are often referred to in Art and Design as 'graphic materials'. Apart from these 'drawing materials', in Art and Design, the graphic work of artists is also used as a term to include their 'printmaking' output.

3 GRAPHIC DESIGNERS

About forty years ago, those who produced 'commercial art' were usually regarded as 'artists'. In the modern world, those who now produce images similar to those of 'commercial artists', as well as a mass of other 'graphic products', are known as 'designers'. If you think of 'graphic designers' being concerned with producing work which 'sells' something, you begin to have a *working* definition of what is meant by 'graphic design'. This will be useful in your GCSE Art and Design studies.

4 COMMUNICATING INFORMATION

Apart from the very obvious 'selling of things', such as posters advertising holidays, or television advertisements designed to sell products ranging from food-stuffs to motor-cars, it is possible to 'sell' other things which are *not* so commercially centred. Therefore it is convenient to think of graphic design being concerned with 'selling', but with a *much wider interpretation* than that usually associated with the exchange of goods and money.

For instance if you *print a poem in a book*, or *hand-letter a poem*, you are 'selling' that poem by '**communicating**' it to others. If you produce a *leaflet* which 'explains' how a product works, or what it offers you, you are 'selling' that product. Therefore it is perhaps better to think of graphic design as being concerned with communicating '**information**'.

A definition such as this allows you to accept that the designer who produces the *credit titles* for a television programme is as much involved with graphic design as the designer who produces the *packaging* to wrap and sell the latest brand of cosmetics.

By accepting the broadest interpretation of what constitutes graphic design you are able to encompass a whole range and variety of Art and Design activities which would otherwise be rejected if your definition of 'graphics' was restricted to 'commercial art', or 'hand lettering', or 'poster design', and so on.

T H E   Q U E S T I O N

For the purposes of this chapter the following 'question' from the 1986 candidates' paper for the LEAG 16+ Joint Certificated examination will be used. As we have analysed that Group's syllabus in Chapter 9, no further discussion of assessment objectives and criteria will take place here.

The question is 'TOWNSCAPE', but this time in the context of graphics.

OUTLINE ANSWER

The thought processes of a student are outlined here. *Examiner* comments are presented in italics.

1 **ANALYSIS** ## BRAINSTORMING DIAGRAM

TOWNSCAPE

■ RE-DESIGNING	■ SELLING	■ HISTORICAL	■ TRAVELLING	■ OTHERS
SHOP FRONTS	ESTATE AGENTS	GEORGIAN	POSTERS	POEMS
HOUSES	HOLIDAYS	VICTORIAN	TRAVEL AGENCIES	PROSE
RE-DEVELOPING	BED & BREAKFAST	EDWARDIAN	RAIL	VIDEOS
ROADWAYS	CONSUMER GOODS	'PRE-WAR'	COACH	LANDMARKS
COMMUNICATIONS		MODERN	CAR	

SIGNS   MODELS   LEAFLETS   PAMPHLETS   BOOKS   PHOTOGRAPHY   ILLUSTRATIONS
DIAGRAMS   PLANS

THOUGHTS

'This is a good theme. There is plenty to do. The difficulty is going to be in deciding what to concentrate on.

From my brainstorming diagram I have so many ideas that I must find a way to develop them in the hope that what I begin to find out will guide me towards what it is I should do.

I think the best way to begin is to try to *list each idea* that I have against the possible *sources and types of information* that I think I might be able to gather.

If I put entries into this system as I think of them, or find out about them, those possibilities which are *strongest* will show in a *visual* way. They will have *most entries* in them.

To do this I need a number of '*categories*' first. These will cover all the possible sources of information. Then I can write against them the *types of information* I expect to be able to find from each.

For my 'sources and types of information' headings I shall use:

- Museums;
- Historical;
- Cultural;
- Books and Magazines;
- Professional;
- Direct Observation.

These should provide me with plenty of information of different varieties, and lead eventually to the "Graphic Design" problem I shall set myself.'

DECISIONS

'I decided to rule out a number of separate *cards*, each headed with an idea which I got from my brainstorming diagram. I found that these "ideas" often put two or three things from my brainstorming diagram together into just one word.

Down the *side* of each card I carefully wrote in each of my information headings.

After I had done that I wrote in as many entries as I could think of against each "information heading", doing one "ideas card" at a time. This seemed to give me plenty of avenues to look into.

The next step would obviously involve first following up some of my possible sources of information, seeing if the types of information I predicted did actually *exist*!

After that the problem of "*selection*" would come in, if my predictions were anywhere near correct! But at least, I now had enough positive things to go and start doing.'

The Cards

Idea: SHOPS

- MUSEUMS — Victorian Shop Front; Food and Products in old wrappings; Methods of selling; Methods of display; Barter; Services which have gone out of fashion, e.g. Cobblers, Wheelwright.

- HISTORICAL — Old Prints; 'Shops' in Paintings, e.g. in works by Utrillo and Van Gogh; Architectural Styles.

- CULTURAL — Change from 'Barter', through 'Shops' to 'Supermarkets'.

- BOOKS & MAGAZINES — Advertisements; History of Photography Books.

- PROFESSIONAL — Modern Shop Fronts; Window Displays; Package Design; Advertising.

- DIRECT OBSERVATION — High Street Shops; Corner Shops; Modern 'Supermarkets'; Market Stalls; Car Boot Sales; Jumble Sales.

Idea: HOUSES

- MUSEUMS — Dolls Houses; Styles of 'Living'; Original versions of Household Aids, e.g. Wash Tubs, Vacuum Cleaners.

- HISTORICAL — Architectural Styles; 'Houses' in Paintings, e.g. Various Views of Venice by Canaletto; Manor Houses; Castles; 'Seaside' Architecture; Country Cottages.

- CULTURAL — Different Planning Ideals, e.g. 'Ribbon' Development, 'Pre-Fabs'; High-Rise Flats; Changes in Living Style; New Standards, e.g. Indoor Bathroom, Car Ownership; Commune Living.

- BOOKS & MAGAZINES — Architectural Magazines; 'Good Housekeeping'; 'Ideal Home'; Photographs – also of other Countries.

- PROFESSIONAL — Architects, e.g. Frank Lloyd Wright, Le Courbousier, Builders and Decorators, Interior Designers.

- DIRECT OBSERVATION — High Streets; Back Streets; Slums; Hotels; Modern Sites; Public Buildings, e.g. Library, Theatre, Town Hall.

Idea: CHURCHES

- MUSEUMS — Old Photographs?

- HISTORICAL — Architectural Styles, 'Churches' in Painting, e.g. Notre Dame Cathedral by Monet.

- CULTURAL — Churches for different Religions, e.g. Catholic Cathedrals, Mosques, Parish Churches, Methodist Chapels.

- BOOKS & MAGAZINES — Church Magazines; Photographs; Articles.

- PROFESSIONAL — Modern Designs.

- DIRECT OBSERVATION — Local Churches; Weddings; Festivals; Services; Graveyards; Interiors.

Idea: TRAVEL

- MUSEUMS — Examples of 'Carriages' and 'Coaches'. Railway Museum, York; Car Museums; Tram Museum; London Transport Museum.

- HISTORICAL — Paintings, Prints, and Drawings with 'Coaches' in them, e.g. 'Mail' Coaches, Stage Coaches, Horse-Drawn Buses; Steam Trains.

- CULTURAL — Changes in reasons for travel; Changes in means of travel; 'it's a small world!'

- BOOKS & MAGAZINES — Holiday Brochures; Colour Supplement Magazines; Specialist Books and Articles.

- PROFESSIONAL — Vehicle Design; Livery Design; 'Stations' and 'Airports' Design; Ticket and Label Design.
- DIRECT OBSERVATION — Railway Stations; Bus and Coach Stations; Vehicles; Waiting Facilities; Eating Facilities; Roadway Designs; Signposting.

Idea: NATURE IN TOWN

- MUSEUMS — Old Plans showing original Open-Spaces; Photographs and Drawings.
- HISTORICAL — 'Garden Cities', such as Letchworth, Welwyn Garden City, Port Sunlight, Bourneville; Royal Parks in London; Zoos.
- CULTURAL — Uses of Open-Spaces; Development of Private 'House Gardens'; Leisure use of Rivers and Canals.
- BOOKS & MAGAZINES — Architectural Planning; Photographs.
- PROFESSIONAL — Botanical Gardens, such as at Kew and in Birmingham; Landscape Gardeners such as 'Capability Brown'.
- DIRECT OBSERVATION — Parks; Roads with Trees in; Front Gardens; Canal and River Banks; Village Greens; Communal Gardens.

Idea: TOWNS IN WORDS

- MUSEUMS — ?
- HISTORICAL — ?
- CULTURAL — ?
- BOOKS & MAGAZINES — Bible; Poems; Prose; Travel Books.
- PROFESSIONAL — Sir John Betjeman, 'Summoned by Bells'.
- DIRECT OBSERVATION — Personal Research at Libraries.

THOUGHTS

'When I had completed the cards they gave me much food for thought. They seemed to come up with plenty of sources and ideas about the types of information I might gather.

"Shops", "Houses" and "Travel" seemed to offer me the *most* sources and types of information, but I did not know where to begin.

I decided to make a start by studying the History of Art and Design. During my course of study I had found that referring back in this way led me into my best ideas for my work.

I had found out that "History" had a way of *repeating itself* in Art, Design and Fashion. For instance, it has been popular in recent years to return first to Victorian times for "design" ideas, then the "Twenties" seemed to reappear. Nowadays there seems to be a nostalgia for the 'Fifties and Sixties'.

Researching history in this way had led me to some good "graphic" ideas for my work, in response to a set design problem.

My trouble is, that so far here, I do not have a "design problem". I am hoping that the historical research will help me to come up with a suitable *problem* as much as a source of suitable material for my *solution*.

The candidates' paper suggested a few ideas for "problems", but I was not sure that I wanted to do one of these. I wanted to "get my own idea" if I could. I had got the references to "Canaletto" and "Utrillo" from the candidates' paper. They had been suggested as good historical sources for any work on the theme.'

Examiner: *In this work so far the candidate has not developed the brainstorming diagram on the diagram itself, but a lot of development of the original 'brainstorming' has gone on in the form of the 'research cards'.*

These are an excellent invention as a form of 'thinking' and stimulating possible avenues of exploration.

Whilst they have not so far turned up a problem to solve, they contain within them the sources of many possible problems.

They also contain the pathway to producing a solution to a suitable problem.

This candidate seems to have been able to do much work without moving out into any 'field studies' so far.

2 > BEGINNING WORK

'I decided to start on three "research" fronts together.

I would:

- conduct some historical research through slides and books;
- go and study the shops in my High Street, both inside and out;
- take a camera to photograph some houses in my Town.'

HISTORICAL RESEARCH

'I started by looking at the work of Canaletto and Utrillo, recommended in the candidates' paper. I found out that Canaletto was an Italian artist who lived from 1697 to 1768. His real name was Antonio Canal, but we was *called* Canaletto because he worked from the canals for his subject matter. He visited England and did some paintings around London.

Utrillo was a French artist who lived from 1883 to 1935. He worked in Paris, around Montmartre. I liked Utrillo's paintings. The buildings looked very "solid" and reminded me of "stage sets". It was almost as if he had "built" them with colour in his works.

But it was Canaletto who "took my eye". I was astounded by his large, panoramic views of the buildings and the canals in Venice (Plate 25). He got every detail into the buildings and the boats. The men in his paintings looked more "sketchy", but it was the buildings and the ornate boats that took the eye.'

Plate 25 Canaletto, 'Venice: Upper Reaches of the Grand Canal'. *Reproduced by courtesy of the Trustees, The National Gallery, London.*

VISITING SHOPS

'On my visit to the shops I became more interested in what was *inside* some of them than I was with the outside of them.

I had seen some old photographs of shops at the beginning of this century. In these the various shops seemed to have most of their stock either hanging on the outside of the shops, or on the pavement itself!

I wished shops were like that nowadays, but I suppose there would be too much "pilfering". I wonder if they suffered from pilfering in the old days? Perhaps the number of staff they had put would-be thieves off!

I spent a lot of time in our bookshop. What attracted me more and more in there were some books by Jan Pienkowski. These are "pop-up" books, but they are not really children's books. They have nearly every kind of "pop-up" and movement you could think of. I spent a lot of time seeing if I could reason out how they worked.'

PHOTOGRAPHING HOUSES

'I decided to try to get a photograph of each period of housing I could identify in my Town. No doubt I will need a book on the History of Architecture, and perhaps the help of my teachers if I am to really place the houses accurately in "History".

As I worked I became more and more interested in the larger, Public Buildings. Some of these looked very impressive and very ornate and reminded me of those painted by Canaletto.

In my Town there is a large Market Square. This is surrounded on all four sides with very old Houses, Hotels, Civic Buildings, and a Local History Museum. The Market Square began to interest me.'

CONTINUING

'Because my preparatory studies coincided with the start of my School Easter Holiday, about a fortnight later I had:

- a set of photographs of buildings in my Town;
- a "pop-up" book by Jan Pienkowski, which I had bought;
- a collection of reproductions of the work of Canaletto;
- some notes of my visit to our Local History Museum.

I also had an *emerging idea* to solve my *problem*. This was,

- to use our local Market Square as the source of my work and problem;
- to try to do something which advertised the attraction of the square in order to encourage tourism.

This emerging problem was partly from the candidates' paper supplied by the Examining Group. In this it was suggested that I might try to:

". . . preserve my town's heritage . . . by projecting the qualities of the town . . ."'

3 › DESIGN PROBLEM

'My design problem is:

To satisfy the need to attract tourists to my town.

I decided to try to do this by communicating some of its fine **buildings** and **qualities**.

- The "buildings" I have chosen to present are those surrounding our local Market Square.
- The "qualities" I have chosen to present are those represented by the Local History Museum.'

INITIAL INTENTIONS

'I have *two* avenues of exploration I have decided to concentrate on. They are,

1 to reflect the very good "toy museum" which is in our Local History Museum. I have chosen to see if I can present the Square in the form of a Victorian "Zoetrope" (Fig 10.1);

2 to present the square in the form of a "pop-up" book.
  Apart from the pop-up book I have bought, there are also some in the toy collection in our Local History Museum.

Each idea will have some "text" in it.

In the case of the Zoetrope I intend to see if the text looks alright set around the outside of the drum.

In the case of the pop-up book I intend to put the text on the pages of the book.

In the rest of my preparatory studies I am going to try to experiment with both ideas. To do so I shall use prints of my black and white photographs. If I do not have to draw my images at this stage it will speed things up.'

WORK PROGRAMME

'My **work-programme** will be:

- experiment with the construction of the Zoetrope Drum;
- test the photographs within the Zoetrope;
- select suitable lettering for the text, on the Zoetrope;
- experiment with the 'cardboard engineering' used in the pop-up books;
- produce a trial page of the pop-up book;
- select suitable lettering for the test in the pop-up book.'

Examiner: *Thanks largely to the open-ended approach adopted in this work, and the fortunate opportunity to use the Easter Holiday, the candidate here is in an excellent position to use the four remaining weeks of the preparatory studies.*

Although it is intended to try to do two different pieces of work, both have obvious links. Both 'models' chosen for the 'form' of the candidate's work come from the Victorian era. This means that it might be that one set of lettering will do for both pieces of work.

It would certainly be a good idea to use just one set in the preparatory studies in this case. If necessary a further set could be sorted out in the controlled test.

The notes in the Outline Answer are already forming a good trace of the candidate's 'critical thinking'.

From now on the candidate's notes come in a drawn as much as a written form.

CONTINUING

'The first thing that I had to do was to go back to my Local History Museum and try to sort out exactly how a Zoetrope was constructed and worked (Fig 10.2). Once I could find that out I could begin to think how I might make a "mock up" of one for my experiment. Some thoughts were emerging by the time I got this far.
  The Zoetrope worked on a "flickering" system, as the slots went round. This reminded me of a few things:

- a "strobe" light has this effect;
- animated cartoons work like this;
- it is the basis of cinematography;
- "flick" books are another example of the system.

Now that I had studied the Zoetrope closely I could see that the "films" used in it were like a "flick" book, but all on one long strip of paper. I thought it might be a good idea to make some of my own films if I get the Zoetrope made.

It seems to me that I shall need to get some form of "animation" into my "film" strip of the Market Square, if I am to capture the essence of the Zoetrope. I might be able to put a man in it, looking as if he is walking round the Whole Market Square.

I think I shall construct my experimental Zoetrope in cardboard. It will be fairly cheap, be easy to work in, and will last out my needs at this stage.

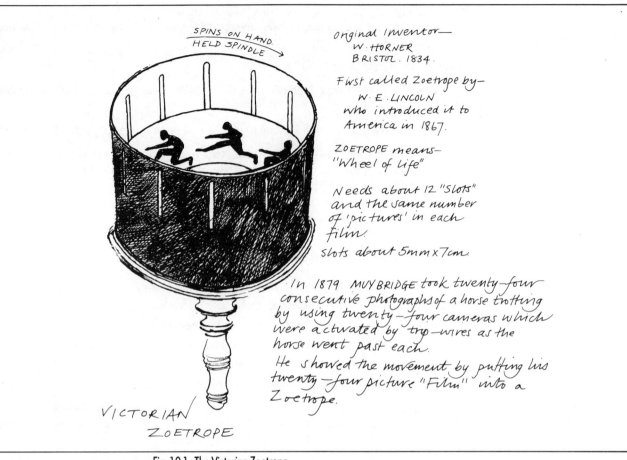

SPINS ON HAND.
HELD SPINDLE

Original Inventor—
W. HORNER
BRISTOL. 1834.

First called Zoetrope by—
W. E. LINCOLN
who introduced it to
America in 1867.

ZOETROPE means—
"Wheel of Life"

Needs about 12 "slots"
and the same number
of 'pictures' in each
film.

Slots about 5mm x 7cm.

In 1879 MUYBRIDGE took twenty-four
consecutive photographs of a horse trotting
by using twenty-four cameras which
were activated by trip-wires as the
horse went past each.
He showed the movement by putting his
twenty-four picture "Film" into a
Zoetrope.

VICTORIAN
ZOETROPE

Fig. 10.1 The Victorian Zoetrope.

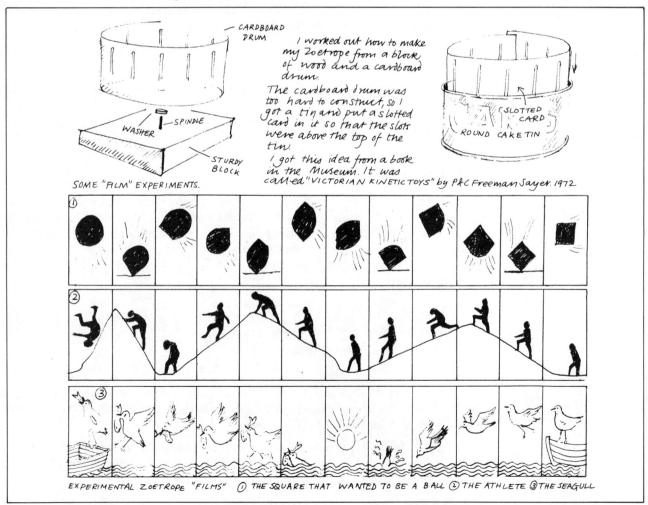

CARDBOARD
DRUM

I worked out how to make
my Zoetrope from a block
of wood and a cardboard
drum.

The cardboard drum was
too hard to construct, so I
got a tin and put a slotted
card in it so that the slots
were above the top of the
tin.

I got this idea from a book
in the Museum. It was
called "VICTORIAN KINETIC TOYS" by P&C Freeman Sayer. 1972

WASHER — SPINDLE

STURDY
BLOCK

SOME "FILM" EXPERIMENTS.

SLOTTED
CARD
ROUND CAKE TIN

EXPERIMENTAL ZOETROPE "FILMS" ① THE SQUARE THAT WANTED TO BE A BALL ② THE ATHLETE ③ THE SEAGULL

Fig. 10.2 Ideas for Zoetrope 'films' and the construction methods for the device.

My next worry is my lettering. It is probably best if I start by collecting a variety of lettering. If I can afford it I will probably use "Transfer Lettering" in my final work, but before I look at the catalogues I will see what I can discover from a variety of sources (Fig 10.3).

I wonder what "Georgian lettering" looked like? It is fairly easy to recognise a "Victorian" sort of lettering. As the Zoetrope is a Victorian toy I think I will stick with "Victorian lettering" in this idea.'

Pop-Up Book

'From my study of the **pop-up book** I had bought, I found out the following':

Lettering

'I shall use **lettering** in my book.

Originally I intended to put it on the flat page, but I think it might be a good idea to make the title of the book "pop-up" as well!

This might mean that the sort of lettering I use will have to be one that allows me to cut it out and make it "pop-up" (Fig 10.4).'

Board games

'On a further visit to the Local History Museum I got interested in the collection of old Board Games they had there. I began to wonder if I could introduce these into my advertising campaign.

Fig. 10.3 Collected lettering samples.

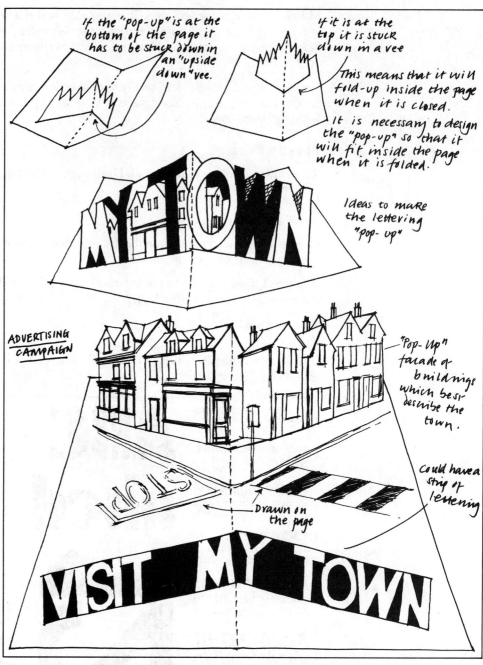

If the "pop-up" is at the bottom of the page it has to be stuck down in an "upside down" vee.

If it is at the top it is stuck down in a vee

This means that it will fold-up inside the page when it is closed.

It is necessary to design the "pop-up" so that it will fit inside the page when it is folded.

Ideas to make the lettering "pop-up"

ADVERTISING CAMPAIGN

"Pop-Up" facade of buildings which best describe the town.

Could have a strip of lettering

Drawn on the page

Fig. 10.4 Ideas for 'pop-up' work.

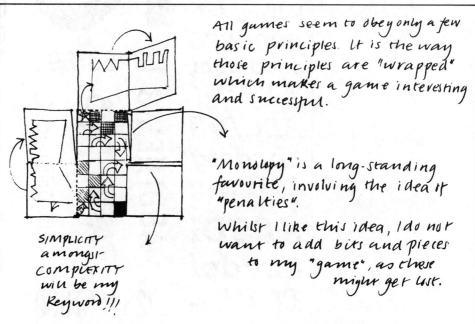

All games seem to obey only a few basic principles. It is the way those principles are "wrapped" which makes a game interesting and successful.

"Monolopy" is a long-standing favourite, involving the idea of "penalties".

Whilst I like this idea, I do not want to add bits and pieces to my "game", as these might get lost.

SIMPLICITY amongst COMPLEXITY will be my keyword!!!

Fig. 10.5 'Pop-up' board game.

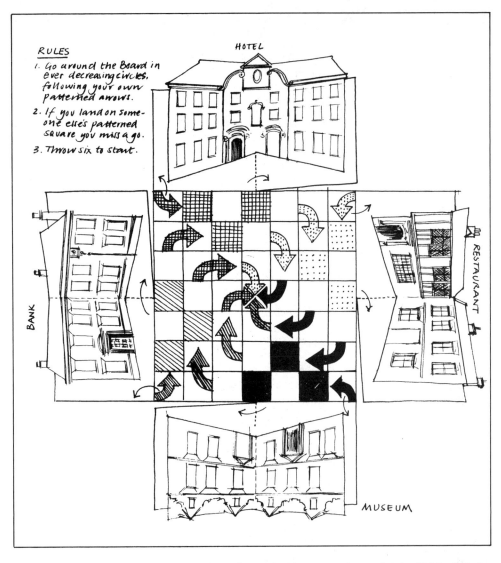

Fig 10.5 (cont)

I had originally planned to do four "folds", or double pages, in my book. If I included a Board Game I would save the time spent doing four "folds" because I would only need one "fold".

I wonder if it is possible to have a single-fold Board Game and still make all four sides of the Market Square "pop-up" (Fig 10.5)?'

4 > CONTROLLED TEST

'I have decided to scrap the idea of the Zoetrope. I enjoyed doing it as far as it went, but I do not think it works very well so far as my design problem is concerned. The work that I did on the Zoetrope will count in my final assessment, so I have not wasted my time.

In my controlled test I am going to make the Board Game, with the four pop-up "wings" in it. I am going to keep the Board Game simple. I shall just fill the board with a "chequers" pattern, using two different coloured sets of sticky-paper squares alternately.

Using sticky coloured paper, instead of painting the squares, will mean that I can get the colour neat and constant.

I shall use Transfer Numbering and Lettering on these coloured squares, to make the "game".

The game will be about going round the "Market Square". If the players land "outside" certain places, such as the Local History Museum, the Hotels, or the Information Centre, they will get bonuses for "visiting and using" the facilities and attractions of my Town.

I shall use the photographs I have already printed in readiness for the "pop-up" wings to the game.

I shall make some counters to play with and include a dice.

If I have time I shall decorate the cover of the "board".'

5 ⟩ CONCLUSIONS

'Things went quite well. Because I had done so much planning I was able to carry out most of my intentions in the time allowed for the controlled test.

Using sticky coloured paper, transfer lettering and photographs was a great help so far as the time went.

I did not have time to decorate the cover of the board, but I did manage to make a label to stick on the outside of the whole thing.

To do this I used a print of the photograph I had taken of the Local History Museum. I added transfer lettering to this, saying,

Step back in History in My Town'

6 ⟩ EXAMINER COMMENTS

This programme of work represents an excellent example of a graphic designer's system of operating.

Whilst pursuing a planned approach at any time, the candidate remained alert and receptive to new stimuluses as they cropped up.

Each of these new stimuluses were taken up, sometimes to be rejected later, sometimes to be included in the work and its development, but nearly always influencing the way that the candidate thought and worked thereafter.

The work grew and grew in its level of ambition up to the time of the controlled test. Then a very sensible appraisal of the relationship between the restrictions of time and the level of ambition took place.

The idea of the cover for the Board Game was a sound approach to take. If time ran out, then it did not get done. If this were to be the case, then the candidate's work would not lose in its value. What had been done would be rewarded according to its level of achievement.

If it could be done, then the likelihood is that the work of the candidate would gain a higher reward, because more was contained in the work.

Doing the 'label' was a good solution to the problem of matching time against ambition. Another possible solution might have been to do a 'sketch design' of the intended cover to the board.

This candidate found out a lot in studying the problem at stake.

What was found out was of obvious interest to the candidate and probably extended the level of the candidate's knowledge and understanding, both relative to the practice of Art and Design and a variety of cross-curricular matters.

History, Social Studies, and possibly Geography came into the work. This is all to the good in terms of the final level of achievement.

For the LEAG examination the candidate certainly dealt with the requirements of the assessment criteria in Group 3, (page 133) and a top grade should result from work such as this.

BIBLIOGRAPHY

PIENKOWSKI. J. (1979). *Haunted House*. London. William Heinemann Ltd.

Fig. 10.6 Alternative studies: lino-cut. This candidate has chosen to interpret a pencil drawing into a lino-cut. The effect of the medium in the lino-cut has already transformed a sincere but limited drawing into a more exciting piece of work of a much higher potential than the drawing alone might have suggested. If the lino-cut was done during the controlled test, then the work is a good example of how your studies might be developed during that test, rather than merely repeated.

CHAPTER

TEXTILES –
ENDORSED

TOPIC AREAS

ASSESSMENT OBJECTIVES

CRITICAL STUDIES

**THE EXTERNALLY SET
EXAMINATION**

ANALYSIS

BEGINNING WORK

CONCLUSIONS

GETTING STARTED

In this chapter we concentrate on the 'Textiles' endorsed certificate. Our case study uses a question from the Welsh Joint Education Committee (WJEC), but what is said here will be helpful to you *whatever* Examination Group you are following.

The question to be answered in this chapter is taken from,

GCSE ART AND DESIGN 1988, WELSH JOINT EDUCATION COMMITTEE

WJEC publishes a very detailed, basic syllabus, which is designed to cover the unendorsed certificate and the five endorsed certificate titles. Further to this basic syllabus, there are *specialised details* included for each of the endorsed titles.

These details explain the activity concerned in each case, but also specify which of the general assessment objectives published in the basic syllabus apply particularly to the endorsed title in question. The study of these specialised notes is very important.

E S S E N T I A L   P R I N C I P L E S

1 > TOPIC AREA

Textiles in the WJEC examination is sub-divided into three 'probable' areas of activity. These are,

a) **Fabric Structure**   Weaving; Knitting; Macrame,
b) **Fabric Decoration**   Embroidery; Surface Printing; Tie and Dye,
c) **Fabric Construction**   Fabric Sculpture; Theatrical Costume; Fashion Design; Adaptation/Embellishment of garments.

Whilst this 'breakdown' and description is not mirrored exactly by any of the other Examining Groups, it presents a sound, *general* framework for you to approach textiles in the GCSE, no matter which Examining Group's syllabus you might be using.

The references to 'Textiles' which the other Examining Groups make differs mostly in quantity rather than content. Remember to look at the syllabus *you* are using, *even if that syllabus is that of the WJEC*.

The 'breakdown' provides you with the means to identify your work in textiles at any time. It also provides you with the initial structure of a vocabulary for you to begin to discuss your work and that of others.

2 > ASSESSMENT OBJECTIVES

The following **assessment objectives** in the WJEC syllabus are specified as being of 'prime' importance for the *Textiles* endorsed certificate.

Candidates will be expected to demonstrate the ability to:

■ show a personal response to a stimulus, e.g. an idea, theme or subject;

■ record from direct observation and personal experience;

■ identify and solve problems and understand and utilise the functions of design in its relationship to all Art and Craft activities (taking account of economic considerations as appropriate);

■ use and compose visual elements, e.g. line, tone, colour, pattern, texture, shape, form, space;

■ select and control materials and processes in a systematic and disciplined way.

These assessment objectives *do not have any order of priority*.

Apart from these five assessment objectives for *Textiles* there are a further five in the *basic* WJEC syllabus.

These further five assessment objectives deal with:

■ sustaining work;

■ independence;

■ analysis;

■ synthesis;

■ critical appreciation.

All ten of these assessment objectives are fairly common to all the Examining Groups. As a consequence you should be reasonably familiar with them and their meaning, no matter what GCSE Art and Design examination syllabus you may be using.

3 > CRITICAL STUDIES

The WJEC syllabus states that 'critical and historical study' is seen as an '**AIM**' rather than an assessment objective when it is part of *another* study. A definite 'critical and historical study', on the other hand, will presumably be measured according to the assessment objectives published in the WJEC syllabus and which apply to *all practical-based studies*.

This all seems to mean that:

It is hoped that acting in a 'critical way', and using the 'history' of your subject in your own work and studies, is something that will become an essential part of your Art and Design activity. However, it will not be **specifically** *assessed, except where you might submit work which is a definite 'critical and historical study'.*

Nevertheless, with the WJEC, as with all the other Examining Groups, adopting a critical stance in your work and studying the history of your subject, can only increase the face-value of your work. This has been said before, and often, in this book, but it is something you should always remember.

The French artist, **Camille Pissarro (1830–1903)**, once said, more or less:

If, without knowledge, you can produce masterpieces, then produce masterpieces. If you cannot produce masterpieces, then get some knowledge!

Acting in a *critical* way, critically studying the history of your subject and becoming skilful at your subject, is one of the surest ways that you might *gain knowledge. Every* examination measures and rewards knowledge so *anything* you can do to increase the *extent and nature* of your knowledge is worthwhile.

4 › THE EXTERNALLY SET EXAMINATION

The WJEC Examination allocates 50% of the marks for the whole examination to the *externally set examination.* You are allowed *fourteen days* in which to carry out your *preparatory studies.* After that you are given a *further* fourteen days, during which you must carry out and complete your *controlled test.*

Whilst there is no set number of hours you should spend on your controlled test, you should obviously use the time the period of fourteen days gives you in an ambitious way. Equally, because you are not working to a specified number of hours in your controlled test, you should obviously *finish* your work in this section of the examination. So you are being given a period of fourteen days preparation to *plan* how to carry out your controlled test and to *decide* what it is you are going to do. This means that you are being thoroughly tested on your ability to plan work and to work independently and successfully within a restricted time limit. With this substantial planning time, you will clearly be expected to *complete* your work for the controlled test in the remaining fourteen days.

THE QUESTION

If you are doing the *unendorsed* Certificate for the WJEC you choose your question in the externally set examination from *any* of the questions in *any* of the *endorsed* certificate titles. There are, however, certain 'controls' in the unendorsed certificate, particularly with regard to the type and content of *coursework* you may have done and its influence on your *choice of question* from the examination paper. You *must* study the syllabus closely in this respect.

In each set of questions there is ample choice given to you. The questions do tend to be 'content' specific. That is to say, they tend to dictate your problem and your subject matter and imagery, but there are plenty of alternative questions in each endorsed certificate title.

For the purposes of this chapter the following question will be used:

Taking a second-hand gent's waistcoat, denim jacket, leather jerkin or a similar item, design and make a decorative garment for casual or fun wear.

OUTLINE ANSWER

The thought processes of a *student* are outlined below. *Examiner* comments at various points are in italics.

1 › ANALYSIS

'In this examination paper there were eighteen alternative questions I could have answered.

These eighteen questions were divided into the three sub-divisions of Textiles, published in the syllabus as:

- Fabric Structure;
- Fabric Decoration;

and

- Fabric Construction.

Each of these sub-sections had six questions. Many of the questions gave me not only the problem to be answered, but the type of things I should include in my answer. I did not mind this because most of the ideas were good and I liked them.

There were other questions which left me to make my *own* mind up about what I would include as my answer. I have chosen to do one of these.

I know that having chosen to work from the sub-division "Fabric Construction", that so far as the syllabus was concerned I should be thinking of:

- Fabric Sculpture;
- Theatrical Costume;
- Fashion Design;
- Adaptation/Embellishment of garments.

I believe that each of these four headings are intermingled with each other. It is therefore difficult to avoid mixing up aspects of all the four in any piece of work.

The question I have chosen to answer is essentially under the heading "Adaptation/Embellishment of garments". But I intend to include aspects of the other three headings in my work.

For instance, if I am going to make a "casual or fun-wear garment", I am instantly involved with "Fashion design". At the same time, the idea of "fun-wear" immediately introduces aspects of "Theatrical Costume" into my work. In turn, if I am going to "adapt and embellish" an already existing garment, I am concerned with a form of "Fabric Sculpture".

I think that I shall use these four headings as part of my "brainstorming diagram".

Apart from these four headings I shall also use "methods", "preparatory studies" and "ideas".

I think that all of these headings will give me plenty of opportunity to write down the possible avenues of exploration I might make, and will help lead me to an appropriate answer.'

BRAINSTORMING DIAGRAM

FABRIC CONSTRUCTION	FABRIC SCULPTURE	APPLIQUE PADDED: FOAM/LAYERS/ WASTE TEXTURE – TOUCH SOUND
	THEATRICAL COSTUME	STUCK-ON COLOURFUL EXAGGERATED DECORATIVE – TEXTURAL HISTORICAL
	FASHION DESIGN	PATTERN CONTEMPORARY HISTORICAL SOURCES STYLE
	ADAPT/EMBELLISH	SHAPE IMAGE EFFECT
QUESTION	CASUAL FUN	LEISURE-PRIVATE WEAR HORROR HUMOUR

METHODS	FANTASY	
	APPLIQUE	
	QUILTING	
	EMBROIDERY	
	COLLAGE	
	SMOCKING	
	KNITTING	
	CROCHET	
PREPARATORY STUDIES	RESEARCH	
	EXPERIMENTS	SAMPLERS
	DOLL?	
	DIRECT OBSERVATIONAL WORK	
IDEAS	MODERN	BIKERS-SPACE-POP STAR
	HISTORICAL	UNIFORMS-ARMOUR-COSTUME
	FILMS	COWBOYS-SURREALISTIC

DECISIONS

'The first thing I decided was to use a denim jacket as the garment I was going to adapt and embellish.

I chose this because I felt that because it had sleeves it gave me more opportunity as something to work on.

The question, so far as I am concerned, suggests that the result should be for a man to wear. Deciding that this is so affects my choice of "subject" for the garment.

I want to give it a male "macho" appearance.

If I use a modern "theme" for the design, the garment will end up looking like what it already is!

I did think that I would use "Cowboy Films" for my design. After all, someone like Clint Eastwood has a "macho" appearance!

Thinking about it more, I felt that the idea of "cowboy" clothes is very much associated with "cap guns" and "little boys" at Christmas.

So, I think I will go back into history for my design.'

THOUGHTS

'As I do not live anywhere near a Museum, I had to conduct my research from books.

My History teacher, my school library and the Librarian at my local Public Library were all most helpful to me.

My History teacher helped me to understand how clothes had changed over the times and some of the reasons why this was so.

The Librarians at school and at the Public Library helped me to find a selection of good books. The school Librarian told me that I could photocopy a selection of the pictures in the books. This was possible because I was only using a selection of them and taking just one copy of each picture. This was apparently legal, because they were going to be used for my personal educational studies.

Choosing *which* pictures to photocopy was difficult. One of the things which was going to control this aspect of my work was the cost of photocopying! I quickly learnt that I could not afford to copy everything I saw and thought might be useful.

I spoke to my Art teachers about this. They advised me to first of all decide on one, or two, *periods* of history that I would investigate. They suggested that it would help if I chose a period where the "shape" of the clothes was very distinctive. They said that it was easier to suggest a historical period through *"shape",* rather than "detail". Detail could follow on, after shape, in my investigation and decisions.

This helpful advice gave me some *reason* to *select* which period I would work from.

I felt that if I chose the *period first*, then it might be more obvious to me *which pictures* I should photocopy.

My Art teachers also said that it would be advisable for me to use just one or two books, once I knew *what* I was going to do.

I could probably borrow these for the month my externally set examination was going to take. If I used them carefully, I could get my ideas from the pictures in them and only photocopy those pictures which I found out in the end had been most helpful in *explaining* my work to the examiner.

I liked this advice. It kept the cost down, but there was also a "good reason" for what I did.

My Art teachers also reminded me that there were plenty of good *examples* of "costume" in paintings from the History of Art and Design.

I felt reassured and ready to work.'

2 >	BEGINNING WORK

'I began, as I was in the Art department, by looking at a copy of Gombrich's *The Story of Art* (1984). In there, on pages 291 – 294, I found some pictures of drawings and paintings which began to interest me.

Three were by **Hans Holbein (1497 – 1543)**. Holbein was a German artist who was commissioned as "Court Painter" to Henry VIII.

I could see in these works what my Art teachers meant by the "**shape**" of clothes. The people in the paintings had large shoulders, caused by cape-like jerkins over fat, padded sleeves (Plate 26).

Plate 26 Hans Holbein, 'The Ambassadors'. *Reproduced by courtesy of the Trustees, The National Gallery, London.*

Plate 27 'Elizabeth I', attributed to
Nicholas Hillyarde. *National
Portrait Gallery, London.*

There was also a portrait (Plate 27) of 'Elizabeth I' by **Nicholas Hillyarde (1547 – 1619)** which attracted me.

This picture had some lovely fine detail of needlework on the Queen's clothing.

I now knew that I was going to do my work based upon the time of *Henry VIII* and *Elizabeth I*.

I was, nevertheless, *not* certain that I had found the "macho" image that I wanted. Then I thought of studying the *Uniforms* and *Armour* of the time. I needed more books for this.'

TEXTILE MATERIALS AND TECHNIQUES

'At the same time that I was researching the uniforms and armour, I began to make a more detailed study of the *textiles materials and techniques* that I had managed to put into my brainstorming diagram.

As these two pieces of research went on, hand-in-hand, i.e. the investigation into uniforms and armour and the enquiry into textiles materials and techniques, I began to see what it was I both *wanted* to do and how I was *going* to do it.'

DESIGNS AND WORK PLAN

'I decided to use the *"visual effect"* of the *armour* I had discovered in some books, linked with the *portraits* by Holbein, Hillyarde and others, if I found them.

My discoveries of "armour" had not all been restricted to the Elizabethan period, or even strictly to armour (Fig 11.1). This led me to decide that, instead of making "imitation armour", I was going to "translate" what I saw in my discoveries into "textiles" in a very "free-wheeling" way.

By this I meant that I was going to try to see *similarities* between the way the *armour and the costumes* "looked", and the way that *different materials and techniques* "looked" when they were worked with. I thought that this was a good way of using the type of source material I had discovered.

Fig. 11.1 Studies relating to armour and decoration.

My "imagery" all came from two-dimensional representations in books. This meant that, whilst they had a strong "visual" impact, they did *not* have any three-dimensional reality. I could not see how "deep" they were, how "textured" they were, how "silky soft" they were, and so on.

However, I *could* experience these three-dimensional and "touch" qualities in the textiles and the techniques and processes associated with their *working*. Nevertheless, I chose to work on the basis of what a particular process "looked like".

In my research on Textiles I discovered an old book in the Public Library. This was:

Newnes Complete Needlecraft (1969). Published by Hamlyn, London.

In this book there were pictures of:

- smocking;
- blackwork embroidery;
- tufting;

- quilting;
- machine embroidery.

All of these techniques seemed to have something to offer my work (Fig 11.2),

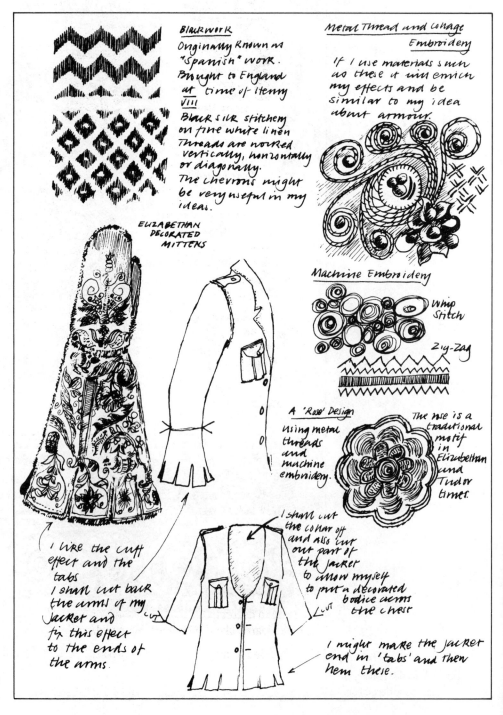

Fig. 11.2 Needlework techniques and design ideas.

white fabric with black, painted-dye stripes

'Quilted' (padded) stripes sewn the direct onto black denim jacket.

A smocking sample I experimented with during my preparatory studies

The shoulder-pads are stuffed with kapook to give them their shape. Gold beads sewn onto these pads.

Held around arms by a gold thong

"shield" done in applique and machine embroidery.

Blackwork embroidery, sewn onto the denim jacket.

Cuffs, Blackwork with Gold Metal Thread edgings

Gold coloured beads sewn on.

Gold metal thread (I have shown the "skirt" as white, but it will be the raw, black denim jacket)

There is a lot of work to do in this design.
Each "Tas" is the same, so I could do one only, to show what I intended.
I also chose to do "pieces" of my design, eg. the smocking sample and the Blackwork, during my preparatory studies.
I felt that as I was 'designing' with these pieces of techniques during the Controlled Test, it was acceptable to do the fabric experiments during my preparatory studies.

Back of jacket kept simple and largely plain, to save time.

Fig. 11.3 Design solution and working techniques to be used.

I also discovered pictures of gloves given to Elizabeth I, and details of cuffs. These both interested me. The book I was looking at said that these items were in the *Victoria and Albert Museum*, in London. I thought I might be able to get postcards of them.

Through a series of drawings and photocopies, made during my preparatory studies time, I was able to design the work I wish to do in the controlled test.

I did most of my drawings and designs at school. When I was at home I experimented with some of the textiles techniques.

During this time I made a *sampler*, using smocking. After discussing that it was alright to do so with my Art teachers, I planned to use some of my experiments in my actual garment during the controlled test.

I planned to decorate the smocking sampler further and to sew this into the denim jacket so that it appeared like a "tee-shirt" worn under the jacket.

I also decided to dye the denim jacket black, so I did this before the start of my controlled test.

My ideas and my designs for my work are shown in the accompanying drawings (Fig 11.3).'

3 > CONCLUSIONS

'When my controlled test was finished I had completed all that I intended to do on the denim jacket.

Apart from the planned time for the controlled test that the art teachers had arranged for me, it meant that I had had to arrange with them to work during some of my lunch-times in order to do all that I wanted to. I did not mind this and was glad that I had. After all, it was *my* examination.

I thought that the result was close to what I intended. I had managed to use the textiles techniques which made my work "look like" the pictures of the armour and costume.

I put the end result on a tailor's dummy and stood it in the school entrance hall for a day. At break-times and during lunch-times I stood there and "trapped" every boy who came past and made them fill in a questionnaire on the jacket.

In my questionnaire I tried to find out if the result was liked and whether it would be worn at a party. The answers I got made me feel that I had a reasonable success in my work.'

4 > EXAMINER COMMENTS

It seemed best to let you read in its entirety the way that this work was thought of, reasoned out, planned and then executed.

Much of the work seemed to go on 'in the head'. This does not matter, so long as what goes on in the head is documented somewhere, as is done in the outline answer presented above.

The candidate appears to be one who knows a lot and has this knowledge fairly firmly imprinted in the mind.

At the same time, the candidate seems to need the reassurance which can be given by teachers. In the GCSE Art and Design there is a tendency for the Examining Groups to try to sort out just how much a candidate requires helping, or 'pushing'.

There seems to be no reason why 'help', or even 'pushing', should always diminish the value of the particular candidate's work. After all, having the ability to take advice, sort out what is valuable in it, and then use it to good advantage, is a valuable and worthwhile attribute to possess.

This candidate seems to have that quality. All the advice has been listened to carefully and then used appropriately.

It is obvious that some of the reward in Textiles will come from seeing and handling the end result. The standard of the 'craftsmanship', and the overall effect, as well as the quality of the ideas, will all need to be taken into account. However, the results of the questionnaire is proof that the idea and the result was successful in the eyes of its potential users.

The work appears to pay no attention to cost, except where the cost of photocopying was concerning the candidate personally.

The work is also rather weak when it comes to 'recording from direct observation', although it is quite good on the matter of 'personal experience'.

Apart from these two aspects of the assessment objectives specifically required in the textiles endorsed certificate, the work seems to satisfy all the other specific assessment objectives as well as most of the other assessment objectives in the basic syllabus.

Doing so makes it eligible, dependent upon the Art and Design standards displayed, for the higher grade GCSE levels with WJEC.

FOOTNOTES

Questionnaire Used

1 Do you like this garment: a lot/it's O.K./not much?
2 What do you think it's for: a pop star/a play/a party?
3 Would you wear it: for school/going out/not at all?

Results

The results were scored,
1 a lot 20%/it's O.K. 57%/not much 23%;
2 a pop star 14%/a play 76%/a party 10%;
3 for school 2%/going out 64%/not at all 34%.

SOME FURTHER ASPECTS

Plate 28 'The Cholmondeley Sisters', British School. *The Tate Gallery, London.*

Plate 29 'John, Baron Craven of Ryton', by a follower of Sir Anthony van Dyck. *The Courtauld Institute Galleries, London.*

The work by the German artist, Hans Holbein, shows the 'shape' sought after by the student in this outline answer.

As was remarked in the text, in Costume Design it is a good idea to concentrate first upon the 'shape' you might wish to create and then later, the details within that shape.

The other work discovered by the student, by the British artist, Nicholas Hillyarde, also shows the 'shape' in question, but contains within the clothing some fine and attractive visual detail.

With these two examples from the History of Painting the student was in a good position to proceed with some work in 'Textile Design'. It is an excellent example of connecting different contexts in Art and Design.

The paintings in Plate 28 and Plate 29 are two further fine examples which might have been uncovered during a candidate's preparatory studies in response to this question. Again, there is some excellent visual detail in the painting of the clothing.

Mention was also made by the student of the examples of 'Cuffs' and 'Gloves' which might be found at a place such as the Victoria and Albert Museum, London.

It might be, as in this instance, that reproductions of the items might be found in a book. Whether this is the case or not, it would be advantageous to arrange to visit a suitable museum in your preparatory studies. You might uncover the most inspirational piece of 'primary source' information.

BIBLIOGRAPHY

(Edited) (1969). *Newnes Complete Needlecraft*. London, Hamlyn.
ROWLAND, K. (1964). *Looking and Seeing. 1. Pattern and Shape*. London, Ginn and Company Ltd.

CHAPTER 12

THREE DIMENSIONAL STUDIES – ENDORSED

GETTING STARTED

It is easy enough to think of **'Three-Dimensional Studies'** as *'Pottery'* or *'Sculpture'*. But do not lose sight of the fact that it can just as easily include *'Modelling'*, *'Constructing'* and *'Assembling'*.

Any of these latter activities could arise naturally and easily out of a course based upon *'Drawing and Painting'*, *'Graphics'*, *'Photography'* or even *'Textiles'*, as much as one entitled *'Three-Dimensional studies'*.

The activities listed in the previous paragraph are not necessarily dependent upon 'Clay', 'Wood', 'Plastics', 'Metal', or similar traditional 'three-dimensional' materials. So even if you *are* studying on a specific 'Three-Dimensional Studies' course, there is nothing to stop you using *'Paint'*, *'Graphic Media'*, *'Photographic Materials and Methods'*, *'Fabrics'*, *'Textiles'*, *'Cardboard'*, and so on in your work.

What is discussed in this chapter about the Three-Dimensional Studies endorsed certificate will apply in general to all the Examining Groups. However for purposes of illustration we will use the Southern Examining Group (SEG) syllabus.

ASSESSMENT OBJECTIVES

DESIGN & EXPRESSIVE ACTIVITIES

BRAINSTORMING DIAGRAM

ANALYSIS

THOUGHTS

PREPARATORY STUDIES

BEGINNING WORK

OUTCOME

ESSENTIAL PRINCIPLES

1 › ASSESSMENT OBJECTIVES

We have already considered the *eight* assessment objectives common for the SEG *unendorsed* certificate and for *each* endorsed certificate. In the case of Three-Dimensional Studies with the SEG, the *specific* assessment objectives are to:

- explore the interaction of the three-dimensional elements indicated in the subject content;
- understand the spatial relationships between various forms and structures and between them and their immediate environment (i.e. the organisation of form within a context);
- gain experience and knowledge by using the skills of investigation;
- understand and use the design process and the expressive process;
- identify problems and seek solutions.

Most of these 'specific' assessment objectives are fairly self-explanatory. However the exception to this is perhaps the penultimate (second from last) objective. This demands that you show your *understanding* of the 'design process' and the 'expressive process' and your *ability to use* these two processes.

For instance, if you are 'expressing your personal ideas and feelings', if you wish these to have any *public credibility*, you must, at the same time, be 'communicating ideas and information'.

In the same way, if you are 'developing your skills in solving problems and testing the results', you would, at the same time, be involved in the 'progressive acquisition of experience, knowledge, skills and values'.

So you can see, the two processes are unavoidably interwoven. In fact, it is probably a weakness in the philosophy surrounding Art and Design that it is often felt necessary to describe the two processes as 'different' activities, and then to spend time stressing their interdependence!

2 › DESIGN AND EXPRESSIVE ACTIVITIES

In this case you need to *find out* what is meant by each of the two processes. This cannot be done by reference to the assessment objective itself.

The Three-Dimensional studies syllabus explains first of all that,

these two approaches are not mutually exclusive.

This really means that you *cannot* do one without the other. However, it is likely that one process will *predominate* in a particular piece of work.

In the syllabus, '**Design Activity**' is described, amongst other things, as:

- influencing the life of all;
- encouraging skills in the use of materials;
- developing skills in solving problems and testing the results;
- communicating ideas and information;
- involving the investigation of aspects of the environment or ergonomic relationships of humans to design problems and their outcomes.

The '**Expressive Activity**' is described as:

- developing the powers of observation and interpretation;
- encouraging first-hand experience through the senses and the intellect;
- providing the progressive acquisition of experience, knowledge, skills and values;
- allowing the expression of personal ideas, thoughts and feelings in visual terms.

3 › EXAMINATION PAPER

When the two 'activities', or 'processes' are laid out side by side like this, you can see that it is almost certainly impossible for you to be involved in one process without being also involved in the other.

In the SEG specimen paper there are ten questions. Some have 'sub-sets' to them, so a wide choice is offered to you. Some of the questions seem to be deliberately aimed at a *particular* material or activity. Two specifically mention 'Sculpture' and one insists on 'Pottery'. There is a question dealing with 'Puppetry' and another with 'Stage Design'.

Despite this, there are opportunities for you to answer questions in *any* material or form you might wish. For instance, one question asks you to make 'a form or body ornament based upon fungi or plants'. There is no reason why you should not use 'Textiles' for this work if you wished. The question on Stage Design allows you to use 'Drawing and Painting' as the basis of your answer. And so on.

WEIGHTING

The SEG externally set examination is allocated 40% of the total marks available for the whole GCSE Examination. Again, the SEG stipulates that the *three* assessment objectives outlined on page 123, will be particularly tested in the *controlled test. Do not think, however, that the other assessment objectives can be ignored.*

THE QUESTION

For the purpose of this chapter the following question from the SEG specimen paper for Three-Dimensional Studies endorsed certificate will be used.

Design and make a decorated lamp base using an internal source of light.

OUTLINE ANSWER

1 > BRAINSTORMING DIAGRAM

BAYONET SOCKET		WOOD
SCREW-IN SOCKET	**LIGHT LAMP**	PLASTICS
BULB		GLASS
PLAIN		CLOTH
PEARL	**MATERIALS**	PAPER
COLOURED		CARDBOARD
		TIN

IDEAS

BASE & LAMP SHADE		COLOUR
BULB IN A CONTAINER	SHAPE?	TEXTURE
HANGING/SUSPENDED	IMAGERY?	FUNCTION=FORM
STANDING		

                        Art & Design Movements   Traditional/materials honesty

De Stijl   The Bauhaus

    Mondrian

KEY: CAPITAL LETTERS=FIRST THOUGHTS
        Small letters=Further Research

2 > ANALYSIS

'Does the way that the question is worded mean that I *cannot* make a lamp-base and a lamp-shade to go on it? I would like to do this, either turning the base in wood, or making it in clay by coiling, throwing, or slab-making.

What worries me is the way that the question says, "using an internal source of light". Is a bulb under a lamp-shade "internal" to the lamp? I do not know.

Nevertheless, I shall sketch out two or three ideas for the base, one in wood and two in two different clay construction methods. I shall then have something to show my teachers, and I will discuss with them my worries about the word "internal".

I liked my sketches. My teachers suggested that I should continue with them, showing my ideas for colour, texture and pattern. I shall do this, including a matching lamp-shade for each base. In these sketches I shall put on them which materials and processes I would use in making each one.

My teachers also suggested that I should think more about the idea I had brought up about an "internal" source of light, although they felt that an "ordinary" lamp could be made to satisfy the idea of the lamp being "internal".'

3 ⟩ THOUGHTS

'On my course I had been shown the work of the two Design Movements from earlier in the twentieth century, the De Stijl Movement and The Bauhaus. All my class had seen slides of the work of these two Movements, had been given notes about them, and had been asked to complete a little appreciation of each.

My work was collected and mounted in two sketch pads. I had designed a cover for each, based upon what I had thought best represented the work of the Movement (Fig 12.1).

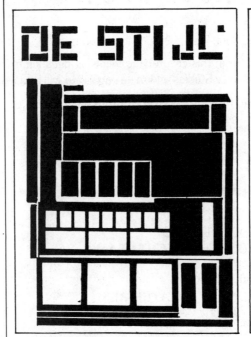 

THE IDEA FOR THIS COVER WAS TAKEN FROM THE SIXTH ISSUE OF "DE STIJL", DESIGNED BY VILMOS HUSZAR.

HUSZAR DESIGNED TWO COVERS FOR THE DE STIJL MAGAZINE, THE FIRST AND THE SIXTH.

THE DESIGN FOR MY COVER WAS TAKEN FROM THE FACADE OF THE RESTAURANT, "CAFÉ DE UNIE".

THIS RESTAURANT WAS DESIGNED BY J.J.P. OUD AND BUILT IN ROTTERDAM, WHERE HE BECAME CITY ARCHITECT, IN 1925.

LIKE HUSZAR, I HAVE TRIED TO MAKE THE WHITE SHAPES AS IMPORTANT AS THE BLACK SHAPES.

THE COVER WAS PRODUCED BY CUTTING THE BLACK SHAPES FROM BLACK SUGAR PAPER AND STICKING THEM ON WHITE CARD. THE RESULT WAS THEN PHOTO-COPIED, AS WAS THE TEXT INSIDE. THIS KEPT A UNITY IN THE PRODUCTION.

FOR THIS COVER I BASED MY DESIGN ON AN EXERCISE WHICH JOSEPH ALBERS USED IN THE FOUNDATION COURSE AT THE BAUHAUS.

I DELIBERATELY AVOIDED CURVES AND CIRCLES IN THE DESIGN, TO KEEP IT AS A PARTNER TO THE DE STIJL COVER, BUT AFTERWARDS I THOUGHT IT WOULD HAVE BEEN BETTER TO INCLUDE THEM.

I COULD HAVE MADE ANOTHER COVER BUT FELT THAT THE IMPORT-ANCE OF THE PROJECT DID NOT DEMAND IT. TO REPEAT THE COVER WOULD HAVE USED TIME FROM ANOTHER PROJECT, WHICH WAS NOT JUSTIFIABLE.

NEVERTHELESS, I DO FEEL THAT THE TWO DESIGNS DO SHOW THE POINTS OF CONTACT BETWEEN THE TWO MOVEMENTS, EVEN IF THEY DO NOT SHOW THE DIFFERENCES.

IT WAS VERY HELPFUL TO BE ABLE TO USE THE KNOWLEDGE FROM THIS PROJECT IN MY EXTERNAL EXAM-INATION.

Fig 12.1 Cover designs for exercises of the de Stijl Movement and the Bauhaus.

I went back to these sketch pads and began to read through my work again.

Amongst examples of other works, I had been shown that by the Dutch artist **Piet Mondrian (1872 – 1944).**

As a result of all this I decided to try to base my work on the *Mondrian* pictures I had been shown earlier.'

4 > **PREPARATORY STUDIES**

'My teachers explained to me that I could not have the same work marked twice for my examination. This meant that I could not submit my two studies, one on the De Stijl Movement and the other on The Bauhaus., for both my coursework and my externally set examination.

As I had done the two studies during my course of study I could only submit them as my coursework. On the other hand I could *use them to develop my preparatory studies.*

If I did this, then any further work on them, or reference to them, would become part of my preparatory studies.

From my earlier studies I knew that **Mondrian** was pre-occupied with "**Clarity**" and "**Discipline**" in his work. As part of this discipline he decided to use straight lines and pure colours.

I knew from Colour Theories, dealt with on my course of study, about such qualities of *colour* as:

HUE	the quality which distinguishes one colour from another, e.g. blue from red, or red from orange. This quality is changed by adding to one colour the colour adjacent to it in a colour-wheel;
TONE	the quality of the degree of "lightness" or "darkness" in a colour. This is changed within one colour by the addition of white or black to the "hue", but colours in their purest state also have different tonal relationships, one to another;
CHROMA	the quality which is the measure of the "purity", or "intensity", or "saturation" of a single colour. This quality is changed by adding to one colour quantities of the colour directly opposite it in a colour-wheel, in order to "reduce" the chroma of the colour.

Returning to my thoughts about the meaning of the word "**internal**" in the question, I began to wonder about a number of things:

- its actual shape; a lamp is like a "box". It is like a box with bits missing and air and space penetrating it;
- a box "contains", therefore a box design would satisfy the term "internal";
- Mondrain's paintings, based on the "rectangle", are like a series of two-dimensional boxes set in relationship to each other;
- I could turn a Mondrian painting into a three-dimensional box, by repeating it five times, four times for each wall of the box and once for the lid;
- if I did I would need to leave some spaces for the light to come out;
- I could let the light out of those rectangles which had the colours with the lightest "tones" in the original Mondrian painting that I used;
- this would be the most simple solution to my self-imposed problem;
- if Mondrian's paintings are a number of "boxes" in two dimensions and in relationship to each other, I could make a construction by making each "box" in three dimensions from a Mondrian painting, and assembling them in a way that reflected the original relationship;
- this would present a problem of getting the light into each separate box;
- if I wanted to have a more complex "assemblage" than a simple box, I could work from the theory that, according to their "chroma", some colours appear to advance whilst others recede.

As a result of all this I now had three alternative ideas to try to sort out.'

Examiner Comments: *This work so far has been an excellent example of using previous experience in new situations.*

The decision to refer back to the earlier exercises on the De Stijl Movement and the Bauhaus was good. There is no point in 're-inventing the wheel' each time you work.

It is not clear from the question if the candidate's concern over the interpretation of the word 'internal' was a justified concern. The likelihood is that the examiner would have happily accepted a well-designed and well-made 'traditional' lamp.

What was important was that the candidate's concern in this respect led on to the consideration of much more interesting design solutions to the problem.

The candidate stated that the idea of the 'traditional' lamp was originally more attractive. However, concern about the word 'internal' has taken the candidate away from this preference into a situation which now deals with solving a real 'problem', rather than making a 'copy' of most other lamps.

5 > BEGINNING WORK

'I decided to start with some *drawings* to try to work out some of my problems (Figs 12.2, 12.3 and 12.4).

I needed to do a number of things in these drawings. These things were:

1 to work out how I would make and construct my lamp each time;

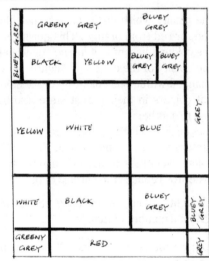

A. Dimensional and Colour Analysis of the original Mondrian painting.

B. Tonal Analysis of the painting

Making these analyses was helpful. They helped me to understand Mondrian's painting a lot more than I did when I first saw it. They also helped to give me ideas of how I might design and make my actual lamp.

I became aware not only of the colours in the painting (c.), but the effect of light and dark (B.) and the size relationships of the rectangles which Mondrian decided on in the first place (A.).

I began to realise that the painting was not as simple or obvious as it first appeared.

c. Rationalisation of the "shades" of each colour into their basic colour.

Fig. 12.2 Various analyses of the original Mondrian painting, 'Composition in Red, Yellow and Blue'.

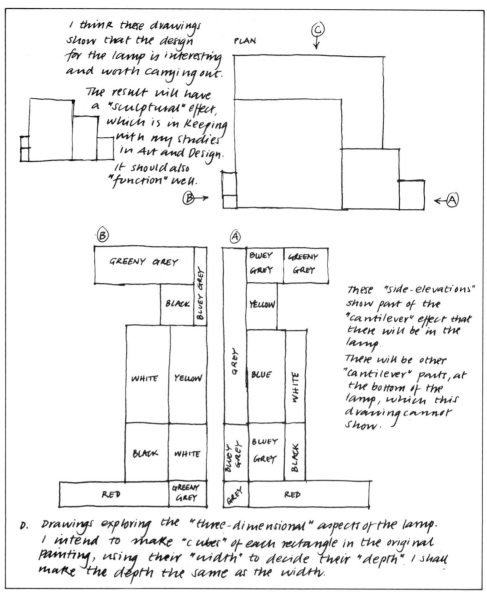

I think these drawings show that the design for the lamp is interesting and worth carrying out.

The result will have a "sculptural" effect, which is in keeping with my studies in Art and Design. It should also "function" well.

PLAN

B→

←A

©

B   A

GREENY GREY	
BLACK	BLUEY GREY
WHITE	YELLOW
BLACK	WHITE
RED	GREENY GREY

BLUEY GREY	GREENY GREY
YELLOW	
GREY	BLUE	WHITE
BLUEY GREY	BLUEY GREY	BLACK
GREY	RED

These "side-elevations" show part of the "cantilever" effect that there will be in the lamp.

There will be other "cantilever" parts, at the bottom of the lamp, which this drawing cannot show.

D. Drawings exploring the "three-dimensional" aspects of the lamp. I intend to make "cubes" of each rectangle in the original painting, using their "width" to decide their "depth". I shall make the depth the same as the width.

Fig. 12.3 Exploring the possible 'shape' of the lamp.

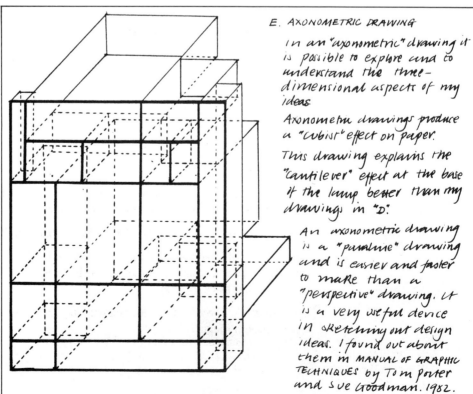

E. AXONOMETRIC DRAWING

In an "axonometric" drawing it is possible to explore and to understand the three-dimensional aspects of my ideas.

Axonometric drawings produce a "Cubist" effect on paper.

This drawing explains the "cantilever" effect at the base of the lamp better than my drawings in "D".

An axonometric drawing is a "paraline" drawing and is easier and faster to make than a "perspective" drawing. It is a very useful device in sketching out design ideas. I found out about them in MANUAL OF GRAPHIC TECHNIQUES by Tom Porter and Sue Goodman. 1982.

Fig. 12.4 'Axonometric' drawing of the lamp.

2 to sort out the "tonal" qualities of the colours in a particular Mondrian painting;

3 to sort out the "chromatic" quality of the colours in a particular Mondrian painting;

4 to analyse a Mondrian painting in order to sort out the relationships between the sizes of the rectangles in that painting.

In order to proceed I decided to use just *ONE* Mondrian painting for *ALL* the alternatives. This would enable me to do all my analyses from the same work. In doing this, I felt that I would get to know much more about the particular painting and be able to get more of its "character" into my work.

To simplify the matter further, I decided to choose my *Mondrian painting* from a book which was freely available to me. I chose Gombrich, 1984.

The painting I chose was,

"Composition in Red, Yellow and Blue". Painted in 1920, by Piet Mondrian. The Municipal Museum, Amsterdam.'

THE SIMPLE FIVE-SIDED BOX

'From my "tonal" interpretation I decided that if I made this lamp I would allow the light to come out of the rectangles coloured WHITE and YELLOW in the original painting.

I thought that I would get a lamp bulb coloured "white" and have a clear "window" where the white rectangles were in the original painting.

For the yellow rectangles, whilst I would cut a window for these, I would then put a transparent material in, coloured yellow, so that the light looked "yellow" through these windows.

I thought that acrylic sheets would probably be best for this lamp, if I could get all the colours I needed.

When I began to experiment with them on a small scale, I found that if I chose an acrylic sheet in the appropriate colour for each rectangle in the original painting, differing amounts of light glowed through each rectangle, according to the tonal density of the colour in each acrylic sheet I had used!

This was a better solution than my original planning, which was to have the light coming from the white and yellow rectangles only. I decided to use this effect if I carried on with this lamp in my controlled test.'

THE ADVANCING/RECEDING BOX

'From my analysis I decided that the colours which Mondrian used made the following scale.

Advancing	RED
	YELLOW
	BLACK
	GREY
	BLUE
Receding	WHITE

In trying to work out how I would have to make this I realised that I would need to construct something like a series of "three-sided boxes".

I decided to use plywood and acrylic for this construction, if I proceeded with it.

I thought that if I used *plywood* for each piece of the lamp which would be either black, or grey, the plywood would give me a good basis to "build" my lamp on. I could paint the plywood either black, or grey.

If I used *acrylic sheet* for the red, yellow, blue and white rectangles, this would allow the light to shine through.'

THE 'LITTLE BOXES' LAMP

'This was the most difficult problem to think about. In the end I decided that it would be best if I built each rectangle in the original painting as a small box made from the appropriately coloured acrylic sheet.

As the red rectangle at the bottom of the painting was the largest, I thought at first that I could put my bulb into this, and by boring holes in each rectangle where they joined and stood on each other, I could get the light to find its own way through the whole lamp.

Of course, this meant that the biggest source of light would be at the bottom of the lamp.

This would not make it a very good lamp. It was usual for a lamp to have its light source high within it. This allowed more light to fall, as well as radiate sideways and upwards. I knew that if I made this lamp I would need to get the bulb higher within the lamp.

The white rectangle was more or less in the middle of the design and was fairly large.

The position of the white rectangle was very suitable as the brightest source of light. I needed to get my bulb up into that box.

I worked out a way, using the idea of the holes bored between the boxes to thread the flex up to the bulb-holder which was to be housed in the white "box".

This meant that I could still get my flex into the lamp at the base. This was something I wanted to do as I did not like the look of a wire going into a lamp halfway up it.

It was also dangerous if it did because it would be easy to pull the lamp over through catching the flex.'

DECISIONS

'Knowing that I had six weeks to complete all my externally set examination, and that I had used three of those getting to the end of my work as described above, I knew that what solution I chose to do would have to depend upon the time I had to do it in.

In the end I chose to do the simple box version of my lamp, and to hope that the examiner would appreciate my other ideas but accept that I was pressed for time at the end of my externally set examination.

The only change that I made to my original plans, was to include sheets of white acrylic for the white rectangles. This development had come from my experimental work with my alternative designs and ideas.'

6 ▷ OUTCOME

'I got the lamp made in the remaining three weeks of my externally set examination (Fig 12.5).

To get more light through the lamp I thought that I would use a "clear" bulb.

This did give more light, but even through the acrylic sheet, I could see the filament of the bulb. I did not like this, so I changed it for a "pearl" bulb. This was much better.

To try to get more light I tried a bulb with a higher wattage. In the end I settled on a 60-watt bulb in the interests of safety.

As I had gone around the shops which sold lamps and bulbs I had noticed that each lamp specified the maximum wattage which could be used with it. When I spoke to the assistants in the shop they explained to me that a bulb gave off a certain amount of heat as it burned and that this could not exceed a level which was well within the safety limits of the material used in the lamp.

With the help of my teachers I worked out the combustion level of the materials I had used in my lamp, and decided on the 60-watt bulb as the safest to use.

My end result "worked" as an idea, but it was not a very "bright" light.

I knew that it would be best if I used either more fire-resistant materials, provided they would let enough light through, or I made the whole thing bigger so that I could get the bulb further away from the materials used in the lamp.

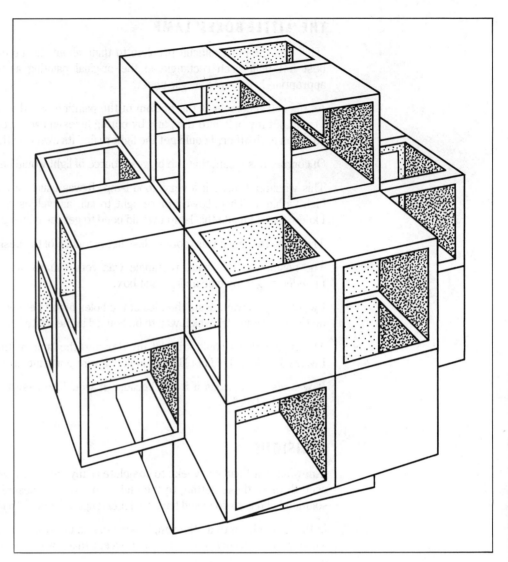

Fig. 12.5 The Mondrian Lamp. In the eventual solution the lamp has gone through a further evolution. This was probably due to the problems and complexities of working with resistant materials and in three dimensions. Nevertheless, the result sustains the excellent preparatory/supporting work.

In both cases I would be able to use a more powerful bulb.

I also thought that it might be an idea to use a fan inside the lamp. This could be operated by the heat from the bulb and would help to cool the bulb down. It could also provide a sense of movement to the lamp, rather like the system used in "artificial coals" in electric fires, which I thought might have possibilities.

For my final presentation I had:

- the extensions and references to my original work on the De Stijl Movement and the Bauhaus;
- the set of early designs for the traditional lamp-base and lamp-shade;
- my research and set of alternative designs based upon the painting of Mondrian;
- the lamp I had made.

I felt that I had worked hard and that my work had turned out different, if not better, than I had intended when I first read the question and decided to do it.'

7 OUTCOME COMMENTS

This whole study turned out to be most worthwhile and valuable to the candidate's level of understanding about solving 'design' problems.

Almost unwittingly the candidate introduced 'concepts' into the problem which meant that from an early stage the work was more involved with solving important 'abstract' problems rather than homing in from the beginning on 'how the lamp would be made'.

These 'concepts' were concerned with the meaning of the word internal, the appropriateness and the inherent qualities of different materials, the effectiveness of a lamp as a means of illumination, and the safety factors which are necessarily involved in product design.

What is apparent in the work, as it went on, is that the materials were used not as a 'means to an end', but that the materials and their qualities produced the type of 'end' which resulted. In many ways this wrestling with ideas and materials led to unspecified 'ends' which the candidate was quick to see and accept for their qualities.

In many ways this is like an axiom associated with the candidate's other earlier study on the Bauhaus, whereby it is often said that 'Form follows Function'. This is rather a bald and often misunderstood quotation which hardly does justice to the fundamental beliefs of the Bauhaus Movement, but the essence of the quotation is apparent in this candidate's work.

Whether the candidate was right to accept the model for the lamp that was finally produced on the basis that it was the 'simplest' solution is questionable. The criterion 'most simple' is not very good unless it can be explained that 'simplicity' itself is a desirable quality in a design solution.

This was not done here. The choice was made on the basis of the 'easiest to do'.

If a criterion such as the 'easiest to do' is to be accepted, then it might be accompanied with the demand that higher technical standards should be displayed in the work. Higher, that is, than work which was more demanding in technical skills, or time.

So, it might have been better to have decided to choose to do one of the solutions which would take up more time after all.

What is apparent in the work as it is described is that the lamp produced might have been a better lamp than the others. That is to say, it might have been a more efficient, attractive, economical and/or easier to clean solution than the alternatives.

If this were so, then any of these other criteria would have been more relevant than 'easy to do', and could result in a higher grade for the same outcome. Nevertheless, the whole of the work was soundly conceived and efficiently carried out.

Whether it satisfied the assessment objectives which were specific to the three-dimensional studies endorsed certificate of the SEG is another matter. If you refer to these, near the beginning of this chapter, you will note that they ask for an appreciation of space, the inter-relation of shapes and objects within space, and the relationship between shapes or objects and their environment.

The lamp produced in this outline answer appears to be very 'flat' on each surface, even though it is a 'three-dimensional' lamp. Therefore, it might be thought that it does not show much understanding and appreciation of 'spatial qualities'.

It is also not very clear that any consideration was made about the environment the lamp was to stand in. This would have been easy to deal with and would have made a valuable contribution to the overall work of the candidate.

It would have been interesting to see the candidate conduct either an interview, or use a questionnaire, with the person, or people, who would have been most directly associated with the use of the lamp and its environment.

For instance, it would be reasonable to assume that the lamp would be used in the candidate's home. It would have been a good idea to conduct an enquiry into the needs of the candidate's family, and then to evaluate how much the various members of the candidate's family liked the final result.

All of this would have put the work even more firmly into the 'design dimension'.

Apart from these reservations about some of the specific assessment objectives, the work seems that it would more than adequately fulfil the majority of the more general 'Art and Design' assessment objectives published by the SEG.

The reservations expressed above would probably mean that the work would not achieve the highest levels of the examination, but would, nevertheless, reach a good grade.

The use of the 'Questionnaire' and the 'Evaluation Programme', described above, and the decision to make either of the two alternative lamps, would have resulted in the best Grades.

ALTERNATIVE STUDIES

Using the same approach, another candidate could have produced a lamp based upon 'Art Nouveau' (Fig 12.6 and 12.7).

This Art and Design Movement can be related to 'Symbolism', which was discussed in Chapter 5. There it was said that gradually Symbolism moved towards 'the shapes in the pictures departing from the natural outlines of the objects they stood for'. Art Nouveau can be seen to be carrying that tendency at least one step further (Plate 30).

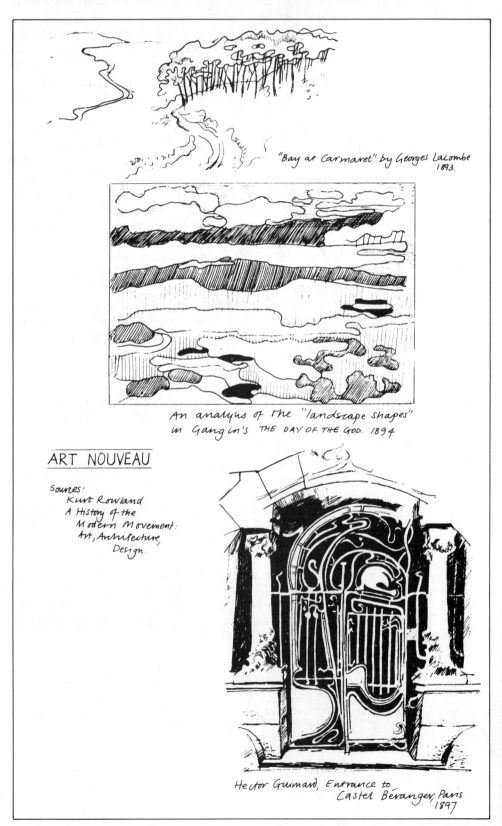

"Bay at Carmaret" by Georges Lacombe 1893.

An analysis of the "landscape shapes" in Gangin's THE DAY OF THE GOD. 1894

ART NOUVEAU

Sources:
Kurt Rowland.
A History of the
Modern Movement:
Art, Architecture,
Design.

Hector Guimard, Entrance to
Castel Béranger, Paris
1897

Fig. 12.6 Alternative studies, for an 'Art Nouveau' lamp.

Plate 30 Paul Gauguin, 'Eda Iheihe'. *The Tate Gallery, London.* In Chapter 5 it was said that the Art Movement known as 'Symbolism' led onto 'Art Nouveau'. In this work by Gauguin you can see similarities between the sinuous, curvilinear lines and formalised representation of nature in Art Nouveau work and the way that Gauguin drew and painted the trees, bushes and fruits in this picture.

Fig. 12.7 Alternative studies: The Art Nouveau lamp. This work has involved 'turning' a bowl. The design in the centre of the bowl is worked in 'marquetry', whereby a picture is made up from different types of 'veneer'. The light source is to come from a circular fluorescent lamp which fits into the rim of the bowl. The whole thing is an excellently conceived and executed piece of work.

PHOTOGRAPHY ENDORSED

SYLLABUS REQUIREMENTS
ANALYSIS
PREPARATORY STUDIES
BEGINNING WORK
CONTROLLED TEST TIME

GETTING STARTED

In most syllabuses, exactly the *same* basic assessment objectives are used to assess your work in *Photography* as are used to assess your work in Painting and Drawing, or Three-Dimensional studies, and so on. So the presence of Photography in Art and Design for the GCSE does *not* mean that your work is going to be examined for its 'scientific' quality alone. Your ability to handle *ideas* and various elements of Art and Design are at least as important, if not more so, as your technical standards of photography. The question used as illustration in this chapter is taken from the Northern Ireland Schools Examination Council (NISEC). The principles involved, however, are relevant to *all* the syllabuses involving photography. NISEC publish a comprehensive syllabus which explains their system of GCSE examination clearly.

E S S E N T I A L   P R I N C I P L E S

At the moment the NISEC system of examination differs a little from the other Examining Groups. NISEC do *not* have endorsed certificates in their examination so far. Instead, they divide Art and Design activities into two major groups, or 'areas'.

These are:

AREA I – FINE ART   Painting, drawing, printmaking, photography, film, video, sculpture or any other medium or combination of media.

AREA II – DESIGN   II.1   Communication Design
                              Photography, film, video, graphic design, illustration, packaging, lettering and calligraphy, display.
                  II.2   Textile and Fashion Design
                              Woven textiles, printed textiles, dyed textiles, creative embroidery, fashion design.
                  II.3   Three-dimensional design
                              Construction (e.g. toys, furniture, models), ceramics, stage design (e.g. sets, costumes, puppetry), interior design, jewellery.

You can see from this that, whilst NISEC might not have 'endorsed certificates' as such, you *can* choose to work in an area of study which mirrors the five endorsed certificate titles approved by the SEC.

Like the other Examining Groups, NISEC divides the work that you do into coursework and an externally set examination.

NISEC is like the WJEC, in that the marks for your GCSE examination overall are divided *equally* between the coursework section and the externally set examination section of the whole examination.

NISEC is like the IGCSE, in that in the externally set examinations both Examining Groups set *two examination papers which you must sit.*

In the NISEC Examination the externally set examination is divided into:

PAPER I – MAIN STUDY (30% of the total marks for the examination)

- Question papers distributed at least six weeks prior to the assessment period.

- During this period you carry out your preparatory studies *and* a twelve-hour controlled test.

- It is possible that you may be allowed more than twelve hours to complete your controlled test. You need to consult your syllabus *and your teachers about this.*

- For your examination you *must* present your preparatory studies with your final piece of work.

- The question paper for this section of your externally set examination will be in two parts. You can choose to work either from a 'Theme', or a 'Set Problem' in both Fine Art or Design areas of activity.

PAPER II – VISUAL ENQUIRY (3 hours: 20% of the total marks for the examination)
           This paper calls for a two-dimensional response to stimuli from *one* of the following areas,
                A   Natural Forms
                B   Manufactured Forms
                C   Human Forms (stationary)

THE QUESTION

As has been mentioned above, the 'specimen paper' for Paper I, Main Study, of the NISEC Examination is divided into *two* sections. The *first section* provides you with a selection of six *'Themes'*. If you choose to respond to one of these you can set your own problem to work on *within the boundaries of the set theme*. The *second section* of the paper has a number of *'Set Problems'*, offering you a variety to choose from, but under the titles of either 'Fine Art' or each of the sub-sections listed above under 'Design'.

There is *one* set problem only for each of the activities under either 'Fine Art' or 'Design'. These activities are in small print in the extract at the beginning of this chapter which explains 'Areas I and II' from the NISEC syllabus. The net result is that you have plenty to choose from in the examination paper.

For the purposes of this chapter the following question will be used,

SET PROBLEM

Produce a set of not more than ten black and white prints of size 203 mm × 254 mm investigating a woodland area.

OUTLINE ANSWER

The thought processes of a *Student* are outlined below. *Examiner* comments at various stages are in italics.

1 > ANALYSIS

'I chose this question because I like photographing the landscape and trees. None of the "Themes" gave me the chance to do this. I know that choosing a "Set Problem" means that there are certain restrictions on what I do. In this case they are:

- I must produce no more than ten prints;
- the prints must be 203 mm × 254 mm;
- I must *investigate* a woodland area.

The "key-word" in this question is "**INVESTIGATE**". When I looked up the word "Investigate" in my dictionary it said,

try to discover the truth about; examine systematically; enquire carefully into.
(*The Penguin English Dictionary*, 1965)

This means, I think, that I cannot just "take some photographs" of a wood!

I have got a good range of references and ideas in my brainstorming diagram.'

BRAINSTORMING DIAGRAM

EMOTIONAL/SENSORY FEELINGS

GREEN LEAFY COOL DAMP DARK FRIGHTENING

WOODLAND

TEXTURES LIGHT & DARK PATTERNS CONTRAST JUXTAPOSITION

VISUAL ELEMENTS

SEE GOMBRICH

ARTISTS	PHOTOGRAPHERS	IDEAS
SAMUEL PALMER	HENRY PEACH ROBINSON	SHAPE OF 'COPSE'
JOHN CONSTABLE	ALEXANDER KEIGHLEY	FOOT OF TREE
GRAHAM SUTHERLAND	J.C.S. MUMMERY	BOLES OF TREES
IVON HITCHENS	P.H. EMERSOM	UNDERGROWTH
JAPANESE/CHINESE	FRANCIS BEDFORD	SHAFTS OF SUNLIGHT
WALT DISNEY	ROGER FENTON	DAPPLED SUNLIGHT
VAN GOGH		SMALL LEAVES

'Landscape with Cypresses near Arles' (National Gallery)

'TEXTURED'
LARGE LEAVES
'SHAPES'

Henri Rousseau

MIST (MORNING)
SKY – THROUGH

Paul Cézanne   'Rockery Scenery in Provence'
   (National Gallery)

BRANCHES

Antoine Watteau   'Fête in a Park'
   (Wallace Collection. London)

CLOSE-UPS
   BARK

Nicholas Hillyarde   'Portrait Miniature'
   (Victoria & Albert Museum)

   FUNGI
   IVY

Jacob Van Ruisdael   'Wooded: Landscape'
   (Oxford. Worcester College)

   FRUIT
   BERRIES
   LEAVES

KEY: CAPITAL LETTERS = FIRST THOUGHTS
   Small letters = Later thoughts

THOUGHTS

'When I had a chance to look at Gombrich I was able to add not only the names of artists who had painted and drawn woodlands in their work, but I was also able to name some *actual paintings* and their *locations*. If I can get to see these I will.

Because I liked landscape and woodlands, I knew from my coursework about some photographers of the past who featured this subject-matter in their work. Part of my research will be to go and look at their work again.

I think that I will try to compile a file on modern "Woodland" photographs. It might mean that I do not always know the names of the photographers, but the Colour Magazine Supplements will provide some of these.

If I can start this "modern" file, I will try to identify the photographers where I can, but I will concentrate on comparing the photographs one with another and also with the work of the photographers of the past who are in my brainstorming diagram. This will give me a relevant critical and historical study to accompany my practical work.'

Examiner Comments: *If you are studying photography as an Art and Design 'endorsed certificate' for your GCSE, it would probably pay you to mix your photographic work with some definite Art and Design studies.*

If you wanted to do a pure photographic examination you would probably be better doing the specialist examinations offered by some of the Examining Groups, such as LEAG, or SEG.

Remember, in an Art and Design based certificate, the likelihood is that you will not be expected to have followed the most rigorous 'scientific' approach to your subject, but you will be expected to show that you can use your camera in a creative way which reflects your understanding about the basic principles in the making of Art and Design forms and images.

Plate 31   Samuel Palmer, 'The Harvest Moon'. *The Tate Gallery, London.* In this work Palmer shows the textural, patterny effect of foliage, amongst other things.

Plate 32   John Middleton, 'Alby, Norfolk'. *The Castle Museum, Norwich.* In this work Middleton demonstrates how bushes, small trees and dark areas build up a composition which leads and entices you into its depths.

2 > PREPARATORY STUDIES

'In the time for my preparatory studies I shall:

- conduct my research;
- take the appropriate photographs for my ideas;
- experiment with some of my ideas;
- decide what I shall produce for my controlled test;
- prepare my negatives for my controlled test.

For my controlled test I shall,

- print the pictures I have planned;
- mount and present the prints.

Thinking more about it I shall definitely get some postcards of paintings of "Woods" done by artists and include them in my critical and historical study (Plates 31, 32 and 33). I have a number of ideas about what practical work to do. In my preparatory studies I shall do the following in this order.

Exercise 1

- Photograph general views in a wood.
- Experiment with some double exposures.
- Experiment with some combination prints in the darkroom.
- Make other experiments in the darkroom as time allows, such as:
    - diffuse prints;
    - distorted prints;
    - multiple image prints.

Exercise 2

Look for examples to photograph which will allow me to show how "line", "tone", "pattern", "texture", "shape", "form" and "space" are present and represented in the wood.

These "elements" come from the assessment objectives printed in my examination syllabus.

Exercise 3

Mark a path through the wood, walk this path, stopping every ten yards.

Each time I stop I shall photograph what is in front of me, behind me, and to my left and my right.

This will give me a form of "documentation" about the wood and its contents and could best fulfil the requirement to "investigate a wood".

I know that this is a lot to do, and that I shall probably not get through everything that I plan.

At least, I can probably get nearly all the exposures I need from two visits to a wood. I shall restrict myself to this in the first instance. After I have developed my films, made some sets of contact prints, and started some of my darkroom experiments, then, if it is necessary, I shall go back to the wood.

Plate 33 Narcisse-Virgilio de la Pena, 'A Clearing in a Forest'. *The Courtauld Institute Galleries, London.* De la Pena was a member of the 'Barbizon School' of painters. Barbizon is a village in the Forest of Fontainebleau. This group of painters worked in the open air, on the spot, to produce their work. At the time this was unusual. Painters worked traditionally in their studio, perhaps from sketches done on the spot. This particular painting is visually similar to many of the photographs of the landscape of the same period, the second half of the last century.

On this next visit, if it comes about, I shall take photographs of the gaps I have identified in my work. If a new idea has come up during my preparatory studies, I shall take photographs necessary for that on this third visit.'

'On my two visits to the wood I took fifty-six exposures. Thirty-six of these were on a film with a speed of 125 ASA. The other twenty were on a film with a speed of 400 ASA. I used an SLR camera which I could 'stop-down' to $f1.5$.

On the first of these visits I took photographs of some general views in the wood (Figs 13.1 and 13.2). The photographs I took used the slower film.

On the second visit to the wood I concentrated on taking photographs which would help me to carry out some of the experiments listed in the first exercise above. The faster film was helpful as I was often focussing closely on dimly lit subjects.

At the same time, largely at home, I began to compile my "Critical and Historical" File (Fig 13.3 and Fig 13.5). When I was at school I photocopied some illustrations from some books which allowed me to show the work of the photographers I had named in my brainstorming diagram.

In the darkroom I developed my two rolls of film.

I made a set of contact prints of each.'

DECISIONS

'For my planned "documented" pathway through the wood I had to make a difficult decision. If I was going to use this in my controlled test, and I could only produce ten prints, I would have to make some careful selections from amongst my photographs.

Studying the contact prints closely I decided that the only way I could best show my work in ten prints, was if I chose ten prints which photographed *in sequence only* what I saw before me when I stopped every ten yards.

I marked these ten prints on my contact sheet and decided that I would not use them in any *other* work I might do.

This left me with a large number of prints, from the two films, to try to sort out the images necessary to do my first and second exercises.

In the second exercise I planned to show "seven elements". I decided to select two prints to show each element.

I made this selection. Again, I decided not to use these prints in any darkroom experimental work I might do which was relevant to my first exercise.

This meant that I had selected so far, twenty-four of my prints. This still left me with over thirty prints to carry out my darkroom experiments.'

DARKROOM EXPERIMENTS

'I could only use the darkroom for a limited amount of time during my preparatory studies. My teachers had to draw-up a rota for its use.

This meant that I could only do a restricted amount of experiments.

I had not taken any double-exposure on my films, so I decided to make some "combination prints" and some "distorted prints" during my time in the darkroom.'

COMBINATION PRINTS

'I chose three negatives. Two were fairly general views of the interior of the wood. The third was taken from outside the wood and showed its "shape" against the sky (Fig 13.4).

Using one of the three negatives I had previously selected, I exposed it onto a sheet of printing paper. I had a "mask" over the centre of the printing paper as I did so.

Fig. 13.1 The 'textural'
appearance of a wood:
photograph.

Fig. 13.2 Inside a wood:
photograph.

Then I covered up the pieces of the printing paper which had been exposed in this way. In the centre of the printing paper I put a smaller "mask" than I had at first used.

I focussed the same negative as before, making it fit inside the "frame" of the first exposure. To do this I used a "safelight filter". Then I exposed the negative for the second time.

After this I took away the central "mask" and added the masking to the outside, to cover both the first and the second exposure.

Again I re-focussed the same negative, so that it now fitted the central portion of the printing paper, so far un-exposed. Then I exposed it.

I did this all again with my other "general view" of the interior of the wood.

Then I did it all again, only this time I used my view of the "shape" of the wood for my outside exposure, the general view which had less undergrowth present in the photograph for my second exposure, and my "densest" general view for the middle of my combination picture.'

Fig. 13.3 Inside a wood: painting.

DISTORTION PRINTS

'At the end of all this I just had enough darkroom time left to make a few "distortion prints".

I made one with the printing paper held in a curve and closely focussed the negative on the crest of the curve. This meant that the centre vertical portion of the print was in fine focus, whilst the edges gradually went out of focus.

I made one or two others by distorting the negative. I effectively "ruined" a couple of my negatives in order to do this, by "heating" them so that they distorted and the emulsion "ran".

I thought that these results, in particular, gave the feeling of "fear" I had first thought of, and I was pleased that I had managed to achieve this.'

Fig. 13.4 On the edge of a wood:
photograph.

Fig. 13.5 On the edge of a wood:
painting.

4 ⟩ CONTROLLED TEST TIME

'I decided that for my controlled test I would, after all, do the set of prints based upon the "elements" of Art and Design.

Part of my reason for this was due to the fact that I was not taking a "pure photography" GCSE. Because I was doing "photography" within my Art and Design Studies, and those studies had introduced me to the principles of Art and Design as well as the techniques of photography, I thought I would carry out the idea which seemed most related to the assessment objectives in my examination.

Another reason was that I did not feel that my alternative ideas were "investigative" enough.

The idea of "documenting" a walk through the wood was defeated by the restriction to 'no more than ten prints'. To carry out this idea successfully I needed to be able to make many more prints than ten. If I were to carry it out, I thought that I might present my results in the form of a "flick book".

The other idea, about using darkroom techniques, whilst it might have been "investigative" of darkroom techniques, it was not sufficiently investigative about the "wood" in my opinion.

The time I could have in the darkroom during my controlled test did not really allow for too much "experimental" work. It was necessary to know what I wanted to try to achieve, and then go in and "do it".

Before the controlled test began I was able to collect together *all* the negatives I had which, in my opinion, dealt with each of the various "elements". I put them together under the title of each element and my teachers allowed me back into the darkroom in order to make sets of contact prints for each "element".

From these contact prints, during my controlled test, I selected two to represent each element and made a 203 mm × 254 mm print of each of them.

Even then I had to reduce the number of my prints from fourteen to ten.

I began this choice by picking what I thought was the best example of each element. This left me room for three more prints. I chose these on the basis of what I thought were the three best quality prints amongst those remaining.

What I was trying to do in doing this was to show my "aesthetic" choice in the first seven selected, and then the level of my "technical ability" in the other three prints.

Doing all this left me with some time left in my controlled test.

Fig. 13.6 Photograph showing the 'line and dot' effect in a wood.

Fig. 13.7 Edge and stick print of 'line and dot' effect.

I decided to make some "edge and stick prints" (Fig 13.7) of what I thought was my best photograph (Fig 13.6) in the series. I chose to do this because it meant that my work would be more related to Art and Design if I did so.

I collected together some pieces of card and thin wood, to give me my "edge" printing tools, and some pieces of dowel, matchsticks, knitting and the like, to give me my "stick" printing tools.

I used these with black lino-printing ink, to compose my picture.

For the presentation of my work I mounted each of my first seven "elements" photographs into an album. I mounted my three "technical ability" prints onto one board, and my "edge and stick" print onto another board.

I put my "critical study" work into another album. This was now a collection of pictures and written work.

In addition I had my photographic work from my preparatory studies. I mounted these in collections on a couple of boards.

I finally made a list of the books I had used for my work. These were Gombrich (1984), Bernard & Norquay (1982), Hannavy (1976), and Hopkinson (1980).'

---

5 ⟩ EXAMINER COMMENTS

This candidate was sensible to combine the Art and Design aspect of the course of study with the photographic.

Doing so gave him access to the fullest range of assessment objectives in the externally set examination.

The choice of what to do finally in the controlled test was well reasoned out. The results were all the better for having so clear an intention. Also, what was done in the controlled test had not been done so far in the work of the candidate. This meant that the work was more likely to achieve a sense of 'freshness'.

A lengthy explanation about 'combination prints' was put down in words. It would have been better, and it would have been easier to understand, if this had been done in a series of 'drawings', perhaps with some written notes included in them.

All of the assessment objectives included in the NISEC syllabus were well attended to in this work, including the one which insists that the relationship should be explored:
'between individuals and their work in the field of Art and Design within the historical, social and environmental context'.

As a result an extremely good grade is likely to result from this work.

The way that the candidate worked and described things, suggests that a lot had been learnt and understood during the course of study. Part of this learning was obviously a familiarity with darkroom procedures and techniques. Whatever the level of technical ability shown in the final prints made during the controlled test, it is likely that the technical skills the candidate knew about and used would have compensated for any 'pure photography' and 'scientific' shortcomings.

SOME ALTERNATIVES

Plate 34 Antoine Watteau, 'Fête in a Park'. *Reproduced by permission of the Trustees of the Wallace Collection, London.*

This work (Plate 34) is by the French artist, **Antoine Watteau (1684–1721)**. It illustrates that in responding to this particular question in your GCSE Examination you could consider the uses to which woods are put, such as picnics, rambles, tree-felling, charcoal burning, wild-life conservation, flora and fauna studies, and so on.

The use of 'focal points' such as these could lead you to some very creditable and worthwhile work in this situation.

Some very good work can be done by studying your subject matter in detailed 'close-up'.

'Close-Up' could have been decided on as a most suitable 'sub-theme' to this question (See Plate 35 and Fig 13.8).

BIBLIOGRAPHY

BERNARD, C. & NORQUAY, K. (1982). *Practical Effects in Photography*. London, Focal Press.
GARMONSWAY, G.N. & SIMPSON, J. (1965). *The Penguin English Dictionary*. Harmondsworth, Middlesex, Penguin Books.
HANNAVY, J. (1976). *Masters of Victorian Photography*. London, David & Charles.
HOPKINSON, T. (1980). *Treasures of the Royal Photographic Society, 1839–1919*. London, Heinemann.

Fig. 13.8 Close up: photograph of
the bole of a tree.

Plate 35 James Sillett, 'Old Oak,
Winfarthing'. *The Castle Museum,
Norwich.*

CRITICAL AND CONTEXTUAL STUDIES: APPLICATIONS

UNENDORSED CERTIFICATE – STILL LIFE PAINTING

ENDORSED CERTIFICATE – DRAWING & PAINTING

ENDORSED CERTIFICATE – GRAPHICS

ENDORSED CERTIFICATE – TEXTILES

ENDORSED CERTIFICATE – THREE-DIMENSIONAL STUDIES

ENDORSED CERTIFICATE – PHOTOGRAPHY

GETTING STARTED

We have considered critical and contextual studies in Chapter 3. Here we take the opportunity of *relating* these studies to the specific questions we have been considering for the various examination groups. This will give you an opportunity to see such studies 'in action', directed to *specific* problems and fields of enquiry. All the Examining Groups expect such studies to form part of your Practical Work during your GCSE course *and* as part of the externally set examination.

ESSENTIAL PRINCIPLES

The outline answer was considered in Chapter 8, pages 125–131. The **critical and contextual studies** could have included:

- references to the history of Still Life painting in Art and Design.

   This was touched upon when the 'Dutch Still Life' Masters were referred to and contrasted with Cézanne. Van Gogh painted still life and so did Gauguin, amongst many others. It could have been worthwhile collecting as many postcards of still life as possible and relating them to their changing times.

   Not all still life paintings were specifically about what is generally and usually regarded as still life subjects. For instance, Van Gogh painted his bedroom: this is a form of still life. Many other artists included tables of bowls and fruit, for example, in pictures of other things. Studying works of art like this will allow you to make deductions about the way that people lived at different times in history.

- illustrations of how 'still life' is used nowadays by other than artists. For instance, the use of still life in advertising.

   If you began to consider this you might question if such modern day use of the subject helps you to understand how people live in your times, or how it is thought they ought to live, or it is pretended they do live!

   You might find out that the graphic designers responsible for some of the advertisements actually use existing, historical paintings in their work. This could lead you to consider not only the 'ethics' of doing this, but also the 'ethical code' necessary in responsible advertising. This is a matter of consideration, if not a problem, for your time.

- examples of how photographers sometimes use still life as their subject-matter.

   You could consider why photographers should choose to use this subject-matter, whether they do more with it than the painters of old, and why any society should need to have still life as part of their culture anyway.

In Chapter 9, pages 132–147, we considered an outline answer for *Drawing and Painting*, looking at the particular theme of **Townscape**. Many artists have painted the landscape and the buildings which man erects in it or gathers together into towns. Again, these paintings help you to understand what things looked like in times gone by.

In addition you might consider:

- what 'buildings' tell you about the social structure of a particular period of history, and not just what they represent as part of the 'History Of Architecture'.

- how man has governed and controlled both his 'dwelling' habitat *and* his total environment. It is interesting to study and use a book such as that written by Hoskins, (1955), which deals with the way that man has 'created' his 'natural' environment.

- the effect of the 'Enclosure Act' and other Land Acts upon the way that the environment appears now.

- the differences in dwelling places in different cultures, climates, and times.

- the differences in Places of Worship which are brought about by differing religious beliefs.

- the differences in buildings which house people and those which house animals.

- the differences in dwelling places which are designed for different forms of employment. For example, the back-to-back houses of the new 'town-dwellers' of the Industrial Revolution and those of the rural agricultural workers of the same period.

- the way that the buildings built for similar purposes look so different as you travel across, or up and down the United Kingdom. Such differences are often 'visual' and come largely from the use of differing building materials in different parts of the United Kingdom. Today, no matter where you are in the United Kingdom, most places are built from the same types of bricks. Does this make all new buildings 'look the same'?

- the effect of new building materials, such as plastic, glass, steel and reinforced concrete upon the design and appearance of modern buildings.
- the differences not only between the 'classical' styles of architecture down through the ages, but also the difference between the 'classical' styles of architecture and 'vernacular architecture'.

3 ENDORSED CERTIFICATE – GRAPHICS

In Chapter 10, pages 148–161, we looked at the same theme of *Townscape*, but this time from the context of *Graphics*. Graphic design, and its fore-runners, reflect the values and beliefs which exist within a society, and provide a clue as to how that society would wish to see itself.

Just by looking at, and comparing, the images and styles the graphic designer uses from one time to another, creates an awareness of the values that each age holds. For instance, if you were to look at a popular magazine published around Christmas in the 1930s, you would be likely to find many advertisements publicising 'hobbies'. There would be illustrations of 'Double-OO' model railways, details about 'Meccano', pictures of 'fretwork' machines. Or there would be pictures of 'teddy bears', 'rag dolls', and so on. Whereas if you were to study the magazines of fifty years later, that is to say, the 1980s, you would be attacked by 'computer games', 'videos', 'Lego', 'talking dolls', and so on.

Apart from the general nature of 'dolls', the only other common factor between the two ages seems to be the 'Meccano' and the 'Lego'. What does this tell you about the two societies? What are the life-styles of each? What values does each hold?

Some of the answers lie in the way the two sets of advertisements are *structured*. In the illustrations and advertisements of the 1930s, the likelihood is that eager-faced young children will be accompanied by their fathers and mothers. In the illustrations and advertisements of the 1980s, it is more likely that the goods will be shown with their young owner *alone*.

Apart, perhaps, from the more personal graphic work of artists, *everything* that comes under the umbrella of 'graphics' provides you with this key to the past and to its social and cultural meaning. This social and cultural meaning 'creates' the sense of 'history' which we come to accept and understand.

It is also interesting to see if, in the past, 'multi-cultural' differences can be identified in the graphic output of different countries. Or has life always been like the ubiquitous 'Coke' bottle, the same the world over!

4 ENDORSED CERTIFICATE – TEXTILES

In Chapter 11, pages 162–174, we considered an outline answer to a question on making a decorative garment for casual or fun wear.

Textiles is well suited to critical and contextual studies. The whole idea of clothing, fashion, and furnishings is culturally and socially constructed. What are 'clothes' for? To keep you warm? Decency? A form of 'body adornment'?

The concept of 'decency' is a *social construct*, otherwise why do some tribes still run around nearly naked? Those that do, live largely in very warm climates, which suggests that clothes are about 'keeping warm'.

If 'decency' was *not* a social construct, but an equally logical requirement like 'keeping warm', then, despite variations in the climate, everyone would wear clothes as a matter of course from the very beginning. On the other hand, amongst such primitive tribes 'body adornment' *is* often an important matter, often in the form of paint or some form of natural decoration.

But of course the 'culture' surrounding clothes has moved far beyond such considerations as warmth, decency and body adornment alone. Clothes are designed and worn for a whole variety of reasons, such as:

- protection at work;
- identification, as in uniforms, team games and activities;
- looking fashionable;
- leading fashion;
- belonging;
- being different.

As well as these personal, group, cultural and social reasons for wearing the clothes that are worn, we can also consider the *technological developments* that have gone on since men and women first wore an animal skin for warmth and protection. In this way you will begin to have an understanding of history as it is represented by the clothes that mankind has worn over the ages.

In the same way, a study of the textiles and fabrics which are used in the *furnishings* which human beings have steadily and increasingly surrounded themselves with, will illustrate:

- the increased wealth that developed societies enjoy;
- the desire to demonstrate that wealth;
- an obedience to fashion;
- the growth of technology.

On the other hand, why is it that *some* societies still maintain the traditions of their culture in the fabric and textile designs they produce and the fabric and textile items they own?

Where this does still happen it seems to be mostly in under-developed societies where, even if there is the will 'to show off', there is certainly not the means.

Does this mean that worthwhile values and 'traditions' cannot be maintained in a modern, and developed industrial world? If this is so, is it a good thing, or a bad thing? Is there some advantage in having an 'International Melting-Pot'?

These and many other considerations could arise out of your critical and contextual studies in the field of Textiles.

5 > ENDORSED CERTIFICATE – THREE-DIMENSIONAL STUDIES

In Chapter 12, pages 175–187, we looked at a question on designing and making a decorated lamp base, as an example of *Three-Dimensional Studies*. What has been said about 'graphics' and 'textiles' can all apply equally to your Three-Dimensional studies.

The three-dimensional products of *any* society reflect the social and cultural values that society holds just as much as the images and the items of adornment it produces. In fact, being three-dimensional, those products perhaps relate *more closely* to the image that human beings hold of themselves. Every three-dimensional object which people produce does, or should, bear a relationship to the three-dimensional shape, size, form, and articulation of human beings, or their association with animals.

Your critical and contextual studies in your Three-Dimensional Studies might involve you considering, for *any* object, the following:

- is it necessary;
- when is it not necessary;
- is it correct that certain buildings, such as churches, should be built 'upwards' on such a scale that they make people insignificant;
- why did this come about;
- do 'gadgets' finally *reduce* the strength of human beings and their ability to express themselves and to communicate;
- are many of a society's three-dimensional products economical, both in materials and energy;
- should they be;
- what atrocities do human beings perpetrate upon the three-dimensional natural world they live in?

6 > ENDORSED CERTIFICATE – PHOTOGRAPHY

These notes supplement Chapter 13, pages 188–201.

Since its invention, photography has provided one of the most immediate and influential means of producing a social document. Photography is like a 'window on an age'. The 'age' since photography is not a very long one, although it has seen, and recorded, the fastest rate of change since the beginning of time.

Photography can appear all embracing, insofar as it picks up and records paintings, drawings, graphic images, architecture, textiles, three-dimensional products, landscape, the surface of the moon, and so on.

Of course, in reality, it does not 'transcend' these other things, rather it *translates* them into something else, namely, a photograph. A photograph translates the *light impulses* coming forth from the objects in front of the camera and *reproduces those light impulses*. It does *not* reproduce, or 'capture' the objects themselves. Having a photograph, you do not own the things it contains within itself, but only that photograph.

What it *does* do so successfully is to *record* the objects, events, standards, values, and so on, of a particular time. But it would be folly to suppose that it does all this in a mechanical and impassionate way.

A human being decides *what* to point a camera at. A human being decides *how* to reproduce the image on the film inside the camera; *what size* it should be; whether it should be *in colour*, sepia, black and white; whether it should have a 'margin' around the final image, or whether it should 'bleed' to the very edges of the print. All of these things influence the way that both the *photograph* and the *subject matter* of the photograph appear!

It is possible to identify the *personal ways* in which photographers approach and view their subject matter. These ways can be used to classify and group 'types' of photographs.

For instance, some of its practitioners have used photography in a **romantic way**. This is a reflection of the perfectly acceptable values that some societies and some members of a society hold.

It is possible to identify the use of photography as a form of '**High Art**'. Fox Talbot can be seen to have engaged himself in this aspect of photography in some of his work. Some early photographers had trained as artists. This is reflected in *their* approach to photography.

A photographer such as P.H. Emerson can be seen to be using photography in a '**Naturalistic**' way. His studies of the Norfolk Broads illustrate this particular use of photography. He wrote about his beliefs in the ability of the camera lens to 'see' better than the human eye, and that in this respect it was able to 'transcend' the human eye!

Other photographers, such as George Davison, were influenced by the '**Impressionist Painters**', and their work reflects this sense of identity.

Photo-journalism is a vigorous and 'critical' use of the medium, whereby photographers 'describe', 'comment upon', 'criticise' and even 'condemn' the events and situations around them. Photographers who go to battle fronts are good examples of this form of photography, but there are just as many who go no further than their immediate environment to find their subject matter.

When you can begin to *classify* and *understand* the photographic images which surround you in this way, you have the means to begin to put them into a '*context*'. Once this is done, you have the means to not only critically evaluate the photographs themselves as 'scientific', or 'aesthetic' achievements, but also to critically evaluate the *world* they reflect. *This is Critical and Contextual Studies.*

EXAMINATION SYLLABUSES

Although it may not be strictly called 'A Critical and Contextual Study', the Examining Groups either insist upon, or provide the opportunity for, this aspect of study in Art and Design.

Table 14.1 tells you whether your Examining Group makes a *specific reference* to 'A Critical and Contextual Study', *what it calls* such a study, and whether it is a *compulsory or an optional* component of the examination.

LEAG	■ Reference made
	■ Called 'Critical and Historical Studies'
	■ Optional, introduced as an Art and Design 'Practice'

MEG	■ Reference made
	■ Called 'Critical and Historical Study'
	■ Optional, introduced as an 'Approach to Study'

NEA	■ Reference made
	■ Referred to as 'Objective 9'
	■ Regarded as *part* of other activities

NISEC	■ Reference made
	■ Called the 'Special Study'
	■ A compulsory coursework unit. The syllabus gives 'Topic areas' for this Study

SEG	■ Reference made
	■ No particular name for the 'Study'
	■ Regarded as an essential part of the 'Content' of each SEG examination syllabus

WJEC	■ Reference made
	■ No particular name for the 'Study'
	■ A compulsory coursework unit

IGCSE	■ Reference made
	■ Called 'Component IV – Art and Design Appreciation'
	■ An optional section of the *whole* of the GCSE course and examination

In the various examination syllabuses available for the GCSE Art and Design, only MEG and NISEC give *examples* of what might be a suitable topic for 'A Critical and Contextual study'. IGCSE is the *only* Examining Group which *publishes set questions* for 'A Critical and Contextual Study' in its externally set examination.

'HISTORICAL' STUDIES

In this book, a 'Historical Study' is deliberately called 'A Critical and Contextual Study' because it is felt that it is most beneficial to you if you regard it in this way. If you think only of the *'Historical'*, the danger is that you will concentrate on the 'history' of the subject, perhaps reducing that history to a list of dates, countries of origin of the artists and designers, and a catalogue of their work.

If you keep the idea of *'Contextual'* foremost in your mind, you will study and understand the work of artists and designers in the way in which such work was largely done. That is to say, you will be aware of the relationship of the work with the *social and cultural,* as well as the *historical* circumstances in which it was done.

Nevertheless, there is nothing wrong in studying your subject in terms of its 'Historical Chronology'. 'Chronology' means giving an event, a situation, a person, and so on, a time and a date, and then *ordering* all those events in terms of their sequence. As has been said, there is nothing wrong in this, but the danger is that it can lead to reciting 'parrot fashion' the names and dates of the Kings and Queens of England, without ever understanding anything about those Kings and Queens and their effect upon the times they lived in, and vice-versa.

You should not however throw this important 'baby' out with the bathwater! Knowing the 'chronology' of your subject does give you a sense of time. But knowing what went on in *other fields* of study and knowledge at the same time, gives you insights into that 'time', and helps to explain it on a variety of levels.

SOME CONCLUSIONS

Throughout this book much emphasis has been placed on the 'critical' and the 'contextual'. This has not been done in order to create more work for you. It has been done because it is believed that;

- the 'critical' and the 'contextual' is an *essential part* of the *successful study* of Art and Design;

- studying the subject in a 'critical' and a 'contextual', as well as a 'practical' way, eventually leads to *much greater enjoyment* in your studies;

- studying the subject in a 'critical' and a 'contextual', as well as a 'practical' way, helps to create a *much deeper level of understanding* of your subject;

- studying the subject in a 'critical' and a 'contextual' way encourages you to *discover and appreciate* the multi-cultural nature of Art and Design;

- *studying the subject in a 'critical' and a 'contextual', as well as a 'practical' way, emphasises that Art and Design is a part not only of a personal or societal life, but of the History of the World.*

BIBLIOGRAPHY

HOSKINS, W.G. (1970). *The Making of the English Landscape.* Harmondsworth, Middlesex, Penguin Books.

RECOMMENDED SOURCE BOOKS

Where specific books have been mentioned in the text throughout this book, they have been included in a bibliography at the end of the appropriate chapter.

A number of other books exist which will be helpful to your studies and some of them are listed here. These are not so much the books you should *read*, as the types of books you should *use*.

The list is not exhaustive and you should be receptive to any source of information which is relevant to your needs, or can guide your responses, at any time.

ASHWIN, C. (1982). *Encyclopedia of Drawing.* London, Batsford.
BERGER, P. & LUCKMAN, T. (1967). *The Social Construction of Reality.* London, Allen Lane.
DAWSON, J. (ed.) (1981). *Prints and Printmaking.* London, Phaidon.
GERNSHEIM, H. & A. (1965). *A Concise History of Photography.* London, Thames and Hudson.
GOSTELOW, M. (ed.) (1982). *The Complete Guide to Needlework: Materials and Techniques.* London, Phaidon.
LAWSON, B. (1980). *How Designers Think.* London, The Architectural Press.
LUCIE-SMITH, E. (1981). *The Story of Craft.* London, Phaidon.
LUCIE-SMITH, E. (1983). *A History of Industrial Design.* London, Phaidon.
READ, H. (1974). *A Concise History of Modern Painting.* London, Thames and Hudson.
ROWLAND, K. (1973). *A History of the Modern Movement: Art, Architecture and Design.* London, Looking and Seeing.
STOREY, J. (1978). *Textile Printing.* London, Thames and Hudson.
THORGESON, S. & DEAN, R. (eds.) (1977). *Album Cover Album.* Limpsfield, Surrey, Dragons World Ltd.

INDEX